REA

**DO NOT REMOVE
CARDS FROM POCKET**

# The Skeleton
# in the Wardrobe

# Other Books by David Holbrook

## Poetry

## Fiction

## On Education

## Criticism

# The Skeleton
# in the Wardrobe

## C. S. Lewis's Fantasies:
## A Phenomenological
## Study

David Holbrook

Lewisburg
Bucknell University Press
London and Toronto: Associated University Presses

Associated University Presses
440 Forsgate Drive
Cranbury, NJ 08512

Associated University Presses
25 Sicilian Avenue
London WC1A 2QH, England

Associated University Presses
P.O. Box 39, Clarkson Pstl. Stn.
Mississauga, Ontario
Canada L5J 3X9


The paper used in this publication meets the requirements of the American National Standard for Permanence of Paper for Printed Library Materials Z39.48-1984.


**Library of Congress Cataloging-in-Publication Data**

Holbrook, David.
    The skeleton in the wardrobe : C.S. Lewis's fantasies : a phenomenological study / David Holbrook.
        p.   cm.
    Includes bibliographical references.
    ISBN 0-8387-5183-0 (alk. paper)
    1. Lewis, C. S. (Clive Staples), 1898–1963—Fictional works.
2. Fantastic fiction, English—History and criticism.   3. Children's stories, English—History and criticism.   4. Phenomenology and literature.   I. Title.
PR6023.E926Z675   1991
823'.912—dc20                                                               89-46400
                                                                                    CIP

PRINTED IN THE UNITED STATES OF AMERICA

# Contents

# References to the Editions of "Narnia"

LWW   *The Lion, the Witch and the Wardrobe.* Penguin Books, 1959. Originally published by Geoffrey Bles, 1950.

PC   *Prince Caspian.* Penguin Books, 1962. Originally published by Geoffrey Bles, 1951.

MN   *The Magician's Nephew.* Penguin Books, 1963. Originally published by The Bodley Head, 1955.

VDT   *The Voyage of the Dawn Treader.* Penguin Books, 1965. Originally published by Geoffrey Bles, 1952.

SC   *The Silver Chair.* Penguin Books, 1965. Originally published by Geoffrey Bles, 1953.

HB   *The Horse and His Boy.* Penguin Books, 1965. Originally published by Geoffrey Bles, 1954.

LB   *The Last Battle.* Penguin Books, 1964. Originally published by the Bodley Head, 1956.

# Preface: Something "Wrong" with the "Narnia" Books?

When I first read the "Narnia" books of C. S. Lewis, I felt there was something seriously "wrong" with them. I then found I was not alone in this. There are parents who feel their children should not be allowed to read them and others who found their children were unduly upset by them. I even heard of one psychotherapist who would not allow his children to read the books because they were "so full of hate."

I felt I should investigate these questions as one concerned with the psychology of culture and with education. Lewis was a serious author, a learned man, a respected university figure, and, evidently, a benign man in his life. He made provisions to give a large proportion of his royalties to good purposes. He wrote Christian apologetics and engaged in theological and philosophical debate at a high level. How could there be anything so objectionable in his stories for children that the books could be condemned? They sold, and still sell, a million copies a year; and thousands of children enjoy them. There is a widespread following of his work.

Indeed, the "Narnia" books are now virtually institutionalized in the world of publishing and bookselling. Penguin Books issued a map of Narnia; the BBC has offered a dramatization of *The Lion, the Witch and the Wardrobe*, and there have been stage presentations. Articles in *The Times* and utterances by bishops offer C. S. Lewis's writings as representative of the intelligent man's Christianity. There is an Anglo-American journal published at Wheaton College, Illinois, that is devoted to the work of seven Christian writers including Lewis: *VII* contains articles about George MacDonald, C. S. Lewis, J. R. R. Tolkien, Charles Williams, Dorothy L. Sayers, and Owen Barfield. In the face of such a coherence of endorsement of Lewis as a Christian writer, it is daunting to embark on a critical reconsideration of the "upshot" of his fantasies, to the extent of doubting their possible influence on sensibility.

9

There is no doubt that Lewis himself regarded even his Narnia books as Christian fables. He asserted that clues to the tenacity of his beliefs would be found in his Narnia books. Of *The Last Battle*, he said, "if anyone thinks I have in any way lost my faith in Christ's promises, will you point them to what I've said in *The Last Battle?*" (In *C. S. Lewis, a Biography* [Green and Hooper 1974, p. 235]).

While some (like Barfield himself) have sometimes had doubts about Lewis's seriousness, this sounds serious enough. Certainly scholars have taken Lewis's theological arguments seriously. He did not, apparently, believe in a power opposite to God; that is, in dualism. As there is no uncreated being except God, he cannot have an opposite. He said:

> The proper question is whether I believe in devils. I do. That is to say, I believe in angels and I believe that some of them, by the abuse of their free will, have become enemies to God and, as a corollary, to us. These we may call devils. They do not differ in nature from good angels, but their nature is depraved. *Devil* is the opposite of *angel* only as Bad Man is the opposite of Good Man. Satan, the leader or dictator of devils, is the opposite not of God but of Michael. (Green and Hooper 1974, p. 193)

He also goes on to say that belief in devils

> seems to me to explain a good many facts. It agrees with the plain sense of Scripture, the tradition of Christendom, and the beliefs of most men at most time. And it conflicts with nothing that any of the sciences has shown to be true.

It is believed by many that Lewis offers a profound critique of science as a form on intellectual pride—even sinfulness since it seems to deny much that belongs to the spirit and the numinous. When the old professor in a "Narnia" book asks what they teach children nowadays, this is taken to mean that Lewis was a champion of the inner life, of the imagination, of recognition of the mysteries of existence, as a pathway to God. In light of this, my Christian friends believe I ought to share his condemnation of the "abolition of man"; and they have urged me not to write this book, if it were likely to undermine his influence. But, as will be seen, while I share Lewis's apprehension about the way the world is going, I do not accept his diagnosis and I certainly do not endorse his remedies, nor the "message" or "upshot" of his fantasies.

Though this is bound to annoy followers of Lewis, I propose to put his Christianity "in brackets." What I propose to do is to examine the meaning of his symbolism as I would with any fairytale, and ask what the "upshot" of each story is in terms of its implicit moral comment on experience. That is, I will make a phenomenological analysis of his stories, applying literary criticism with a basis in philosophical anthropology as I have done elsewhere with the background in subjective philosophy such as I have explored in my books on this subject.

As will appear, Lewis himself thought that perhaps there might be some kind of psychological explanation for some of his proclivities. In my examination of his work I shall invoke psychoanalytical modes of interpretation of his meanings. It seems clear that some of his preoccupations were so private that he would not have liked them to become part of a general assessment of his work—though he sometimes wrote quite clearly about them: about masturbation, for example. Of particular interest are his misogyny, and his enthusiasm for fantasies of whipping. It is perhaps worth recording that I had virtually completed my studies of his fantasies before I came across the revealing passages uncovered in the letters to Arthur Greeves that confirmed my doubts.

What I have struggled to do is to *understand*, in the process of critical discrimination. As so often, when one does, what one finds is an unhappy child beneath the surface of the confident adult, in dread of its own weakness, trying to compensate. It is in this compensation that the false solutions, as I see them, lie.

The crux of my argument appears if I open up Lewis's Christianity to critical analysis and suggest that his Christ is too severe an authoritarian power to whom one needs masochistically to submit. There are, of course, the problems of submission posed by the Book of Job and the story of Abraham and Isaac. But my problem, if I think about Lewis's version of Christ, is that his representation of Him as Aslan seems too full of magic and the impulse to control. These are not on my part religious doubts, but doubts that arise if I examine his meanings as a creative writer within the Christian tradition.

Here, therefore, I can hardly expect much sympathy from the Christian community that respects Lewis. Even as I write, I find a parish magazine thrust through the letter box, with an insertion from the Bishop's Palace that tells me:

If your children have not yet been introduced to Aslan, it is high time they were: he could accompany them for the rest of their lives. And beyond. . . . It is hard to believe that there are many Christians in this country at all who need an introduction to the land of Narnia: to Aslan the lion, or the children who journey to those wonderful, if sometimes perilous regions. . . . (Jim Rose, *The Sign*)

Some Christians, it would seem, almost offer these stories as a sacred text, outlining a spiritual journey, the modern equivalent of *A Pilgrim's Progress*. They endorse the message of Lewis's fantasies, and the values inherent in them. When the Narnia books were televised, no less a figure than Walter Cronkite commended the Narnia books in glowing terms:

. . .these classics present human values often lacking in today's television: loyalty, courage, caring, responsibility, truthfulness, and compassion. . . . (Bulletin of the *New York C. S. Lewis Society* no. 97 [November 1977], p. 17. Quoted in Sammons 1979, p. 9)

It must seem futile to challenge such an institution: When I was once interviewed for a religious television program, the team were representatives of "Aslan Services Limited," a subsidiary of "Lion Publishing." Today there seems to be a huge commercial boom in Lewis's work. However, I hope that in my first chapter I may be able to convince my readers that there are some puzzling moments in Lewis's fantasies about which it seems sensible to attempt to pursue debate, while his overall message needs some questioning.

I propose to develop my subsequent explorations as follows. I will try to register my initial response to the most famous of Lewis's fantasies, *The Lion, the Witch and the Wardrobe*— because the solution to the phenomenological puzzle seems to be all there, even in the title. I will allow my doubts and associations free range in discussing that book. I will turn to the question of the basis of my approach in the various disciplines of phenomenology. I will then turn to Lewis's life, to how, I believe, the foundations were laid for his particular kind of *Sehnsucht*, his lifelong quest, through symbolism, to solve his psychic problems. Then I will turn back to "Narnia," to the "adult" fairy tales, and lastly to *Till We Have Faces* and try to examine whether in them, in the "upshot," there are offered true or false solutions to the problem of life.

# The Skeleton
# in the Wardrobe

# Part 1
## The Man and His Problems

# 1
## Insights and Misgivings

It will be necessary to take each story by Lewis to ask about its overall implications. This might seem foolhardy to some, especially with fairy tales, at a time when there are modes of criticism that deny any connection between art and life. However with Lewis it seems legitimate, because the stories are offered by the author and others as fables with an improving meaning: they are homiletic.

There are benign episodes in Lewis's Narnia stories, such as the concern of the boy Digory in *The Magician's Nephew* when he confronts danger (not least that of a witch figure) to bring his sick mother the Apple of life.

> . . . Digory took a minute to get his breath, and then went softly into his Mother's room. And there she lay, as he had seen her lie so many other times, propped up on the pillows, with a thin, pale face that could make you cry to look at. Digory took the Apple of life out of his pocket. (MN, p. 166)

This episode will appear as greatly significant as we proceed—not least because it is linked with the origin of the Narnia books themselves.

> And just as the Witch Jadis had looked different when you saw her in our world instead of in her own, so the fruit of the mountain garden looked different too. There were of course all sorts of coloured things in the bedroom; the coloured counterpane on the bed, the wall-paper, the sunlight from the window, and Mother's pretty, pale blue dressing jacket. But the moment Digory took the Apple out of his pocket, all those other things seemed to have scarcely any colour at all. Everyone of them, even the sunlight, looked faded and dingy. The brightness of the Apple threw strange lights on the ceiling. Nothing else was worth looking at: indeed you couldn't look at anything else. And the smell of the Apple

17

of Youth was as if there was a window in the room that opened on Heaven.

"Oh, darling, how lovely," said Digory's Mother.

"You will eat it, won't you? Please," said Digory.

"I don't know what the Doctor would say," she answered. "But really—I almost feel as if I could."

He peeled it and cut it up and gave it to her piece by piece. And no sooner had she finished it than she smiled and her head sank back on the pillow and she was asleep . . . a real, natural, gentle sleep . . . the thing in the whole world that she wanted most. . . . (MN, p. 167)

Digory looks round him: "whenever he looked at the things about him, and saw how ordinary and un-magical they were, he hardly dared to hope." But the Apple is magical, and has been given him by Aslan, and so the mother is cured. Behind the episode is the child's fervent wish that he had magic enough to deny ordinary reality, and restore the dying mother to life by magic—which as we shall see was the child Lewis's predicament.

When Digory's mother has eaten the Apple of life, "That evening he buried the core of the Apple in the back garden" (p. 160). Towards the end of the book we are told "The tree which sprang from the Apple . . . lived and grew into a fine tree. . . ." Because it was growing on English rather than Narnian soil, it did not produce magic apples; but "there was still magic in it now." There was a great storm, and the tree blew down. The professor who owned it couldn't bear to have it chopped up into firewood:

So he had part of the timber made into a wardrobe, which he put in his big house in the country. (p. 171)

The children discovered the magic properties of this wardrobe: "This was the beginning of all the comings and goings between Narnia and our world. . . ." Surely, it is clear that by this Lewis is virtually telling us that the magic-of-going-through-the-wardrobe, which is the essence of the Narnia fantasies, originated in an impulse to restore the mother to life, and that this has something to do with *restoring the mother's body*, which is itself the Tree of Life made into a wardrobe?*

---

*The logic of the fantasy here is a poetic logic. (As a matter of interest,

Lewis's fantasies have a great deal to do with belief in the "Emperor's magic": the magic by which Christ and God can alter the world for goodness. The world Narnia is to be "all right" when Aslan comes in sight: if only we can sustain our belief in Christ, then this world will come right, too. Benign animals like the Beavers, Father Christmas, and other agents help the forces of good throughout Lewis's tales.

However, as I shall try to demonstrate, our difficulties arise from the sense that the solutions Lewis offers are not in the end benign. The main discipline by which the good is promoted in Narnia and the worlds of the other stories is assertiveness—which word is not enough: the word has to be aggressiveness. Take the end of *Prince Caspian*, in the chapter entitled "How All Were Very Busy."

> The roar of the Telmarshes rose like the noise of the sea. "Now, Miraz" they yelled. "Now. Quick! Quick! Kill him." But indeed there was no need to urge the usurper on. He was on top of Peter already. Edmund bit his lips till the blood came as the sword flashed down on Peter. It looked as if it would slash off his head. Thank heavens! It had glanced down on his right shoulder. The Dwarf-made mail was sound and did not break. . . . (PC, p. 165)

> . . . It was most humble and most magnificent. . . .

> Glozelle stopped to stab his own king dead where he lay: "That's for your insult this morning," he whispered as the blade went home. Peter swung face to face Supespian, slashing his legs from under him and, with the back-cut of the same stroke, walloped off his head. . . .

> Many a Telmarine warrior that day felt his foot suddenly pierced as if by a dozen skewers, hopped on one leg cursing the pain, and fell as often as not. If he fell, the mice finished him off; if he did not, someone else did. (p. 167)

If we attend closely to the language, we may note its excited enthusiasm: "it was most humble and most magnificent." There is a fascination with certain kinds of "stroke" and an excitement

---

I decided that the wardrobe was the mother's body before reading *The Magician's Nephew* which so plainly confirms the insight.) I daresay Lewis was not even conscious of it. Gaston Bachelard, the critic of surrealism, interprets symbols of cupboards and chests as representing the mother's body. See Bachelard 1964.

with certain kinds of sadistic gloating as when Glozelle whispers to the king he kills, and over how when the mice didn't "finish him off," "someone else did."

This particular note will be attended to in a moment. Further questions are raised by how this scene progresses. Peter's army wins the day. In the meantime Aslan has been leading a party consisting of Bacchus and his Maenads, "leaping, rushing and turning somersaults," "Silenus and his donkey bringing up the rear." (p. 169) They reach the Bridge of Beruna where out of the water appears a River God, who asks for his chains to be loosened. The wood of the bridge grows into gay hedges and trees and then collapses into the river so that it becomes the Ford of Beruna again.

Perhaps the reader of classics may find associations in all this; but it must be remembered that the band of revellers with Bacchus and company is led by Aslan, who is Christ. We are told: "Everyone in the streets fled before their faces. . . ." The battle against the forces of darkness has been won; the followers of Miraz have fled. There seems to be some kind of spiritual revolution.

What exactly is radically changed?

> The first house they came to was a school: a girls' school, where a lot of Narnian girls, with their hair done very tight and ugly tight collars round their necks and thick tickly stockings on their legs, were having a history lesson. . . . (p. 170)

This lesson (it is dull history) is being conducted by a Miss Prizzle who is punitive towards her pupil, Gwendolen, among others. A row interrupts her.

> The walls became a mass of shimmering green, and leafy branches overarched overhead where the ceiling had been. . . . (p. 171)

Miss Prizzle finds she is clasping a rosebush rather than a desk.

> Wild people such as she had never even imagined were crowding round her. Then she saw the Lion, screamed and fled, and with her fled her class, who were mostly dumpy, prim little girls with fat legs. (p. 171)

What are we supposed to make of this? The Bacchanalian, it seems, is being revived, with Aslan-Christ's help: "nature" replaces sterility and tedium. But what is Miss Prizzle's offense and that of her "dumpy" girls, that a Christ figure should frighten them so? Some kind of liberation is going on, but what is its goal? Gwendolen hesitates.

> "You'll stay with us, sweetheart?" said Aslan.
> Instantly she joined hands with two of the Maenads who whirled her around in a merry dance and *helped her take off some of the unnecessary and uncomfortable clothes that she was wearing.* (p. 171; my Italics)

How much may she take off? Why is she excused from being a victim? How far can a Maenad go? Surely in some historical periods the Maenads went into frenzies, inflamed by drink as servants of a Bacchanal? Did they tear people to pieces? Did they perform religious sexual acts? How seriously can we take all this and what does it signify?

It is true that there is a general coming-to-life:

> At every farm animals came out to join them. Sad old donkeys who had never known joy grew suddenly young again. . . . (p. 171)

But then we have a revealing image:

> At a well in a yard they met a man who was beating a boy. The stick burst into flower in the man's hand. He tried to drop it, but it stuck to his hand. His arm became a branch, his body the trunk of a tree, his feet took root. The boy, who had been crying a moment before, burst out laughing and joined them. (p. 172)

Here I believe we may have a glimpse of a further source of Lewis's magic and his vision of Aslan's power: Aslan is a personal creature who can remedy a certain deathly element in the school atmosphere and who can stop the adult beating the child and so restore joy and life to the world when it was blighted by suffering and sorrow. We shall see the significance of this later.

As the revellers go on, they find a "tired-looking girl. . . . teaching arithmetic to a number of boys who looked like pigs." Aslan stops right under the window to look at her. The boys notice and look out of the window with "their mean little faces."

> Bacchus gave a great cry of *Euan, euoi-oi-oi-oi* and the boys all began howling with fright and trampling one another down to get out of the door and jumping out of the window. And it was said

afterwards (whether truly or not) that those particular little boys
were never seen again, but that there were a lot of very fine little
pigs in that part of the country which had never been there before.
(p. 173)

Again, one is not clear of the connection between Bacchus and
Christ: but here both are involved in frightening children they
take a dislike to, who (with an ambiguous disclaimer) are said
to have turned into pigs. It is comically said, but the comedy
seems cruel and we are invited to laugh at a humiliation. Meanwhile, Aslan-Christ takes over the tired teacher: "Now, Dear
Heart," said Aslan to the mistress; and she jumped down and
joined them.

In the next breath Aslan revives Caspian's old nurse, assisted
by Bacchus, who gives her water from the well which turns
into wine: ". . . the richest wine, red as red-currant jelly, smooth
as oil, strong as beef, warming as tea, cool as dew" (p, 174).
The old woman jumps out of bed; "Ride on me" says Aslan.
And so, "with leaping and dancing and singing," they come
to the place where the defeated army is surrendering "and Peter's
army, still holding their weapons and breathing hard, stood
round them with stern and hard faces." (p. 174)

The revival of the old woman, like that of Digory's mother,
gives another clue to the phenomenological meaning of Lewis's
fantasies of magic: Bacchus, the wedding at Cain, Christ, everything that Lewis can muster from myth is invoked to prevent
the mother from dying, and to restore the world to life which
had been blighted by depression and grief—intensified by being
beaten. But I anticipate. . . .

Here I simply want to draw attention to the fate of Miss
Prizzle, the dislike of the "dumpy" little girls and the boys
who look like pigs—so they are turned into pigs, or at least
are severely frightened. We are invited to be glad of this—and
throughout Lewis's fantasies *we are encouraged to be glad at
the humiliation of others.* It may be they are "bad" others, and
everything is arranged so that they "deserve" their humiliation.
However, to gloat on the humiliation even of "bad" characters
is not an attractive indulgence—and it is at such moments that
one cannot but have doubts about Lewis's fantasies, not least
when they are offered as "Christian."

At the end of *The Silver Chair*, there is a very powerful scene
in which King Caspian is restored to life by a thorn being thrust

into Aslan's paw: an evident piece of symbolism to do with the power of Christ's blood to resurrect. There follows a solemn discussion of life and death: most people have died (that is, have lost their faith) and people go from one world to another. Caspian wants to glimpse the children's world, and this includes "Experiment House." This is presumably a school developed on humanistic, rational, non-Christian principles.

*Aslan leads a punitive attack on this school*: he specifically directs a process of physical assault:

> "Daughter," said Aslan to Jill, "Pluck a switch off that branch." She did; and as soon as it was in her hand *it turned into a fine new riding crop*. (SC, p. 204; my italics)

The purpose of this weapon? To chastise Experiment House:

> "Now, sons of Adam, draw your swords," said Aslan. "But only use the flat, for it is cowards and children, not warriors, against whom I sent you." (SC, p. 204)

Aslan is not joining them, and they are only to see his back. We may notice, however, that the implication is that it is acceptable to use the flat of a sword on "cowards and children" if one hates their methods of education.

Again, one is invited to join in a *righteous humiliation*, performed in part by the symbolic embodiment of Christ: "Then Aslan roared so that the sun shook in the sky and thirty feet of the wall fell down before them . . . (SC, p. 204). Then Aslan "breathed upon them, and touched their foreheads with his tongue"—commending their attack on a kind of Dartington. However doubtful one might be of experiment in education, or even atheistical education, can we believe Christ might have roared in threat to it "so that the sun shook in the sky"? And how seriously can one take the combination of solemn Biblical language with a tone like that of Frank Richard's school stories?

> Most of the gang were there—Adela Pennyfather and Cholmondely Major, Edith Winterblott, "Spotty" Somer, Big Bannister and the two loathsome Garrett twins. But suddenly they stopped. Their faces changed, and all the meanness, conceit, cruelty and sneakishness almost all disappeared in one single expression of terror. For they saw the wall fallen down, and a lion as large as a young elephant lying in the gap and three figures in glittering clothes with weapons

in their hands rushing down upon them. For, *with the strength of Aslan in them*, Jill plied her crop on the girls and Caspian and Eustace plied the flats of their swords on the boys so well that in two minutes all the bullies were running like mad, crying out, "Murder! Fascists! Lions! It isn't fair!" (SC, p. 205; my italics)

It would be interesting to hear those who commend C. S. Lewis on his straight Christianity, on this method of dealing with enemies, even supposing them to be as mean and bullying as Lewis does. How are problems of prejudice, justice, and tolerance implicitly offered?

The head of the school has hysterics and goes to the police; but Aslan restores the wall and when the police arrive they find nothing except the head "behaving like a lunatic." So, in the interests of Christian triumph, even Christ, apparently, is willing to lend himself to the destruction of evidence and perversion of justice.

From that day forth things changed for the better at Experiment House, and it became quite a good school. (SC, p. 206)

The head is made an inspector "to interfere with other heads."

And when they found she wasn't much good at that, they got her into Parliament where she lived happily ever after. (SC, p. 206)

How serious is Lewis? As we have seen, people take him seriously; but surely here we have an example of that kind of lapse that made Owen Barfield accuse him of a *voulu* quality. There are disturbing shifts of tone, which surely must raise doubts. However, there is one thing about which Lewis is *always* solemn and serious: the need to chastise. Throughout all his work there are passages that invite the enjoyment of hurting and humiliating others:

At the sight of Aslan the cheeks of the Telmarine soldiers became the colour of cold gravy, their knees knocked together, and many fell on their faces. (PC, p. 175)

"Then take that, "said Reepicheep, "and that—to teach you manners—and the respect due to a knight—and a mouse—and a mouse's tail—" and at each word he gave Eustace a blow with the side of his rapier, which was thin, fine dwarf-tempered steel *and as supple and effective as a birch rod*. Eustace (of course) was at a school where they didn't have corporal punishment, so the sensation was quite new to him . . . it seemed to Eustace that the rapier as well as the pursuit was hot. *It might have been red-hot by the feel* . . . [he] went to his bunk. *He was careful to be on his side.* (VDT, p. 35; my italics)

Aslan can turn his enemies into donkeys:

"The hour has struck," said Aslan: and Rabadash saw, to his supreme horror, that everyone had begun to laugh.
They couldn't help it. Rabadash had been wagging his ears all the time and as soon as Aslan said, "The hour has struck" the ears began to change. They grew larger and more pointed and soon were covered with grey hair . . . everyone laughed louder and louder (because they couldn't help it) for now what had been Rabadash was, simply and unmistakably, a donkey. . . . (HB, p. 183)

Can one imagine Christ taking such a magical revenge? Early in the book the horse Shasta "feels glad" when the voice of Aslan tells him it was He who wounded Aravis and terrified Shasta. Is it the message that one should be glad to be chastised?

In *The Magician's Nephew* Uncle Andrew is not a pleasant character; he has made guinea pigs explode by his experiments. His humiliation at the hands of Narnian animals is characteristic:

. . . the Elephant walked quietly to the river, filled her trunk with water, and came back to attend to Uncle Andrew. The sagacious animal went on doing this till gallons of water had been squirted over him, and water was running out of the skirts of his frock coat as if he had been for a bathe with his clothes on . . . we must leave him to think over his wicked deeds (if he was likely to do anything so sensible). (MN, pp. 123-124)

How is it that Lewis's incitements to enjoy what, after all, seems to be cruelty has come to be accepted as a religious message, and good children's fiction? Because, I believe, it is offered as having a "corrective" message; and also because it is especially directed to those who *don't believe*. In a way it represents a kind of militant fundamentalism.

In *The Last Battle* we shall follow an orgy of conflict, and in the adult fantasies the feeling expressed by the protagonists is that in conflict they find their deepest sense of meaning and satisfaction. In *The Last Battle* the view is expressed that a warrior's life is infinitely superior to the life of peace. Jill declares ". . . I'd rather be killed fighting for Narnia than grow old and stupid at home and perhaps go about in a bath-chair and then die in the end just the same" (LB, p. 88).

Is this really a good "message" for the modern world?

In *The Voyage of the Dawn Treader* we shall look at the meaning of what is perhaps the most disturbing episode in Lewis's Narnia books—the "peeling" of Eustace, by Aslan, who removes from his body the flesh that he has acquired when he turned into a dragon. Here the problem is the disturbing feeling of self-loathing, of the loathing of being in the flesh, that the episode conveys.

These are some of the disturbing moments in Lewis's fantasies that seem to have a sadistic element, but we must link them with wider problems. Why is it that in his fables, effort in life, in relation to the conflicts in the inner world, has always to do with strengthening oneself:

> . . . If you must weep, sweetheart (this was to Jill) turn your face aside and see you wet not your bowstring. . . . (LB, p. 112)

Is it true that the world is full of threatening figures against which one must continually strive? And is it true that the only hope one has of winning against these powers is by frightening, threatening, controlling, or destroying them?

And hardening oneself to do so?

# 2

## The Lion, the Witch and the Wardrobe—The Way into "Narnia"

A phenomenological investigation of the modes of symbolism and consciousness reveals many things we take for granted—take for granted so much that we often don't stop to ask. Suppose we do? A title like that of Lewis's first fable for children offers a challenge—how do we connect a lion, a witch, and a wardrobe? It is the kind of challenge a preacher characteristically makes, and has done since the use of the *exemplum* in the Middle Ages (see Owst 1933). There is a tacit understanding between author and listener that these objects are offered as metaphors—just as objects in dreams and visions come as metaphors. The mode belongs to a long tradition in which moral and spiritual aspects of "the journey of life" are examined in terms of a journey as in *The Plain Man's Pathway to Heaven* or *Pilgrims Progress*. As a literary man, of course, Lewis knew many such allegories; and one can find in his fable writings elements from Spenser, medieval literature, the accounts of voyages of ancient saints (for example, Brendan) and so on.

As we have seen, Lewis himself tells us what the connection is between the wardrobe and the witch. As one of the illustrations in the Penguin edition makes clear, Digory takes the apple from the tree of life where a witch lurks to prevent him. He could only take this apple with the authority of the lion.

The Christian will see that as a test of obedience having to do with the forbidden fruit, Eden, and the Fall of Man. But who is the witch? If we put the Christianity in brackets and invoke psychoanalysis, we could argue that in going through the wardrobe the children are going through the mother's body as through the birth passage into another world, where the dead mother is to be found. She is there, in that world, and she has blighted it. The impulse to go into that world has to do with restoring her to life; but the problem is that since she is still the mother who rejected the child by dying, what happens if she is encountered, given new life, or brought back into this (real) world?

In exploring the possible meaning like this, I am also taking into account the meanings (as I see them) of George MacDonald's fantasies—fantasies that much influenced Lewis and that involve many processes of this kind. MacDonald, like Lewis, lost his mother as a young child; and all his work, I believe is compelled by the quest for the dead mother. MacDonald's work "baptized" Lewis into this phenomenological mode, as we shall see.

There is a whole literature that examines cases in which an individual's life is blighted by the presence in the inner world of an internalized *rejecting mother.*

In many psychoanalytical studies, human beings are found to have an unconscious fear of woman. In many case histories, in patients' reports of their dreams and fantasies, and in their drawings, there lurks a "phantom woman" who is often terrifying; and who threatens their well-being. This phantom woman is found in much literature—as, for instance, in the work of D. H. Lawrence (see, for example, the dreams of the character Somers in *Kangaroo,* Chapter V).*

This internalized hostile woman has to do with the natural processes by which we internalize the mother: we learn from the mother what it is to be human, and what it is to be feminine in our nature. But from the infant logic of our earliest experiences, we retain a fear of dependence on her. Once we were totally dependent upon this woman who had the power to bring us into life. Could she not have an equal power to take that life away? As Jungians believe, woman has a number of functions in our life—she creates us as mother, then she is our mater; and finally, as Mother Earth, she receives us back into her body, in death.** In Jungian studies there exists in the unconscious a dark side to both men and women, the Anima in men which can be negative and the Animus in women. Jungian studies of the witch in human symbolism see her embodying the opposite dynamics to those by which woman creates the child

---

*Cf. also *She, The Return of the Native, The Fairy Queen,* the myth of Melusine, Morgan le Fay, the *Medea, Macbeth,* and the myths of Lilith. See also my analysis of the phantom woman in the plays of James Barrie in *Images of Woman in Literature,* 1990.

**See Rosemary Gordon on D. H. Lawrence, *Journal of Analytic Psychology* 23, no. 3 (July 1978): p. 259.

(and we can glimpse this witch figure in a character like Lady Macbeth). This "Phantom Woman of the Unconscious," according to D. W. Winnicott, lies at the heart of much unfairness to woman throughout history (see also the work of Ann Ulanov, Bibliography).

Where individuals have had seriously disturbed experiences of the mother, or have had traumatic experiences of maternal bereavement, the phantom woman of the unconscious may haunt their lives. I first encountered this problem with the creative writing of a bereaved child: everything this girl of fourteen wrote in her English lessons was about the loss of her mother; and her fairy story was about confronting the internalized "bad mother" who had been left in her memory, thereby darkening her life (see *English for the Rejected* (Holbrook 1964), the case of "Rose"). In Marie von Naevestad's marvelous account of a patient dealing with a bad internal mother-imago, *The Colours of Rage and Love* (1979), the drawings show the woman patient thrusting good and modifying elements in her psyche "into mother." Until she can exorcise the ghost of a bad mother, she cannot fulfil herself as a woman. In an amazing case history described by Roland Kuhn in *Existence* (May et al., 1958), a butcher's boy, Rudolph, who had shot at a prostitute, was found to be impelled by fantasies about his dead mother. He had experienced an appalling upbringing, and had had as an infant, a traumatic experience of his mother's death. Many of his acts, some of them delinquent and criminal, had to do with his life-long need to find his mother again, and to experience "reflection" from her eyes. He was obsessed with glittering objects, for example, which symbolized the mother's eyes. His primary need was to complete mourning; but his deepest dread was that, by his acts which sought to refind the mother who was in the world of death, he would actually bring her from that world, and bring her out of fantasy into the world of reality. When the prostitute with whom he was spending his time undressed, he saw her genital as the gate to the other world, and so he had to try to kill her to prevent the phantom woman from entering reality, coming into this world.

Similar symbolic problems may be traced in the work of George MacDonald, by whom Lewis was so much influenced. MacDonald seeks to refind the dead mother, but is appalled at the prospect that when he does find her, she may turn out malignant. The impulse is to find the mother as the source of being, but when she is encountered in the world of death

she may be the same mother who offered the ultimate rejection—
by dying. All these phenomenological analyses help us to answer the question of who is the white witch, and they will
be expanded below.

But what then of Aslan? The answer perhaps is that the situation when the mother is lost the child's world is so dangerous
that a substitute authority is needed to deal with reality. Lewis,
like other individuals who suffered this trauma, was left with
a profound hunger to find the mother in order to complete
"being." The need is tremendous; and since it is an oral need,
to love and be loved—hence, a fierce lion is an appropriate
figure. Aslan doesn't eat anyone, but he growls and shows his
teeth. He has claws and he lacerates and unpeels people. The
oral element in Aslan's love must be seen in complex with
other oral elements in Lewis's work—Aslan sings the world
into being; Lewis himself feared to eat certain foods because
they might arouse sexual feelings; sin is eating Turkish Delight;
beatitude is eating heavenly food. Then there are creatures like
the Harfangs and odd references as to "eating a baby." But as
we shall see, Aslan's particular kind of minatory authority seems
to me to come from another source, from the internalization
of a figure *in loco parentis*.

The title of the first fable we examine virtually means, by
my phenomenological analysis, "the strong (oral) authority I
needed to invoke in my search through the birth-passage into
the world of death for my dead mother who, I feared, might
be a witch." The very fact that the fable is offered in terms
of such symbolism actually invites such an interpretation, and
to interpret is quite legitimate—as Lewis hinted he believed.

There are many common or archetypal features of this
kind of symbolic story—passages, books, mirrors, changes of
landscape—indeed a whole topography (as in Bunyan or Carroll's *Alice*) with metaphorical features with a body-meaning
significance, or a spiritual significance. There are castles, dun-
geons, lakes, seas, and, of course, *other worlds*, often approached
by holes in the ground, or through attics or passages. Besides
the Alice stories of Lewis Carroll, there are MacDonald's
*Phantastes* and *Lilith*; in the latter, a protagonist goes through
a mirror and by a stairway into such a world. A possible source
of the opening of the Narnia books is suggested in the biography
of Lewis by Green and Hooper, where they point out that Lewis
seems clearly to have echoed a short story written by E. Nesbit
that appeared in *Blackie's Christmas Annual*, 1908.

The story concerns a little girl who overhears an adult conversation and tries to put a situation right by mistaken efforts: she cuts flowers out of the greenhouse and sticks them in the flowerbed. For this, she is sent to Coventry, and "this time she would stay there."

> She was to spend the whole day alone in the best bedroom, the one with the fourpost bed, and the red curtains, and the large wardrobe with a looking-glass in it that you could see yourself in it, to the very ends of your strap shoes. . . .

She finds a strange kind of timetable, and in it she finds strange stations: "WHEREYOUWANTTOGOTO" is one and another is "BIGWARDROBEINSPAREROOM." She goes through the wardrobe, to another world, where she is complimented for her good deed and is reconciled to her aunt. The story is called *The Aunt and Annabel*. In *The Lion, the Witch and the Wardrobe*, the Faun speaks of the far land of "Spare Oom" and "the Bright City of Wardrobe"—and these suggest reminiscences of E. Nesbit's story. We know that Lewis was much influenced by E. Nesbit, and those who read the story will recognize elements in it that remained in Lewis's memory—the wish-fulfilment element (Annabel is faced with buttons you press which read WHATYOUWANTTOEAT,    WHATYOUWANTTODRINK,    and WHATYOUWANTTOREAD); the purified nature of things in the other world, such as a train made entirely of crystal with white satin cushions; and the way in which we return from the dream of a transformed world in the end. At the end Annabel and her aunt "are now the best of friends"; they do not speak of their meeting in the other world, "but of course they both know they have when you and they alike belong to the PEOPLE-WHO-UNDERSTAND."

As in many of the fantasies I have referred to about "other" worlds, the quest in these books often seems to be for *understanding*, however playful the mode. Whenever we get "there" and find what we are seeking, we shall *know*. Narnia is the realm where spiritual battles are fought; in the end it is the place where (everlasting) life begins. If indeed Lewis did read Nesbit's story in *Blackie's Christmas Annual*, at the moment when he was grieving for the death of his mother, what he picked up from it was the element of this achievement of understanding. (It must be said Lewis shows no sign of remembering the story as an adult.) In any case, the implicit search to understand the mystery of life (and death) by making one's way into another world is an element that appeals greatly to children.

At the beginning of The Lion, the Witch and the Wardrobe, Lucy has been in the "other" world; but the others do not believe her. What is Lewis's point here? He obviously believes that it is very important that we should recognize the existence of spiritual reality. This is something he aspires to teach us. But is he trying to teach us to be more imaginative, more insightful, or more "religious"? Lucy can move easily between the world of the spirit (I would say the "unconscious") and the world of everyday; but those who belong to the world of the common light-of-day are not able to accept reports from that "other" world, and are, indeed, hostile to its recognition:

> "Come on," said Peter, "that's going a bit too far. You've had your joke. Hadn't you better drop it now?" (LWW, p. 28)

Looked at realistically, "there is nothing but the back of the wardrobe." The others are imprisoned in the limitations of the materialism that cannot find the spiritual dimension:

> The others who thought she was telling a lie, and a silly lie too, made her very unhappy. (LWW, p. 29)

The implication of this (at the level of parish magazine theology) is that Christians know that there is a spiritual reality beyond that recognized by scientific positivism. Yet when they protest as much, they may be mocked. At the end of the book, the old Professor even suggests that they don't talk over much to one another of their experience of Narnia, and implies that one cannot get into it by the same route more than once, nor by will. But at the beginning Lucy is the one true believer, who suffers from the skepticism of the others:

> The two elder ones did this without meaning to do it, but Edmund could be spiteful. He sneered and jeered at Lucy and kept on asking her if she'd found any other new countries in other cupboards all over the house. (LWW, p. 29)

If we take the didactic implications, the problem now arises about how much we believe about the other world Lucy enters. Are we being asked to allow fantasy to explore all kinds of other possible worlds? Or are we being asked to accept that there is a special kind of actual spiritual world? George Macdonald wrote in *Lilith* (1895)

> Ah! the two worlds! So strangely are they one,
> And yet so measurelessly wide apart. . . .

To him the "other world" was the spiritual world. To me, that other world is the world of the unconscious. Much depends on what you believe here. Both Christian and phenomenologist can agree that "inner reality" is a primary preoccupation in human experience.

When the children ask the old Professor about the other world, he says "I wonder what they *do* teach at these schools." This is surely meant to imply that Peter and Susan find it hard to allow themselves to recognize "other worlds," because they have been given too rationalist and too literal an education: the kind of education Lewis fears may be given at Experiment House.

> "But do you really mean, Sir," said Peter, "that there could be other worlds—all over the place, just round the corner, like that?"
> "Nothing is more probable," said the Professor, taking off his spectacles and beginning to polish them. . . . (LWW, p. 49)

With Lewis in this vein, we might be inclined to agree, in an Arnoldian way, feeling that the apprehension of such "other" realities may be a source of sweetness and light. But Lewis's purpose is more straightforwardly homiletic: he wants to save us, and to save "England," and her children, by pressing upon us the literal reality of the Christian faith as we shall find it. To him the "other" world is not the world of imagination or the subjective life—it is a literally real spiritual world more primary (as it was to T. S. Eliot) than "this" world. We must submit ourselves completely to that world.

In the biography by Hooper and Green, a phrase is quoted about how we feel in Narnia, "a sensation not of following an adventure but of making a myth." Lewis himself spoke in lectures of how he felt "a fairy tale addressed to children, was exactly what I must write—or burst" (p. 237). The New Narnia at the end of *The Last Battle* is, as we shall see, Heaven:

> . . . putting out from the mountains of Aslan are all the *real* countries, one of which is that inner England which, Lewis believed, will never be destroyed. (Green and Hooper 1974, p. 25)

Lewis's was a very personal Christianity, with its own topography and idiosyncracies, and it is as literal as (say) the Christianity of the Jehovah's Witnesses, who also literally believe in demons.

Lewis's use of a lion to portray Christ perhaps developed out of certain theological discussions he had engaged in.* His biographers quote a letter from Evelyn Underhill on the subject of animal pain. Lewis had argued that the tame animal is the only natural animal, and Evelyn Underhill commended to his attention those animals that live in complete adjustment to nature apart from man: "I feel your concept of God would be improved by just a touch of wildness" (Green and Hooper 1974, p. 189).

So, when one of the children asks in The Lion, the Witch and the Wardrobe if Aslan is "safe," the reply is "safe? Who said anything about safe?" "Course he isn't safe. But he's good." "Aslan is a lion—the Lion, the great Lion."

In the "Narnia" books the Christian mythology centers in Lewis's portrayal of Christ as Aslan. Those who read attentively, however, may from the beginning be troubled by cerain doubts. For one thing, the outcome of the Apocalyptic story is predetermined: we learn of an ultimate magic that can never be overcome. No doubt this may raise problems within Christian belief, but do these fables not rely too heavily on this magic? While Aslan embodies love (albeit of a wild kind) and playfulness, he is also menacing. Throughout, his capacity to "puts things right" has a minatory quality, as when he shows his claws. That is, he is an absolute athoritarian figure who puts things right more by power and command than by eliciting inner redemption:

> Wrong will be right, when Aslan comes in sight;
> At the sound of his roar, sorrows will be no more,
> When he bares his teeth, winter meets its death,
> And when he shakes his mane, we shall have spring again.
> You'll understand when you see him.
>
> (LWW, p. 75)

---

*See Lewis's remarks on "The Place of the Lion" by Charles Williams in the letters to Arthur Greeves: "The lion of strength appears in the world" (p. 479, 26 February 1936). Martha Sammons points out that "Aslan" is the name for a lion in Turkish.

Significantly, Lucy asks, "Is—is he a man?"

> "Aslan a man!" said Mr Beaver sternly, "certainly not. I tell you
> he is the King of the Wood and the son of the great Emperor-beyond-
> the-sea. Don't you know who is the King of Beasts? Aslan is a
> lion—*the* Lion, the Great Lion." (LWW, p. 75)

At this level Aslan is the central figure in a didactic Christian
tale; the response of the children is that of a straightforward
Sunday school parable:

> "Ooh!" said Susan . . . "I shall feel rather nervous about meeting
> a lion. . . ."
> "I'm longing to see him," said Peter, "even if I do feel frightened
> when it comes to the point." (LWW, p. 75)

There is another prophecy:

> When Adam's flesh and Adam's bone
> Sits at Cair Paravel in throne,
> The evil time will be over and done.
>
> (LWW, p. 76)

The children are "sons of Adam and daughters of Eve." None
of this race have been in Narnia before. "So things must be
drawing near their end now he's come and you've come." Presumably Christians see this as a parable of the Second Coming?
The end of Adam's curse?

In trying to develop any kind of phenomenological interpretation, it seems sensible to be on the lookout for meanings in
Lewis's names, which evidently have a significance for him.

Some of the names defeat me: I cannot find any clues to
"Narnia" itself.* Other names seem more open to interpretation.
Surely "Cair Paravel," the palace of the Kings of Narnia, is
a place of beatitude. The words are charming coinages, and
obviously products of a literary mind. "Cair" suggests "Care"
while the "para" (as in *parapluie* and *parasol*) suggests protection; the name certainly has a flavor that suggests a state of
being happily cared for, a state of benignity, where "all manner
of thing shall be well." In such imaginings we can see the benign

---

*According to Marjorie Wright, Narnia is the name of an Italian town men-
tioned by Livy. See Sammons 1979, p. 147. She also points out that a "Court
Paravail" is one in position below another.

dynamic in Lewis's quest, for a curative magic, with elements derived from MacDonald's fantasies. In a short story by George MacDonald for instance that is a magic fluid called Carasoyn (= care + soin [Fr.]: see The Carasoyn in The Gifts of the Christ Child).

I am also interested, as I have said, in the topography, which as so often in such stories, seems to have a *bodily* meaning—much of which springs from unconscious memories of the mother's body—memories of infancy—as, for instance, with the Witch's palace:

> It seemed to be all towers; little towers with long pointed spires on them, sharp as needles. They looked like huge dunce's caps or sorcerer's caps. (LWW, p. 85)

These shapes, we may say, belong to the antithesis to the appropriate characteristics of woman; instead of the soft breast they seem to offer a threatening, spiky character with the power to humiliate. Instead of a female power they symbolize a bad male power, a power to *impinge*—the significance of which word will become clear later.

She has the power to *petrify*. In the courtyard of the witch's palace there are people turned to stone. Edmund is very frightened of a big stone lion—until he realizes it *is* stone. He supposes it is Aslan petrified. Being a bad one, he draws graffiti spectacles and a moustache on it, and jeers: "Yah! Silly old Aslan! How do you like being a stone? You thought yourself mighty fine, didn't you?" This is very much the kind of defensive insult one might find oneself offering as blasphemy in a nightmare. And then Edmund enters the palace as one might in a nightmare: almost at once he encounters the wolf Maugrim who takes him to the queen. These scenes in which Edmund moves seem full of menacing images of hate of a magical kind and the havoc it can wreak—as by dehumanizing people (and animals) and turning them into stone. The wolf (a symbol of oral voraciousness) seems to be some kind of vicious emissary from the queen with such menacing powers. She is a parental figure capable of unleashing the most menacing oral powers: the Castrating Mother, in short.

By contrast, the Beavers are what Winnicott called "the ordinary good home," good parents. They relax in their cave, and it is in their world that the snow is beginning to melt. This is the world of the benign father. *Father* Christmas arrives (whose significance is more in that he is *father* than *christmas*).

He was a huge man in a bright red robe (bright as holly berries) with a hood that had fur inside it and a great white beard that fell like a foam waterfall over his chest ... they felt very glad, but also solemn. (LWW, p. 98)

The witch's magic is weakening, under Aslan's power:

And Lucy felt running through her that deep shower of gladness which you only get if you are being solemn and still. . . . (LWW, p. 99)

Father Christmas distributes presents which are presumably meant to be symbolic of the potentialities Christianity offers:

"These are your presents" . . . "and they are tools not toys. The time to use them is perhaps near at hand. Bear them well!" With these words he handed to Peter a shield and a sword. The shield was the colour of silver and across it there ramped a red lion, as bright as a ripe strawberry at the moment when you pick it. (LWW, pp. 99–100)

Susan, Eve's daughter, is given a bow and a quiver full of arrows and a little ivory horn; Lucy a little bottle and a small dagger. The bottle contains a cordial made of the "juice of the fire-flowers that drew in the mountains of the sun."
The presents are meant to be benign, as the references to ripe strawberries and fire-flowers implies; but it is of significance that most of the gifts are instruments or weapons. Apart from Lucy's bottle, they seem (in psychoanalytical terms) phallic.
It is true that Father Christmas expresses some hesitancy about Susan or Lucy being involved in battles.

"Why sir?" said Lucy, "I think—I don't know—but I think I could be brave enough."
"That is not the point," he said.
"But battles are ugly when women fight. . . ." (LWW, p. 100)

As we shall see, the girls in Lewis's fables do become involved in battles, and they are warned not to cry because this is likely to wet their bowstrings; that is, to incapacitate them by emotion. The gifts include the restorative powers Lewis feels it necessary for the Christian to have. All the same, the gifts given to these children in the world of Narnia are for a coming battle; and as we shall see, Lewis's central concern throughout his fables is to present the world as a threatening place for dealing with which you have to prepare yourself with weapons and determination.

So Father Christmas, that is, does not give the children equipment to be *creative*, to love, or to triumph by reason, insight, or reparation, or means simply *to be*, in the world enjoying it.* What they are, in fact, given, is the equipment to solve one's problems by inflicting pain and death: in our modern jargon, defence weapons to be used in a Holy War, for which one has to toughen oneself.

Of course, in many fairy tales, if there are to be adventures there needs to be some kind of menace—giants or witches—and such fantasies hold the attention by creating an atmosphere of fear that echoes the child's fears. In many such tales the emphasis is on cunning, or on teaching bad characters to frustrate themselves, or on the power of love. Lewis's books nearly all end in battle, against enemies, by bravery.

There is no doubt in Narnia about the kind of threat the White Witch presents: "'. . . Kill whatever you find there,' she cried, sending off a wolf to the beavers' house." She turns a party of revellers to stone, and gives Edmund a "stunning blow on the face." She and her dwarf drive Edmund on; and they encounter signs of her spell of blight breaking, of springtime. The dwarf cries

> "This is Spring. What are we to do? Your Winter has been destroyed I tell you! This is Aslan's doing."
> "If either of you mention that name again," said the Witch, "he shall instantly be killed." (LWW, p. 112)

Leaving aside for the moment the question of what (in the Christian mythology) the White Witch represents, we can say that the positive impulse of the first "Narnia" book is to redeem the world that has been blighted by her and in which she offers the threat of annihilation. In this world, there are magical forces to rely upon: a robin who leads the children and Father Christmas. Edmund, however, raises the question of how human nature may be trusted; he is susceptible to temptation, and with him arises the question of the nature of sin. Only Edmund,

---

*For example, paint brushes, distaffs, flowers, musical instruments, sources of wisdom like books, or any earnests of "fertility." The exception is the juice, but even that is an instrument of healing to be used under battle conditions.

for instance, is doubtful of the benignity of the Beavers; and with him we encounter the problem of sin.

The episode with the Beavers is one of the most benign episodes in *The Lion, the Witch and the Wardrobe*. The Beavers represent a warmhearted, kindly domesticity such as a child may feel deprived of at a prep school, and may yearn for. Indeed, we may say that the Beavers are *love*. The Beavers are good parents, and their house, built on a dam, is the product of considerable labor, in relation to natural beauty and fecundity:

> ... where the water had been trickling over and spurting through the dam there was now a glittering wall of icicles, as if the side of the dam had been covered all over with flowers and wreaths and festoons of the purest sugar. (LWW, p. 66)

Such images of benign plenty are the best things in Lewis's Narnia fantasies. The Beavers work hard and their house is an "enormous beehive." It is counterset against the distant hills, where Edmund supposes the White Witch's house to be. With the Beavers we glimpse the reparative element in the story. One aim is to free the inner world, that other country of blight— to neutralize the White Witch so that the Pevensie children may become rulers there in allegiance with the "Good Powers" so that the child self may come into its own. Mrs. Beaver is an image of the Good Mother, working her sewing machine; she has been expecting the children: "So you've come at last!" she said. "At last! To think that ever I should live to see this day. . . ." The children are to become kings and queens of Narnia, and the talking animals know this is prophesied.

There is, however, one odd aspect of this world of the Beavers where Lewis perhaps shows himself oddly unaware of the child's feelings about eating things:

> ... all the children thought—and I agree with them—that there's nothing to beat good freshwater fish if you eat it when it has been alive half an hour ago, and has come out of the pan half a minute ago. (LWW, p. 70)

In the context of the benignity of the Robin and the Beavers in the fairytale mode in which these (talking) creatures are the children's friends, it seems odd to introduce a note of relish about eating other creatures (the nontalking sort). We may compare the insights of Lewis Carroll. When Alice speaks of her cat catching mice and birds to the animals in Wonderland, the animals are shocked; and Alice realizes her remarks have been in the worst possible taste. As I have already suggested, eating or taking things into oneself (like the Witch's Turkish Delight) have a profound significance throughout Lewis's tales. In truth children often have severe difficulties over things like catching and eating a fish, and here perhaps Lewis shows an odd insensitivity.

This leads us to the question of what is (morally) wrong with enjoying eating? It is a mark of Edmund's capacity for corruption that he enjoys the White Witch's Turkish Delight. This is his "sin"; and as a consequence, he becomes treacherous and betrays the Faun. What can this possibly mean in Christian mythology? Edmund is contaminated in his soul:

> The Queen took from somewhere among her wrappings a very small bottle which looked as if it were made of copper . . . she let one drop fall from it on the snow beside the sledge. Edmund saw the drop for a second in mid-air, shining like a diamond. . . . it was something he had never tasted before, very sweet and foamy and creamy, and it warmed him right down to his toes. . . .
> The Queen let another drop fall from her bottle . . . and instantly there appeared a round box, tied with green silk ribbon, which, when opened, turned out to contain several pounds of the best Turkish Delight. Each piece was sweet and light to the very centre and Edmund had never tasted anything more delicious. . . . Edmund . . . thought only of trying to shovel down as much Turkish Delight as he could, and the more he wanted to eat. . . . (LWW, p. 36)

Edmund is so busy eating that he doesn't see he is being interrogated. "She got him to tell her that he had one brother and two sisters, and that one of his sisters had already been in Narnia and had met a Faun there. . . ." This is, of course, to betray them to death.

The Queen has soliloquized to herself: "A door from the world of men! I have heard of such things. This may wreck all. But he is only one, and he is easily dealt with." Edmund has entered from the real world into the world of fantasy. Lucy, at the end of the chapter is on the side of the fauns and the animals, while Edmund is "more than half on the side of the Witch." He intends to keep his secret in spite of having spoken to the White Witch, even though he knows that she is hated, turns people into stone, and does "all kinds of horrible things."

Elsewhere in Lewis's fantasies the symbolism of hunger for the breast is clear, as in Perelandra. There is symbolism of intense oral hunger behind the fantasies, and here the liquid of-

fered by the Witch seems like (magic) breast-milk ("very sweet
and foamy and creamy"). As we shall see, at the end of all
the Narnia stories, the children feed on heavenly food; and
again, this seems like the breast. What is the difference between
enjoying the Witch's breast and the breast of heaven? The answer
must be given in Kleinian terms of the difference between Good
Breast and Bad Breast.

Bad breast has the same kind of vengeful magic by which
the White Witch destroys people. "Mr Tumnus," the faun, has
suffered magic petrifaction:

> "There's not many taken in there that ever comes out again. Statues.
> All full of statues they say it is—in the courtyard and up the stairs
> and in the hall. People she's turned"—(he paused and shuddered)
> "turned into stone." (LWW, p. 73)

The children want to tackle the problem of the fate of the faun.
But is it any good *their* trying? However, now "Aslan" is "on
the move." Who is Aslan?

> "He's the King. He's the Lord of the whole wood, but not often
> here, you understand. . . . But the word has reached us that he
> has come back. He is in Narnia at this moment. He'll settle the
> White Queen all right." (LWW, p. 74)

He won't be turned to stone: "If she can look him in the
face it'll be the most she can do. . . ." So, the whole adventure
is conceived from the start in terms of confrontation, between
forces threatening annihilation or petrification, and those standing for "life": Aslan has a counteracting magic.

But what is *wickedness*? How should we take Edmund's corruption, by the White Witch's temptation? Is is that a pagan
greed and selfishness (*Turkish* Delight) will make us treacherous
to our own natures and to others? Edmund's badness, it should
be noted, doesn't come from within: it is introduced into him.
Edmund has been poisoned in his mind:

> "He had the look of one who has been with the Witch and eaten
> her food. You can always tell them if you've lived long in Narnia;
> something about their eyes. . . ." (LWW, p. 80)

The last phrase is interesting, because there is a schoolboy
legend that if you masturbate it can be seen in your eyes. We
shall later look at a poem of Lewis's about how Lilith tempts
one to masturbate. Edmund's sin, though it is not made plain,

is to be seduced by the Witch into self-indulgent pleasure as one is tempted to masturbate. This is *sin*. And although Peter says "He is our brother after all, *even if he is rather a little beast*. And he's only a kid. . . ." Edmund is now presented as virtually a different kind of creature: a baddie through and through. He is now an "enemy" and is treated as if he were wholly black (except that Aslan talks to him privately while the author tells us he need not reveal what Aslan said). Sin for Lewis thus seems to be something thrust into one by bad "forces," which sets one apart (and yet Christ is prepared to die for us).

Edmund does not enjoy the Beaver's dinner because of his indulgence in Bad Breast: "There's nothing that spoils the taste of good ordinary food half so much as the memory of bad magic food." He imagines the others are taking no notice of him and are trying to give him the cold shoulder: "They weren't but he imagined it." So the Witch's food makes Edmund paranoid. But he isn't yet totally malevolent.

> You mustn't think that even now Edmund was quite so bad that he actually wanted his brothers and sisters to be turned to stone. (LWW, p. 82)

Yet the bad magic food is powerful enough to prompt Edmund to something more than sibling rivalry:

> He did want Turkish Delight and to be a Prince (and later a King) and to pay Peter out for calling him a beast. . . . (LWW, p. 82)

> And he thought about Turkish Delight and about being a King ("And I wonder how Peter will like that?" he asked himself) and horrible ideas came into his head. (LWW, p. 67)

What exactly is the nature of Edmund's "sin?" One of the reader's problems is to find the right sense of proportion. Did Christ die to save small boys from peccadillos? Behind Edmund one senses a serious preoccupation with guilt, and betrayal. But elsewhere the tone lapses, and the language and development of events sinks to the level of Greyfrair's School stories or E. Nesbit.*

---

*Astonishingly, the biographers call her "a slipshod writer where style was concerned," and one who delighted in clichés. I find E. Nesbit a much more sympathetic writer than Lewis; her writing has more realism, charm and originality.

The White Witch " . . . was jolly nice to me, anyway, much nicer than they are." There is a Sunday school kind of moral parable: "Deep down inside him he really knew that the White Witch was bad and cruel." But beneath the childish story there is a sinister preoccupation with Edmund's treachery that has a gravity that is not only didactic. The threat of petrifaction and death feel menacing, while what we thought was a mere child's tale takes on an ominous quality, in the tone of the author's voice. As we go on reading Lewis's fantasies, we shall find similar difficulties in our response to Aslan. The Beaver introduces him: "They say Aslan is on the move—perhaps has already landed."

This produces one of Lewis's poetic enconiums on the magic of Christ-the-Lion's influence:

> And now a very curious thing happened. None of the children knew who Aslan was any more than you do; but the moment the Beaver had spoken these words, everyone felt quite different. Perhaps it has sometimes happened to you in a dream that someone says something which you don't understand but in the dream it feels as if it had some enormous meaning—either a terrifying one which turns the whole dream into a nightmare or else a lovely meaning too lovely to put into words, which make the dream so beautiful that you remember it all your life and are always wishing you could get into that dream again. (LWW, p. 65)

The language and the manner of telling are appropriate to the age of ten; the acceptance of "Aslan" is expressed in terms of delicious sensations and childish feelings. It is significant that for Peter the effect of the name Aslan is to make him feel "brave and adventurous":

> At the name Aslan each one of the children felt something jump in its inside. Edmund felt a sensation of mysterious horror. Peter felt suddenly brave and adventurous. Susan felt as if some delicious smell of some delightful strain of music had just floated by her. And they got the feeling you have when you wake up in the morning and realise that it is the beginning of the holidays or the beginning of summer. (LWW, p. 65)

The scenes that develop with the children involve the strange mixture of classical and Christian mythology already noted: there are the Tree-Women and Well-Women (Dryads and Naiads); centaurs, a unicorn, an eagle, and a great dog. But the most serious prose is still reserved for the description of Aslan:

> People who have not been in Narnia sometimes think that a thing
> cannot be good and terrible at the same time. If the children had
> ever thought so, they were cured of it now. For when they tried
> to look at Aslan's face they just caught a glimpse of the golden
> mane and the great, royal, solemn overwhelming eyes; and they
> found they couldn't look at him and went all trembly. . . . His voice
> was deep and rich and somehow took the fidgets out of them. . . .
> (LWW, p. 117)

Phrases like "took the fidgets out of them" and "went all
trembly" are somewhat coy and avuncular; and we have the
sense of an older man writing for children, imagining how children might feel about a religious hero for themselves—with
a touch of didacticism. For instance when the question of
Edmund crops up, Peter confesses his past; and "something"
makes him say "That was partly my fault, Aslan. I was angry
with him and I think that helped him go wrong. . . ." "All shall
be done," said Aslan, "but it may be harder than you think."
Lewis is clearly trying to convey to children his own brand
of Christian homiletics—improving human nature may be more
difficult than one imagines; grace does not come easy.
A sterner note is struck, over the symbolism of Aslan, when
it comes to his "wildness":

> The Lion shook his mane and clapped his paws together. ("Terrible
> paws" thought Lucy, "if he didn't know how to velvet them.") (LWW
> p. 118)

The enthusiasm for being inspired by Aslan leads to a certain
enthusiasm for that impulse to be brave and adventurous. Aslan
is concerned that Prince Peter should win his spurs. Above
all it is this kind of choice and action which C. S. Lewis endorses
(and makes Aslan preeminently endorse) in his young protagonists. At a certain dramatic moment, a Wolf leaps into the pastoral scene—and Peter uses his sword.

> As it was—though all this happened too quickly for Peter to think
> at all—he had just time to duck down and plunge his sword, as
> hard as he could, between the brute's forelegs into his heart. Then
> came a horrible, confused moment like something in a nightmare.
> He was tugging and pulling and the Wolf seemed neither alive nor
> dead, and its bared teeth knocked against his forehead and every-
> thing was blood and heat and hair. . . . (LWW, p. 120)

Susan comes down the tree. "She and Peter felt pretty shaky when they met and I won't say there wasn't kissing and crying, on both sides. But in Narnia no one thinks any the worse of you for that."

As we shall see, such moments are the highest *spiritual* achievements in Lewis; but they are also expressed in a language which gives them a kind of excitement, about pain, struggle, cruelty and execution, about which we shall become increasingly doubtful.

In the above fight Peter has won his spurs, but then there is the insistence from Aslan that *he must clean his sword.* This particular preoccupation becomes quite·obsessional throughout the "Narnia" books:

> "You have forgotten to clean your sword." It was true. Peter blushed when he looked at the bright blade and saw it all smeared with the Wolf's hair and blood. (LWW, p. 121)

In Lewis's fantasies, people experience a special kind of euphoria when killing. Afterwards, while they are not guilty about the killing, they do blush to see the blood and hair on their swords. This guilt has to be overcome and the cleaning of the sword is also a guarantee that one won't allow oneself to be vulnerable if surprised in the future. The girls on their part have to be careful not to wet their bowstrings—as by weeping. In the private world of Lewis's personal mythology these almost fetishistic preoccupations have considerable importance, as we shall see.

From first reading The Lion, the Witch and the Wardrobe, the reader becomes aware of a wide variety of styles, and finds a great contrast between a tone appropriate to a tale for children, and a much more serious, grim note that seems to belong to another kind of fantasy altogether. At times, the child reader is clearly in view: "She knew it was very silly to shut oneself up in a wardrobe, even if it is not a magic one."

When the children find themselves in Narnia, because it is cold, they put on the fur coats that are in the wardrobe:

> The coats were rather too big for them so that they came down to their heels and looked more like royal robes than coats when she had put them on. (LWW, p. 54)

At best this tale-telling mode conveys a paternal respect for children and an admiration of their energy and courage. At times, unfortunately, this mode lapses into the use of a "prep-school" language and ethos. When Edmund reveals his treachery to Lucy, for instance, the language and emotion sinks to the level of *The Magnet* and *Gem*:

> There was a dead silence. "Well, of all the poisonous little beasts—" said Peter, and shrugged his shoulders and said no more.... Edmund was saying to himself, "I'll pay you all out for this, you pack of stuck-up, self-satisfied prigs!" (LWW, p. 55)

Then there is a different note altogether, as when he describes the discovery of the Faun's victimization. The language takes on a new gravity and the fantasy a certain grim intensity:

> The door had been wrenched off its hinges and broken to bits. Inside, the cave was dark and cold and had the damp feel and smell of a place that had not been lived in for several days. Snow had drifted in from the doorway and was heaped on the floor, mixed with something black, which turned out to be the charred sticks and ashes from the fire. Someone had apparently flung it about the room and then stamped it out. The crockery lay smashed on the floor and the picture of the Faun's father had been slashed into shreds with a knife. (LWW, pp. 55–56)

The same is true of the scenes of the humiliation of Aslan, before his "crucifixion":

> "Stop!" said the Witch. "Let him first be shaved."
> Another roar of mean laughter went up from her followers as an ogre with a pair of shears came forward and squatted down by Aslan's head. Snip—snip—snip went the shears and masses of curling gold began to fall to the ground.... "Why, he's only a great cat after all!" (LWW, p. 139)

It seems clear at such moments that Lewis has touched on a deeper vibration in himself, at the level of his own nightmares. The scene is disturbing, because of an undercurrent of very deep anxiety, which we shall examine. The author is evidently aware of the problem of how powerfully he can disturb his readers. He even says in one place there were ". . . other creatures whom I won't describe because if I did the grown-ups would probably not let you read this book." The beastliness of the crowd calling, "Puss, puss! Poor pussy," at the humiliated lion, is evidently intended to call out anger in the child reader—an anger that is later invoked and directed against the evil mob: encouraging them rather to hate them than to forgive them in the spirit of "they know not what they do." Under the surface, one detects a seething rage, in which Lewis seeks to involve the child reader.*

Grim, too, with the attempted execution of Edmund in the background, is the actual stabbing of Aslan:

> The Witch bared her arms as she had bared them the previous night. . . . It looked to the children, when the gleam of the torchlight fell on it, as if the knife were made of stone, not of steel, and it was a strange and evil shape. (LWW, p. 140)

In Lewis's conscious mind, the shape is that of the stone daggers of prehistoric cults. But there is another unconscious element in that phrase about "a strange and evil shape": surely what must be aroused in the child's mind is the unconscious fear of parental intercourse, in which there are dangers of the destructive phallus?** If we read the episode carefully, and bear in mind psychoanalytical interpretations, we must surely recognize here the *Primal Scene*; and see that the fear it arouses is related to the fear of talion retribution from the combatants as in the infant's frightening fantasy of the "combined parents"? What these terms mean will become clear later. Here it is sufficient to say that the powerfulness of these scenes has to do with the element in them which evokes infantile fantasies of parental sexual intercourse, full of dangers and threats at the unconscious level. What we may note here, I believe, is that such episodes have a sadomasochistic and sexual undercurrent that we certainly do not feel as we read the story of Christ. They are a special element in the private mythological fantasy of the unconscious that the facade of "Christian fable" conceals.

A phenomenological analysis reveals that the very disturbing castration scene here is grave in tone because it derives from the fear of death. In Freudian and post-Freudian discourse, the word *castration* applied to fantasies really means something more like *annihilation*. As we have seen, in these grimmer areas of Lewis's fantasies a certain paranoid-schizoid tension develops around a fear of going out of existence.*** Such episodes thus

---

*The same effect on the reader is prompted by a diabolical jeer about Christ's last cry, in *Perelandra*, to justify a particularly sadistic incident. See below p. 236.

**If this is thought to be exaggerated, let the reader compare the symbolism in D. H. Lawrence's *The Woman who Rode Away* where the heroine is put to death by a huge stone phallus.

***In Lewis's fantasy for adults, *Till We Have Faces*, there is an actual castra-

take on a nightmarish quality. I believe the force of these scenes
is only explicable in some such terms as those of Melanie Klein's
accounts of infant fantasy. They arise (as I believe) from the
child Lewis's perplexities over what killed his mother. Was it
sexual intercourse? And may not the same danger (of the Primal
Scene and the combined parents) turn on him?

The castration theme becomes clear in *The Lion, the Witch
and the Wardrobe* when the White Witch prepares Edmund's
sacrifice, at the beginning of Chapter 13 (*Deep Magic from the
Dawn of Time*).

> "Then," said the Dwarf, "we had better do what we have to do
> at once."
> "I would like to have it done on the Stone Table itself," said
> the Witch. "That is the proper place. That is where it had always
> been done before." (LWW, p. 123))

Edmund is now reduced to "it":

> "Now?" she said, "we have no table—let me see. We had better
> put it against the trunk of a tree." (LWW, p. 123)

As we have seen, the White Witch has the power to turn people
to stone at once—since it is instantaneous, there is no groaning
or screaming and so it is merciful. Here it is obvious that she
intends to do something sadistic to Edmund, almost certainly
cut his throat, while he is divested of personal qualities by
being called an "it."

The moment is very frightening, and resembles moments of
symbolic castration in the James Bond thrillers of Ian Fleming.
Examined carefully, the appeal of such fantasies lies in the
way they touch on our deepest (schizoid) fears of depersonalization and annihilation. Here the prose takes on an unusual excitement, quite different from the child's adventure or Sunday
school parable mode. There is a particular emphasis on naked
flesh, and whiteness:

> He saw the Witch take off her outer mantle. Her arms were bare
> underneath it and terribly white. Because they were so white he
> could see them, but he could not see much else, it was so dark
> in this valley under the dark trees.

---

tion, while terrible mutilations are common in those adult fantasies of his.
In *The Last Battle* I believe there is a cosmic scene of the "combined parents."

"Prepare the victim," said the Witch. And the Dwarf undid Edmund's collar and folded back his shirt at the neck. Then he took Edmund's hair and pulled his head back so that he had to raise his chin . . . Edmund heard a strange noise—whizz-whizz-whizz. . . . It was the sound of a knife being sharpened. (LWW, p. 124)

Edmund is rescued in the nick of time. The Witch becomes "an old stump" and the dwarf a boulder. They are depersonalized in their turn:

If you had gone on looking you would gradually have begun to think there was something odd about both the stump and the boulder. And next you would have thought that the stump did not look really remarkably like a little fat man crouching on the ground* . . . the stump and the boulder were simply the Witch and the Dwarf. . . . (LWW, p. 125)

Though the Witch is in her turn castrated by becoming a "stump", we may also note that she holds onto her power (in Freudian terms, hold onto her penis, her magic male phallic power**): "She has kept hold of her wand, so it had been kept safe, too." The whole episode, we must point out again, is redolent with unconscious castration anxiety; and, indeed, it is very frightening, because of this.

One's doubts about Lewis's episode here are not, of course, merely directed at the fact that it is frightening (many fairy tales are). What one is interested in are the words and images which arise from the underlying obsession with the hints of sexual maiming: the whiteness, the dark valley, the woman's arms, the throat, the knife, the stump. But the "creative" question is—is the underlying fear of being annihilated resolved? Is the nightmare modified by any reaching out toward insights that humanize it? Or is the dread aroused for other purposes?

The scene that follows was obviously regarded by Lewis as a high moment. His language becomes quite "Shakespearean": "Here is your brother," he said "and—there is no need to talk to him about what is past."

---

*This is an odd sentence: should it not have been "you could have wondered—did not the stump look really . . . "?
**See below clues to this phenomenon when Jadis tears a crossbar from a lamp post to attack Aslan with. It falls to the ground and (appropriately) begins to grow into a new lamp post.

That is, by certain archaisms ("what is past," "Sire," "craves audience") Lewis seeks to raise the dramatic tension, though much of his language here hardly rises above banality ("It'll be all right." . . . "Fall back, all of you," said Aslan). So we are never quite sure at what level to take the incident, even though by his "comic relief" (remarks by Mr. Beaver), Lewis shows he wants it to be solemn.**

Of course, in terms of the Christian parable, presumably what is happening is that Edmund, because he has eaten Turkish Delight, is Fallen Man. The White Witch must have blood:

> ". . . unless I have blood as the Law says all Narnia will be over-turned and perish in fire and water."
> "It is very true," said Aslan, "I do not deny it." (LWW, p. 129)

There is a "deep Magic" that cannot be questioned. ("'Work against the Emperor's Magic?' said Aslan, turning to her with something like a frown on his face. And nobody ever made that suggestion to him again.") This is God's plan for the world. The White Witch is aware that this ultimate will cannot be thwarted, even by Aslan:

> "Fool," said the Witch with a savage smile that was almost a snarl to the Bull, "do you really think your master can rob me of my rights by mere force? He knows the Deep Magic better than that. . . ."
> (LWW, p. 129)

This magic, which the "Emperor put into Narnia at the very beginning," laid down that ". . . Every traitor belongs to me as my lawful prey and that for every treachery I have a right to kill. . . ." She is really the Emperor's hangman in a sense (as Mr. Beaver pronounces, to be told "Peace, Beaver" by Aslan). Aslan's authoritarian manner should be noticed and the implicit reliance on an *absolute* control by the powers of heaven.

How possible is it to reconcile the Christian story with the adventure?** One might say that the great achievement of the Christian religion is its emphasis on inwardness; grace, and

---

*The way in which his tone and language can let him down is evident on p. 132: "Of course everyone was dying to ask him how he had *arranged matters* with the Witch" (my italics). This, about the pact between Aslan as Christ and the White Witch, to undergo crucifixion!

**Stephen Prickett sees the incident as "artistically fraudulent" because of its theological naivety; the White Witch doesn't know some of the hidden rules. See *New Universities Quarterly* 33, no. 3: pp. 263–64.

redemption; but attention to inward grace is scanty in Lewis's fantasies. His morality is essentially black and white. Take Edmund's treachery, for example. Edmund has foolishly betrayed his siblings—but for a child to do so, when so ignorant and immature, is this so serious? (He didn't *want* his siblings to be turned to stone.) How does this amount to a crime that deserves a death? And how is it an analogy, leading to Christ's sacrifice for Fallen Man? (Do we really see it as a restatement of the doctrine of Atonement by substitution?) Was Christ's sacrifice a ransom paid to the devil?

Edmund's treachery did lead to the petrifaction of the Faun. In some way his greed and moral weakness have led to at least one castration by the powerful Witch. The hostile magic by which she is equipped can, it seems, even overcome the male strength of Aslan. In her presence, the dread is deep: "Though it was bright sunshine everyone suddenly felt cold. . . . " No one is at ease—except Aslan and the Witch. "It was the oddest thing to see these two faces—the golden face and the dead-white face. . . . "

We see (in the illustration in the Penguin edition) Aslan and the Witch walking together in conversation: unconsciously the artist has drawn them (appropriately) like mummy and daddy. Aslan is seeking to save Edmund from the Witch. How does he do that? By offering himself to be crucified, in a bargain that is actually a cheat because the Witch doesn't know the deepest rules?

If we take seriously the church's injunction to study the Narnia books as vehicles of heavenly truth, we may have a number of perplexing questions to ask. Was Christ's sacrifice occasioned like this by some Lilith force that demanded a quota of blood—without the payment of which the world must end? Would a child's peccadillo (such as would be hardly sufficient in our society to bring him before a headmaster, let alone a magistrate) make it necessary for Christ to suffer crucifixion? Surely in terms of the artistic quality of the story, the concept of wickedness here is inadequate? Here there is no pride, arrogance, cruelty, viciousness, or malevolence such as man is capable of: only a child's petulant sulkiness, his touch of prep-form beastliness, and his betrayal of his brothers and sisters by ignorance, and lack of forethought while he is in a state generated in him by some kind of poison, with which he has been seduced. In fact, all the time everyone is, in any case, under powerful magical influences from a very cunning White Witch. Can we accept the message that Christ's agony was a price to be paid for such petty lapses, in a heavily controlled situation, even in a story for children? The concept of sin seems very limited; and there are few insights into human weakness, such as are one often encounters in Grimm or Andersen.

If we examine the analogues with the Gospel stories, the fable seems a bit thin: thinner than it need be even for a naive readership. In Chapter 14 we are supposed to see Aslan's gloomy mood as the mood of Christ in the wilderness. If one remembers this anguish as rendered by Handel or Bach—or even the simple medieval mystery plays—the level of language and art here is too callow: "I've a most horrible feeling—as if something were hanging over us. . . ."

There are even echoes from the Garden of Gethsemane:

"Oh children, children, why are you following me?"

" . . . I should be glad of company tonight," he says.

"Yes, you may come, if you will promise to stop when I tell you, and after that leave me to go on alone." (LWW, p. 135)

The scenes are an odd mixture of this feeble kind of story for children, and another mode that develops a deep emotional energy:

After a lot of working at it (for their fingers were cold and it was now the darkest part of the night) . . . they succeeded. And when they saw his face without it they burst out crying again and kissed it and fondled it and wiped away the blood and the foam as well as they could. And it was all more lonely, and hopeless and horrid than I know how to describe. (LWW, p. 143)

A crowd of mice come and nibble at the lion's bonds, and so the scene is an odd combination of fairy story and nightmare. And, yet again, the tone and language lapses into banality: "It's too bad—they might have left the body alone" (p. 146).

Lewis seeks both to insist that his myth is true ("Jesus lives!"); but yet resorts to magic, with the assertion that the Emperor's magic is superior. The stone table breaks and Aslan reappears, shaking his mane, which has immediately grown again. He isn't a ghost: he is real: "Oh, you're real, you're real! Oh, Aslan!" As Aslan explains, everything is brought about by superior forms of magic overcoming not-so-superior magic: "Though the Witch knew the deep Magic there is a magic deeper still which she did not know." Death itself is now "working backwards" because the Witch only knew as far back as the dawn of time:

> But if she could have looked a little further back, into the stillness and darkness, she could have read there a different incantation. (LWW, p. 148)

This duplicity is encountered throughout Lewis. He believed (as we shall see) Christianity to be the one myth that was true. So even as he tells a fairy tale in which miracles happen by magic, he assumes a tone and manner which have behind them a conviction that these things are real and true (as with his belief in demons).

But in the unconscious mythology of the tale, I believe we have reached a crisis, too. The tables have been turned on the Witch by putting Aslan, whatever he stands for, to the ultimate test. So now it is safe for the girls to indulge in libidinal play with the lion. What is interesting is the intense sensuality of this romp. At first it might seem "sexual," but we may remember W. R. D. Fairbairn's suggestion that to the infant the feeling should really be described as "sensual."*

> Then he made a leap high over their heads and landed on the other side of the Table. Laughing, though she didn't know why, Lucy scrambled over it to reach him. Aslan leaped again. A mad chase began. Round and round the hill-top he led them, now hopelessly out of reach, now letting them almost catch his tail, now diving between them, now tossing them in the air with his huge and beautifully velvetted paws and catching them again, and now stopping unexpectedly so that all three of them rolled over together in a happy laughing heap of fur and arms and legs. It was such a romp as no one has ever had except in Narnia; and whether it was more like playing with a thunderstorm or playing with a kitten Lucy could never make up her mind. And the funny thing was that when all three lay together panting in the sun the girls no longer felt in the least tired or hungry or thirsty. (LWW, p. 148)

When I first studied that, I thought it was an analogy with sexual intercourse, ending with the girls and Aslan lying "together panting." There follows a ride ("You must ride on me.". . . . "the most wonderful thing that happened to them

---

*"Fundamental Principles of Psychoanalysis," *Edinburgh Medical Journal*, June 1929, pp. 340–41: see on this Guntrip 1961, p. 258.

in Narnia") ecstatically described, and this ride takes them to the Witch's Castle which is "all pointed towers." All of this could well be interpreted in a Freudian way as an episode of the sexual act, but I believe it is more insightful if we try to understand it in terms derives from post-Freudians like Winnicott. It has something to do with *the need for play*, the need to reexperience the mother's body and response (a theme which persists throughout George MacDonald's fantasies by which Lewis was so influenced).

At any rate, this play experience leads to a new potency in the engagement with experience—the Witch's victims, for instance, are now to be released from petrifaction. A Jungian critic sees the episode as symbolizing triumph over the *mother's* power. There is perhaps some truth in this because the White Witch has been allowed to do her damndest, and yet the protagonists have survived. They have been released to play, and so to begin to learn *to be*. But I believe we should approach certain aspects of the Narnia books, the romps with Aslan, the weapons given by Father Christmas (including the "ramping" strawberry on Peter's shield) and even the violence in battle as forms of play—sometimes perhaps desperate play—direct at completing certain processes, as in infancy and infant play, of "finding reality."

In exploring Lewis's symbolism, as I have said, I am putting his Christianity "in brackets." This is most helpful over the main symbolic character, Aslan. From my phenomenological viewpoint, he is rather seen as a big guide dog or powerful pet. There are two curious things about Aslan. One is that he is a male. The other is that he is an animal. How do we account for these features?

The play scenes just discussed reveal Aslan as a kind of pet. In a children's story this is wholly appropriate: children find it difficult to deal with the deepest human problems in terms of whole human beings. In their dreams and culture they do, however, love to explore human characteristics, and the dynamics in their own human nature in terms of animal symbols (wolves, dogs, dragons, robins and so on). In dreams, such animal figures represent elements in their intrapsychic world; and they act out the dreams of the soul for us. Aslan and the Faun both emerge as prominent figures in the fantasies of Lewis who was, as we know from biographical evidence, very strongly affected by dreams and nightmares.

"Narnia" itself began, he tells us "with seeing pictures in my head." "At first they were not a story, just pictures. *The*

*Lion* began with a picture of a faun carrying an umbrella and parcels in a snowy wood. The picture was in my mind when I was about sixteen. Then one day when I was about forty, I said to myself, 'Let's try to make a story about it.' Later, the lion 'bounded in': He pulled the whole story together, and soon he pulled the other six stories in after him" (Green and Hooper 1974, p. 246).

Both the Faun and Aslan offer qualities which are of the kind sought for, in the child's fantasy, in seeking love in pet objects. In thinking about Aslan and his role in this fantasy, I felt there were clues in a case history discussed by John Bowlby in his work on attachment and loss. He discusses the case history of a child who had lost his mother at the age of five, and was unable to show any emotional reactions to those near him. In analysis, Bowlby's child patient

. . . described how through several years of later childhood he used to leave his bedroom door open "in the hope that a large dog would come to him, be very kind to him, and fulfil all his wishes." (Bowlby 1967, p. 149)

Associated with this fantasy was a vivid childhood memory of a bitch which had left four puppies alone and helpless when she had died shortly after their birth. The child had seriously hostile memories of the mother and in consequence he "grew up gravely impoverished." As Bowlby argues, there is a need in such cases to complete the process of mourning, so that the person may be restored to a life of feeling and attachment.

Lewis reports that as he began on the first book, "suddenly Aslan came bounding into it. I think I had been having a good many dreams of lions about that time. Apart from that, I don't know where the Lion came from or why he came" (Green and Hooper 1974, p. 240). It is interesting that Lewis gives Aslan a capital 'L' thus indicating he believes Aslan "is" Christ. The lion surely bounds out of Lewis's own subconscious, like the dog in the wish-fulfilment dreams of the bereaved child of five discussed above: an animal that would "be very kind to him, and fulfil all his wishes." In this is the the origin of Lewis's heavy reliance on Aslan as having unlimited powers of *magic*.

The other aspect of Aslan is his tactile quality, with his mane, and his creative powers (as when he "sings" Narnia into being). In my "bracketted" terms, he is less Christ than a substitute for the lost mother and here one might make analogies with the North Wind in George MacDonald's *At the Back of the North Wind*: she is a manifestation of MacDonald's intense need for further *experience of the mother's body* (especially her hair). (She is also stern and sometimes implacably cruel.)

All this explains how the relationship between the girls and Aslan develops a sensual undercurrent that seems sexual. Aslan moans:

> "Are you ill, dear Aslan?" asked Susan. "No," said Aslan. "I am sad and lonely. Lay your hands on my mane so that I can feel you are there and let us walk like that."
>
> And so the girls did what they would never have dared to do without his permission, but what they had longed to do ever since they first saw him—buried their cold hands in the beautiful sea of fur and stroked it, and, so doing, walked with him. . . . (LWW, p. 136)

As we have seen, fur has a special meaning in the first story. Fur in the wardrobe is the feel of the mother's body. The children take on the fur coats like royal robes. These are fantasies of moving into adult maturity. Tumnus the faun is hairy, and he represents adult sexuality. Aslan's mane has a powerful sensual quality throughout the books. So the girls here are learning to be libidinal: in this Aslan represents the Good Mother with whom the bereaved child needs body-play still, of a sensual (infant) kind. But as we shall see, this mane has another more sinister origin, for Aslan is also the internalization of a cruel bearded schoolmaster who gave Lewis a dreadful kind of security in the intensity of his grief, at the very moment he was mourning his loss.

The last section of The Lion, the Witch and the Wardrobe is, in Lewis's terms, about resurrection. The petrified victims of the White Witch are brought back to life by Aslan's breath. Here, color is significant, in contrast to the white, dead world of the Witch:

> Instead of all that deadly white the courtyard was now a blaze of colours: glassy chestnut sides of centaurs, indigo horns of uni-corns, dazzling plumages of birds, reddy-brown of foxes, dogs and satyrs yellow stockings and crimson hoods of dwarfs: and the birch girls in silver, and the beech-girls in fresh, transparent greens, and the larch girls in green so bright that it was almost yellow. (LWW, p. 153)

Dominating the assembly is a big giant, called Rumble-buffin, who knocks down the wall of the queen's palace, and opens it to life:

[I]t was odd . . . to see through the gap all the grass and waving trees and sparkling streams of the forest. . . . (LWW, p. 157)

The castle, another symbol of the bad mother's body, is explored, and the world is restored to life by the resurrection of the petrified creatures inside it. The moment—in all its fairy-story comedy—could be compared with the great moment of reparation in *The Ancient Mariner*, when the protagonist, "unawares," blesses the water-snakes. But such a comparison tends to reveal the difference between a great creative achievement and Lewis's very limited engagement with the problem which lacks reparative power, or, to use the Christian term again, "grace." What Lewis seems to offer is a rather childish coherence of triumph among those *who are sure they are right*: his solution is not an embracing of ambivalence, but greater defensive amouring; and of assertive whiteness against blackness. The happy cameraderie among the "goodie" forces remains childish and childishly didactic:

> But most pleased of the lot was the other lion who kept running about everywhere pretending to be very busy but really in order to say to everyone he met "Did you hear what he said? *Us lions* That means him and me. *Us lions.* That's what I like about Aslan. No side, no stand-offishness. *Us lions.* That meant him and me!" At least he went on saying this till Aslan had loaded him up with three dwarfs, one dryad, two rabbits, and a hedgehog. That steadied him a bit. (LWW p. 158)

And now, characteristically, it soon becomes plain that the achievement of a temporary benignity progresses towards preparation for a final triumph of aggression for *battle*. As so often in Lewis, the solution to the spiritual problem is conceived of in terms of the assertion of a self-righteous hostility to enemies who are completely black, unremitting evil. Moreover, the solutions are exclusively "male" ones. I have pointed out that the gifts offered the children symbolize male attributes: the animals released from stone are mostly male—giants, centaurs, fauns—apart from the diaphanous Dryads (who only seem to exist to set off the maleness around them\*). If, as I do, we take the story to be a quest for fresh modes of being, then we must surely

---

\*Lucy is mistaken by the giant for a handkerchief. The faun keeps her handkerchief, we remember. "Never met a nicer handkerchee. So fine, so handy" says the giant. A handkerchief is the female role in Lewis's world.

see that it is conceived as one of aggressive (male) domination. This goes with the whole conception in Lewis of the spiritual problem as an exciting macho conflict against hostile enemies. Excitement now mounts as the battle resembles a fox hunt:

> The noise was like an English fox-hunt only better because every now and then with the music of the hounds was mixed the far deeper and more awful roar of Aslan himself. (LWW, p. 159)

Soon the children come upon the engagement, and horribleness is emphasized by reference to the *deformity* of the enemy.

> Horrible creatures . . . they looked even stranger and more evil and more deformed . . . horrible things were happening wherever she looked. (LWW, p. 159)

The children, it seems, must be properly "blooded." Aslan orders the children off his back and his roar shakes all Narnia "from the western lamp-post" to the sea. Then Aslan attacks the Witch:

> The giant beast flung himself upon the White Witch. Lucy says her face lifted towards him for one second with an expression of terror and amazement. The Lion and the Witch had rolled over together but with the Witch underneath. . . . (LWW, pp. 160–161)

In psychoanalytical terms, what is this again but the primal scene?

As always, when excited, what Lewis likes most is a fight, in which the bad forces are put to flight by a ("good") use of the weapons of pain and assault learned at school:

> . . . dwarfs with their battleaxes, dogs with teeth, the Giant with his club (and his feet also crushed dozens of the foe), unicorns with their horns, centaurs with swords and hoofs . . . the enemy squealed and gibbered. . . . (LWW, p. 161)

Peter is now more than blooded: his aggression is endorsed by Aslan, and it is a mark of maturity:

> The next thing that Lucy knew was that Peter and Aslan were shaking hands. It was strange to her to see Peter as he looked now—his face was so pale and stern and he seemed so much older. . . . (LWW, p. 162)

Edmund had turned out well, ratifying the traditional belief that to make a man out of a delinquent son, the best thing to do is to put him in the army:

> When he reached her he had the sense to bring his sword smashing down on her wand instead of trying to go for her directly and simply getting made a statue himself for his pains. . . . (LWW, p. 162)

So he castrates the White Witch.

But Edmund is "terribly wounded" and now has to have some magic liquid from Lucy's bottle, which she had from Father Christmas—Good Breast for the boy wounded in the fight with Bad Breast, so to speak, if we put it in Kleinian terms.*

At this point there is one of those odd disproportionate moments, a lapse. Aslan is angry with Lucy for attending so to Edmund. It seems an odd argument to come from a symbol of Jesus; but is supposed to show that Jesus-Aslan is not "safe" but continually challenging: "daughters of Eve," said Aslan in a graver voice, "others also are at the point of death. Must more people die for Edmund?"

But—if Lewis's emphasis on magic is to be believed, Aslan, surely, could use his own magic to restore them? And didn't Christ die for Edmund willingly, anyhow? Lewis's world, however, is not consistent. It is only consistent within his own strange unconscious mythology. This mythology is even given a kind of intellectual "point": it is all due to experimental education! Edmund must be excused because he went to such a bad school; and he must be excused the worst knowledge:

> She found him . . . looking better than she had seen him look—oh, for ages; in fact ever since his first term at *that horrid school which was where he had begun to go wrong.* He had become his real self again and could look you in the face. And there on the field of battle Aslan made him a knight.
>
> "Does he know," whispered Lucy to Susan, "what Aslan did for him? Does he know that the arrangement with the Witch really was?"
>
> "Hush! No. Of course not," said Susan.
>
> "Oughtn't he to be told?" said Lucy.
>
> "Oh, surely not," said Susan. "it would be too awful for him. Think how you'd feel if you were he." (LWW, p. 163, my italics)

---

*See Klein 1932.

In short we ought to jolly well know that Christ died for us. The implications are that anyone who doesn't believe in Christ's atonement is a fool—the homeletic here takes on a characteristic minatory tone. Yet half the energy is directed against humanist-vegetarian schools as so often the lapse reveals in Lewis's sensibility a strange lack of proportion. Soon we shall see why *schooling* plays such a predominant part in his myth here.

Of course, a Christian would argue that these horrible creatures represent "sins" or even "demons": sloth or cupidity or envy. How, in any case, do they menace the children? They offer them pain, petrifaction and death—all of which (in the light of Christian morality) are nothing, since they cannot touch one's soul. In any case, Aslan could restore the victims by magic. But the "wrong" thing surely is that none of the sins can be redeemed. They are so horrible, moreover, that there is never any question of the children being tempted to join the world of the "bad side" (even when Edmund eats Turkish Delight he is aware that the Witch is unattractive and knows deep down that she is evil). So where is temptation, in the exercise of choice and "ethical living"? Where is the spiritual conflict? Since there are no real problems, the triumph is all too easy: they are armed with magic weapons; Aslan is all powerful; and the outcome has been decided anyway, by the deeper magic from the Dawn of Time. Now, by the same magic as in a child's day dream, they are made kings and queens.

The price to be paid for such an easy victory is an absence of the problem of responsibility to one's own conscience. The victory belongs to manic defence: a failure "to recognise sadness, guilt and worthlessness and the value of reacting to this which belongs to personal inner or psychic reality" (Winnicott [1958], it should be noticed says this in *defence* of religion, p. 135).

Instead of the acceptance of one's reality one has an encouragement to be fortified in one's complacency. Aslan, in Narnia, is "not a *tame* lion" (p. 168); and the lesson is that one *must not be ashamed of one's self-righteous aggressiveness.* To be aggressive is to be like the Wild God. There is no question of the redemption of the enemy: he is nonhuman, and there is no call to extend pity to him. Evil is not to be understood and countered by the strength of love—it must *be stamped out:*

> . . . all that *foul brood was stamped out* . . . they made good laws
> and kept the peace and saved good trees from being unnecessarily

cut down, and liberated young dwarfs and young satyrs from being sent to school, and generally *stopped busybodies and interferers and encouraged ordinary people who wanted to live and let live.* (LWW, p. 166, my italics)

This last petulant bark is characteristic as is the banality of the decline of tone in the paragraph. We thought we were dealing with resurrection; then we are urged to exterminate sin; now we find ourselves urged against bureaucrats and state officials in the tone of a letter from an irate authoritarian to the editor of the *Daily Telegraph.* As a juvenile program, to be inculcated into defenseless child minds, it seem to me unfortunate. But besides this ethical flaw, it appears that there are serious artistic flaws too.

This book ends in a fantasy coda, in which, after years of benign reign, the children rediscover the lamp post, and are reborn back into the world—minus the fur coats. You can't apparently get back into Narnia by the same route twice: "Indeed, don't *try* to get there at all. It'll happen when you're not looking for it. . . ."

We may take Narnia as "the Spiritual World" if we wish, and we may agree with Lewis that it is a good thing to slip into this other world when we least expect it, but surely everything depends on what you learn while you're there?

# 3
# How Do We Read a Parable?

I have tried to give a "reading" of *The Lion, the Witch and the Wardrobe* in my terms, taking account of the presentation of it as a Christian parable; but then also looking at it from a more open phenomenological point of view. At this point I ought to put my cards on the table and say in detail what I think C. S. Lewis's fantasies are about, if we put the Christianity in brackets.

We may start from the main problem which must arise—who is the White Witch?—since she is the great difference from the Christian myth. She may have antecedents in Eve and Lilith; but she is a much more familiar figure in the psychoanalytical case history (see Stern, 1966 and Winnicott, 1965, p. 164). Here, for the purposes of my analysis of the meanings of Lewis's works, I propose to take for granted the truth of certain insights from object relations and existential psychoanalysis especially to do with gender and becoming. Children learn to be male and female by identifying with the mother and father; but it is more complicated than that, since both mother and father have both male and female aspects. In the mother especially we find capacities to respond to the infant in ways which he or she may make use of. These are the powers of "being for" that enable the mother to draw out the human identity and consciousness as it grows. Winnicott postulated a certain state of being in the pregnant woman he called "primary maternal preoccupation"—and he talked of "creative reflection." The infant looks into the mother's face and sees himself, or herself becoming in her response: she/he looks in the mother's mind and discovers what kind of image she has of him or her. Through responsive exchange and play the mother creates a favorable environment in the context of which the developmental processes in the infant can complete themselves.

Of course, these processes can go wrong; and at times (as with the processes of physical development), they go "wrong" in everyone: growing up itself depends upon imperfections in the process. So, we discover our mother is not ourself, that the world is not perfect, that our love for her and her love for us can be destructive, or can turn threatening. We can fear that our intense oral love (the wolf) may eat her up. We may fear that her benign power to create us could also destroy us, that she might be a witch (like Lady Macbeth). *If she dies this fear may seem to have come true*—for she has offered us the worst kind of rejection.

I have already pointed out that Lewis found inspiration in the fantasies of George MacDonald, and I believe this was because he found in his writings the clues he needed to how to tackle his own inner problem by symbolic effort—how to work on them. MacDonald, too, lost his mother as a child and spent his adult creative effort trying to find her again. Only there are significant differences between Lewis's modes and MacDonald's. For instance, MacDonald's relate very much to weaning. Lewis's by contrast, tend to take an aggressive stance against menaces. In both we find the powerful presence of the phantom woman who is both sought after, and yet who threatens the world. And in both, while the loss of the mother by death is important, there are other earlier problems—in MacDonald the sudden traumatic weaning; in Lewis, as I shall postulate, a deficiency of *play* and a deficiency of the experience of *creative reflection*, causing some confusion of fantasy and reality—as in his literalism about Christian mythology.

There can be no confirmation of the biological realities behind such questions. My only excuse for making such postulations is the way in which, if one makes them, they illuminate the symbolism (as they have done, for me, in understanding the meanings of other writers.) Often one finds startling confirmation in further texts, as in the evident symbolism of rebirth and the breast in C. S. Lewis's adult "space fiction."

Lewis himself points out that in Freudian language kings and queens stand for mothers and fathers. In "Narnia," then, let us say, we have a bad mother who has destroyed the world, and a good father who is opposing her. The children, as we later find, are to become kings and queens. So, in one sense, the fairy story is a fable of gender identity, and fulfilment of one's role.

I will look later at certain biographical details of Lewis's life; but here I will postulate a degree of inadequacy of the sense of being in him, from the formative years of early infancy. As with the fantasies of George MacDonald, Lewis's fictions are about a deep need to find the mother again, and to complete the processes of creative reflection with her.

There is another experience that Lewis shared with MacDonald: the loss of his mother by death when he was a child. Behind the need to fantasize lies a deep and urgent problem of mourning. The "Narnia" books are an attempt, through symbolism, to complete a process of mourning that began when his mother died when he was nine and three-quarters. The quest was bedeviled by his earliest experience of the mother, which I deduce to have been unsatisfactory to a degree; and compounded later by the cruelty he experienced as a child at preparatory school while he was grieving and his world had collapsed. His frequent odd references to schools and schooling spring from this traumatic source.

The infant (and in the fantasies of both George MacDonald and Lewis we are following the dreams of an infant spirit) who has suffered the ultimate rejection by the mother, by her death, may believe that if only he can penetrate into the world of death, where the mother is, he can in some way reexperience the original processes of love and being. He can redeem the world, and *begin to be*.

But because the world into which he wishes to penetrate is the world of death, and the mother there may still be the ultimate "Rejecting Mother," the quest is terribly dangerous. The yearned-for Good Breast may turn out to be Bad Breast; and instead of filling you with goodness, may thrust badness into you, "implode" you, or annihilate you.

What about the father? Here there are more dangers. For one thing, what is it that has killed the Mother? In MacDonald's *Phantastes*, often, once the (dead) mother is found, there is an even more terrible figure who menacingly appears—clearly the father.

Why is the father so dangerous? Because, in the passionate sexual relationship between father and mother, there are powerful (oral) feelings in which the infant feels involved. There is Oedipal jealousy—the desire to have the mother to himself which brings him into conflict with the father. And there are those intense oral feelings for the breast which have (in infant fantasy) at times threatened to eat up the mother and the world. In their sexuality, the parents seem to be likely to (dangerously) eat up one another; or, if the infant becomes excitedly involved, as in his Oedipal envy, the combined parents may turn on him and eat him up. The fantasy of the "Combined Parents," Melanie Klein found to be the most terrible of all infant fears (Klein 1932).

Once the male element is introduced into the fantasy of the Quest for the lost mother, terrible dangers arise. Although the male principle or element offers security and strength, it is also bound up with serious threats as of castration and annihilation—fears that are commonly symbolized in fairy stories, with their ogres and wolves, their beheadings, and poisoned garments.

This explains the grim and ominous note in the description of the Faun's wrecked room. The slashing of the father's picture points to the underlying meaning. At this point the White Witch's name is given as "Jadis"—a jade, a (night)mare—making clear the connection between the bad mother and Lewis's lifelong nightmares. Many of his fantasies seem to be about the terrible dangers that lurk behind sexuality, as we shall see (and we may here recall his fear that certain foods promoted sexual urges—indicating an oral element). This we may link with the wider issue of what is inside one, what is inside others, and how one's oral hunger may affect others (as with Maugrim the Wolf, the Harfangs, etc.—*maws* and *fangs* being menacing). To the child, sexuality is a powerful oral energy like a form of eating. This is why sexuality is so dangerous to the infant psyche. So, sexual hunger is one possible answer to the haunting question, why did the mother die? Here, we need to examine infant logic: Lewis's mother died of cancer, and he was possibly aware that this meant a growth in the mother's body (as we shall see, there is a phenomenological connection in his symbolism between the wardrobe and the mother's body). This might well seem to an infant like a terrible pregnancy. So, when, in the infant fantasy, we go through the mother's body into the "other" world where the dead mother is—we shall find evidence there of the father's phallic presence, which is just what we do find at the beginning of the "Narnia" stories. Beneath all these strange elements in the fantasies lies an infant belief that it is *sexual intercourse that has killed the mother.*\*

Those who know Bachelard's work on symbolism (see

---

\*These interpretations may be paralleled in an approach to the fantasies of George MacDonald from which Lewis learned so much.

Bachelard 1964) will have no difficulty in recognizing the wardrobe as a symbol of the mother's body. The mirror is a little more difficult, until we have absorbed Winnicott's essay on *The Mother's Mirror Role* in *Playing and Reality* (Winnicott 1971, p. 111).

In the first "Narnia" book, the room is

> empty except for one big wardrobe: the sort that has a looking glass in the door. There was nothing else in the room at all except a dead blue-bottle on the window-sill. . . .
> "Nothing there!" said Peter. (LWW, p. 11)

The repetition of the word "nothing" and the word "empty" should alert us, as should the dead blue-bottle. There are, as we shall see, some disturbing moments for Lewis around the appearance of beetles; and this blue-bottle is the kind of detail which, to a child, might well be disturbing. The world of SPARE ROOM has vibrations for Lewis, and we may recall one of his comments on grieving:

> Grief in childhood is complicated with many other miseries. I was taken into the bedroom where my mother lay dead; as they said "to see her," in reality, as I at once knew, "to see *it*." (*Surprised by Joy*, p. 25; my italics)

The blue bottle is a faint echo of mother made, by death, into in inanimate object: as we shall see, fear of being turned into an inanimate object was a persistent fear in Lewis. He had terrible nightmares of depersonalization.

The room through which the children go into the "other" world, then, is a room full of nothing but strong memories of the mother being turned into nothing. There is also a *looking glass* in the door—and we will recall how significant are the mirrors in *Alice* and MacDonald's *Lilith* as pathways to another world. The mirror is the mother's eyes, in which the child hopes to see his being reflected.* Here the phenomenological insight is much illuminated by the above-mentioned case of "Rudolph," who sought the mother's eyes everywhere in glittering objects, and looked into the eyes of animals he killed to see through into the "other" world (of death).** The children go through the mother's body (associated with her eyes) into the world where she is now.

---

*See "Mirror-role of Mother and Family in Child Development," in Winnicott 1967.
**May et al, 1958, p. 365ff.

The main feature of the world in which Lucy finds herself is a lamp post. This is, in its most obvious symbolism, a marker or beacon that offers illumination and protection. It will enable Lucy to find the entrance and come back to the world. But, however delicate one needs to be about making crude "Freudian" interpretations, one must not overlook its phallic significance. I was myself very hesitant at first about emphasizing the phallic significance of the lamp posts in Narnia until I found in *The Magician's Nephew* the grotesque fantasy of the witch who is clearly the "Castrating Mother," who tears a bit off a lamp post, which is thrown to earth—and grows into a new lamp post! There would seem to be no doubt then that the lamp post is the father's fertile penis. The "bad" dead mother has taken the father's penis with her into the world of death.

Other genital imagery in the "Narnia" books includes the monopods which are detached part-objects—feet, which are by displacement, surely penises; the silver chair (Fr., *chair* = flesh) which is a trap-like female genital; the hairy mirror on the magician's wall; the various doors through which people magically pass; the ring on Eustace's arm; the projection on which it eventually rests; Tumnus himself; the Witch as an old stump; and many other forms. In some cases the illustrations unwittingly confirm the genital meaning, as in the Penguin editions, where the artist has often picked up the sexual symbolism.

The two symbols of phallic sexuality which Lucy meets as soon as she enters Narnia are the lamp post and Tumnus the faun.

The lamp post plays a significant part in one of the later books and continues to signify maleness in its broader aspects. In *The Last Battle* we learn there is a whole lamp post waste, where the Calormenes are cutting down the trees by the false instruction of a false Aslan (that is, castrating them.)

The faun is different: he is quite clearly a libidinal phallic force with his black hairy legs. An unwittingly erotic image in the illustrations to the Puffin version shows this (we even have Bacchus with an erection made from one of the faun's horns).

Here we surely have a theme quite different from the "Christian message":

From the waist upwards he was like a man, but his legs were shaped like a goat's ["the hair on them was glossy black"] and instead of feet he had goat's hoofs. He also had a tail, but Lucy did not notice that at first because it was neatly caught up over the arm

that held the umbrella so as to keep it from trailing in the snow.* . . .
(LWW, pp. 14–15)

Here I believe a straightforward Freudian interpretation is
justified (an umbrella can be "put up" and so is capable of
erection).

A parallel topographical symbolism may be found, in the hills,
and the Witch's castle. Again, the illustrator picks up the unconscious meaning; and we find a spiky phallic object like a growth,
between two breast-like hills. What I am analyzing are infant
body symbols. In my terms (as will be seen), the spiky castle,
like many other manifestations of the White Witch, represents
what Winnicott calls a "collection of impingements," a spiky
cluster of experiences of "male doing" where one might expect
"female element being" between the breasts. That is, it symbolizes the infant's experience of a "male" type of handling from
the mother, which he could not make use of when he needed
creative reflection and "being for" of a feminine kind. As
Winnicott says, such unsatisfactory handling is experienced as
*hate*: we can say that the White Witch menaces with her (phallic)
hate.**

If we become aware of the nature of infant fantasy of this
kind in fairy tales, we may find corroboration throughout the
"Narnia" books. I have suggested that there is a fear that the
mother died from sexual intercourse: that this kind of sexual
implosion had corrupted her body, so her cancer itself could
seem to be the father's penis, or a kind of pregnancy caused
by it. The faun's name is Tumnus, the origins of which name
now seem clear: *Tumesco*, to swell; *Tumidas*, big, protuberant;
*Tumor*, a bump or bunch; also perhaps *tum* "at that time": and
perhaps just the infant's "tummy." Perhaps Tumnus is the father's penis inside the mother which became a cancer? Certainly,
the faun has a powerful sexual quality, which is presented as
if seen by a child; and this sexuality brings at once the fear
of mutilation and death.

In the faun's bookcase are a number of books, one of which
is *Nymphs and their Ways*. The faun is charming, domestic,
and benign:

---

*The tail is "not noticed" by Lucy because the penis is under a heavy taboo,
just as Peter says there is "nothing" in the room containing the dead blue-bottle
mother.
**Jungians would perhaps talk about the Witch's (mother's) animus, her preda-
tory male "side."

He had a strange, but pleasant little face, with a short pointed beard and curly hair, and out of the hair there stuck two horns one on each side of his forehead. (LWW, p. 15)

The faun "looked as if he had been doing his Christmas shopping"; later the blight on the world is thawed by *Father* Christmas, and the faun seems to belong to that paternal benignity.

There is, however, from the first, a tension and an ambiguity between the libidinal dynamics for which the faun stands, with all their dangers, and his tea-time benignity. There is a hint of the (paranoid) sense of mortal danger. The faun's problem of loyalty is felt to be serious. The faun, we discover, is in fact supposed to be working for the White Witch. He at first intends to hand Lucy over to her—presumably to be put to death. The White Witch is later to torture the faun and petrify him, discovering (by finding Lucy's handkerchief) that he has been fraternizing with a human being. We needn't draw the parallel with the handkerchief in *Othello* but there is a distant sense that the Witch's response is a sexually jealous one. Throughout the Narnia books we tend to have references to experiences that would be sexual if the whole atmosphere did not belong to what Freud called the "latency period."

Is it appropriate to arrive at such conclusions? Well, surely, may we first agree that the interpretation of symbols is in order? There can be no doubt that Lewis's fairy-story books demand to be taken as parables with a double meaning: the topography is offered as having a meaning,* and so do the characters. They are offered like that as in Bunyan. The stories are of interest because of the complex ambiguity of this metaphorical mode. When a boy is turned into a dragon for having "dragonish thoughts," this is offered as symbolism; and we are obliged to interpret it in terms of a parable as when Edmund is given "Turkish Delight" by the White Witch. But if we begin to interpret, we may also find an unspoken, unacknowledged meaning to be arrived at in terms of which the author was unconscious.

Why pursue this theme of underlying meanings at all? I believe we are forced to do so because Lewis himself informs us that he is *instructing* us by his fantasies, and because some

---

*So, too, for instance, does the description of the castle of Sir Bercilak de Hautdesert in *Sir Gawaine and the Grene Knight* though we may go on arguing about the meaning of "pared out of paper purely." This kind of symbolism has a long ancestry.

take his work to be good instruction. Indeed, there is a sense in which he turns minatory, if we do not accept his fables in this way, for he promises us some kind of cosmic disaster if we do not listen. Yet the world Lewis invents is a very frightening one, not least when it is related to our world. Worlds come and go. For example the old world of "Charn" has passed away. Lewis makes it plain in many places that we should reflect on worlds that pass away, and so try to find meanings and values that transcend the mutability of reality. He is warning us to pay attention to "truth," and then he offers us solutions based on this truth. If we do not accept his truth, our world may pass away, too. But suppose his "truth" is false? Not least in deciding whether or not to follow his injunctions, we need to inquire into this question. As will already be clear, I take and examine the topography of Narnia as the topography of Lewis's "psychic tissue." It is the Geist-body-world of Lewis himself. The protagonists—children, witch, lion—I take to be dynamics of his inner self: the stories I see as dramas of endopsychic conflict, like our dreams. He offers them as characters in Christian myth; I approach them as figures in the dynamics of his psyche, and judge them as enactments of subjective human truth.

The "other world" has affinities with the world we seem to move about it, in dreams, which is often clearly enough our body and also our mind—it has cliffs of fall, corridors, blankness, and chasms. This other world Lewis saw as the world of the spirit; to me it is the embodied world of the mind, great tracts of it being the "unconscious" mind, the world of the body as we experience it subjectively and remember it from infancy. I take clues here from many writers, of course, from Freud to Winnicott and R. D. Laing. In one critical book I notice (Lord of the Elves, by Richard Purtill [1974]) the critic says that, in Lewis's Narnia, a character like Tumnus the faun has "no significatio." This will not do: everything produced by the human consciousness has a significatio (and as we have seen, Tumnus certainly has). In every writer's consciousness is a unique topography with its structure and system. In every human being there seems to be a sense of one's own right "shape." In the historical memory of each of us, of body-life and psychic parturition—of growth towards oneself in the family, then inevitably, archetypal patterns begin to emerge, which relate to common human experiences, of good and bad, positive and negative, male and female. These, in their turn, relate to eventful experiences in the individual psyche, being born and raised, being a member of this or that kind of family, and discovering one's identity and gender. Such aspects of symbolism are now commonly recognized (see, for instance, Derek Brewer's *Symbolic Stories* [1980]) in which he traces aspects of family pattern behind fairy tales and other imaginative works).

When an individual has a profound feeling of incompletion of identity, he may feel deep down that he has never been born. So, he may yearn to go back to the beginning again, to reexperience birth. This is often a symbolic element in the impulse behind fantasies. The symbolism of rebirth is also found in fairy stories. There are many symbolic moments in *Alice in Wonderland*, for example, in which Alice is clearly going through birth experiences, floating in the amniotic fluid, or passing down long passageways, or changing shape dramatically. Similarly, the way in which Tom progresses in *The Water Babies*, especially his journey into the sea, seems a fantasy of rebirth. In George MacDonald's *At the Back of the North Wind*, the child Diamond crawls through between the legs of the North Wind; and there are other images in this author's work which suggest rebirth.

All such fantasy events, I take it, symbolize a need to go back to the beginning, and to reexperience a new start, especially a new experience of those creative processes which can enable us *to be*, and to fulfil ourselves. There is a symbolic element of this kind, of course, in Christianity, in which death can be a rebirth, and the Crucifixion is followed by Resurrection into another world and another state. In both George MacDonald and C. S. Lewis there are recurrent passages into that "other world," which they take to be the spiritual world but which I take to be a renewed state of being.

So, to return to the moment when the children in the "Narnia" books go through the wardrobe, this may be understood as symbolic of "going through the mother's body" into another world, in order to find her, and there to complete the work that has never been done on "being"—but then finding, in that other world, all kinds of dangers associated with the phantom woman. If a child finds himself by looking into his mother's mind, then if she is lost, he may feel he no longer exists, just as an infant may fear that he no longer exists if his mother is not looking at him (see *Feeling and Perception in Young Children* [Chaloner, 1963]). Certain kinds of reflecting and glittering objects can, phenomenologically speaking, as Kuhn's case (of "Rudolph") shows, represent the mother's eyes which are desperately sought, so that they may reflect the self that is hungry for confirmation of being.*

We may link these symbolic eyes with everything psychoanalysts like Melanie Klein and Winnicott call "breast," which really means all the infant's experience of the mother's body and being. Tremendous existential feelings are associated with the breast, because it is the focus of the development of the sense of being, and of reality as well as considerable envy, because of the sexual (sensual) excitement and satisfaction involved. There is a magic about eyes, and about breasts. In one of Lewis's stories, as we shall see, we have another "breast" symbol in the magic rings in The Magician's Nephew. Significantly, these magic rings are the means by which one may pass from one world to another. The mother's eyes and her breasts are magic in that they are the focus for that play and interchange by which the infant becomes himself, and finds the capacity to relate to the real world.

The children's movements in the "Narnia" books through the wardrobe are like being born. When Lucy enters the wardrobe, she has agreeable body feelings: "there was nothing Lucy liked so much as the smell and feel of fur" (LWW, p. 12). When she comes out the other side, the strange world of Narnia is cold and bleak.** The moment is similar to one in Sylvia Plath's novel The Bell Jar. There the heroine curls up in a space in the cellar in a failed suicide attempt and comes back to life: "through the thick furry darkness a voice cried, 'Mother!'"— a clear indication of rebirth. In George MacDonald's fantasies there are many such images that come from reminiscences of the mother's body; and in the girls' play with Aslan, we have again a symbol of the refinding of the mother's body, as I have suggested.

Bringing all these insights from phenomenology together, when, I suggest that as Lewis leads us through the wardrobe into Narnia, we have a central motif of ultimate regression— going back through the womb, into another world, where life is to begin, by rebirth from the refound mother.

At first, such phenomenological interpretations may seem bi-

---

*"All his life George MacDonald loved the flash of precious stones: lady admirers once gave him an opal. In the beauty of colourful clothes and jewels, he saw God's loving hand." Wolff 1961, p. 6. "Rudolph's" case is in May et al, 1958.

**See below the experience of coldness after "rebirth" in the symbolism in Perelandra, p. 241.

zarre; but what proves interesting is that, in their own symbolism and meaning, the stories confirm them. As often in these matters, if we study closely what the author says, he will tell us himself what his symbolism means. We have looked at the important clue in *The Magician's Nephew* to the whole impulse of the "Narnia" books; that is, Digory's struggle to restore his mother to health. This is surely a reminiscence of Lewis's childhood experience of his sick mother, and it explains the source of the belief in magic in the "Narnia" books. In *The Magician's Nephew* he allows himself a boyish fantasy of having omnipotent power to bring the mother back to life ("Mother" has a significant capital "M"). This magic power in *The Magician's Nephew* is given by Aslan, of course, so we may see it as a manifestation of Christ healing—a miracle. We may remember that as a boy Lewis prayed for such a miracle:

> when her case was pronounced hopeless I remembered what I had been taught; that prayers offered in faith would be granted I accordingly set myself to produce by willpower a firm belief that my prayers for her recovery would be successful; and, as I thought, I achieved it. When nevertheless she died I shifted my ground and worked myself into a belief that there was to be a miracle. The interesting thing is that my disappointment produced no results beyond itself. The thing hadn't worked, and I thought no more about it. (*Surprised by Joy*, p. 26)

It would seem that Lewis is here deceiving himself: he obviously thought about it so much that he needed to reconsider the failure of his attempt to bring about a miracle, in middle age, by writing many books about the problem.

Where did the apple from the Tree of Life itself come from? We shall look more fully at *The Magician's Nephew* below: it is a very revealing book in the series in many ways. The apple comes from a tree in a garden that resembles the Garden of Eden and is from the Tree of Knowledge of Good and Evil. We shall look carefully at the topography of this garden, which is on a steep green hill. But, as so often, the drawings give us a clue. The green hill is shaped like a breast; and it is set among cruel, spiked, mountainous country and is only accessible by flight (on the winged horse Fledge). The spiked country resembles the spiky castle of the White Witch's castle in *The Lion, the Witch and the Wardrobe*. There, the castle is between two hills—as I have suggested, "entre deux seins," a "bad breast" (or false male breast) among good breasts.

We may, I believe, interpret this symbolism thus: Digory's quest is that of Lewis himself, to find "good breast," to find the mother's benignity, and to repair the inadequacy in his psyche with this benignity. This has to be sought in the face of the bleak domination of his world by the "bad" mother, and among the spiky points of his experience of her early bad "impingeing" (too "male") mothering. Later, of course, he experienced her death. His struggle is to restore a real and creative relationship between the self and the world: *to begin to live.* At the end of *The Last Battle* he asserts he has reached this point. Later we shall have to decide if he is successful.

There is one further clue in Lewis to this theme of engagement with the shadow mother. When his mother died, something dropped out of Lewis's world—a whole continent:

> With my mother's death all settled happiness, all that was tranquil and reliable, disappeared from my life. There was to be fun, many pleasures, many states of joy; but no more of the old security. It was sea and islands now; the *great continent had sunk like Atlantis.\** (*Surprised by Joy,* p. 27; my italics)

Let us return to *The Magician's Nephew.* The children go into the other world where they find the Tree of Life by the use of magic rings. Where are these rings first found? The box in which these rings lie was Atlantis: "it came from the lost island of Atlantis" (p. 4):

> They were no bigger than ordinary rings, and no one could help noticing them because they were so bright. They were the most beautifully shiny little things you can imagine. If Polly had been a very little younger *she would have wanted to put one in her mouth.* (MN, p. 17; my italics)

This last phrase is a clear reference to the oral stage. It is surely now clear that the rings belong to the mother's body and are her eyes or nipples; or, rather, those centers of infant attention at the breast which are the focus of his discovery of self and world: hence the magic. The world "Atlantis" makes the (oceanic) connection plain.

In the story, the rings are more like playthings; that is, they have become "transitional objects," those symbolic playthings

---

*Compare the symbolism of land and floating islands on Venus in *Perelandra,* one of Lewis's space fiction stories.

that take the place of the breast and mother, and are the means towards a full creative engagement with reality, and a personal culture.* Their powerful magic is that of all those processes by which, by her "creative reflection," the mother creates being. Yet, of course, this magic can go wrong.

These rings are the way to the Garden of Eden; but whenever the children penetrate to this source of life, there lurks the White Witch. Again, as in MacDonald's stories, even as the goal of the existential quest is approached, danger threatens from the Phantom Woman.

I hope I have established, by my interpretation of symbols, that the "Narnia" books have to do with the dead mother, and that they are an act of mourning. The goal is that of finding the dead mother, with the hope of exorcising her, and embracing her—internalized as part of oneself—so that self and world may be whole. Then, once the reality of the world is found, to let the real mother go, and thus complete the mourning process. This, I believe, was the aim of Lewis's creative efforts in his fairy tales.

There is evidently a dichotomy, between what Lewis thought he was doing, and what at the unconscious level was happening as he created his fantasies. It is this dichotomy that makes for the extraordinary unevenness, and the frequent inappropriateness in his modes of writing.

For instance, as we have seen, Lewis seems to be recommending a naked Bacchanalian mode of freedom to schoolgirls. He obviously cannot really mean orgiastic behavior. So, in his editions, the illustrations coyly avoid the embarrassing fact that the fauns and centaurs would be "entire"—even though to the Greeks this was surely the whole point.**

While the dynamics of adult sexuality are missing, however, and the libidinal potentialities are treated with a somewhat coy playfulness, the same is not true of the violence. The castration

---

*Transitional object—the teddy bear or corner of the blanket which is the child's first symbol of his union with the mother. See *Playing and Reality* (1971), D. W. Winnicott and also his *Collected Papers* (1956). For the many forms transitional objects may take, as the origin of culture, see *Between Reality and Phantasy, Transitional Objects and Phenomena* (1978). Play begins at the breast, and then moves on to the transitional object, and then to symbolic culture. See also Tustin 1981 on the way symbolism is the infant's way of holding experiences together. She interprets the infant's first disillusionment as "the Fall."

**"Writing 'juveniles' certainly modified my mode of composition . . . [it] excluded erotic love . . ." *Letters*, p. 307. Why, then, the Bacchanalia?

and annihilation of the faun are presented in a quite different and serious tone:

> "I've pretended to be your friend and asked you to tea, and all the time I've been meaning to wait until you were asleep and then go and tell *Her*."
> "Oh, but you won't, Mr. Tumnus," said Lucy. "You won't will you? Indeed, indeed you really mustn't."
> "And if I don't," said he, beginning to cry again, "she's sure to find out. And she'll have my tail cut off, and my horns sawn off, and my beard plucked out, and she'll wave her wand over my beautiful cloven hoofs, like a wretched horse. And if she is extra and specially angry, she'll turn me to stone. . . ." (LWW, p. 24)

This contrast, between the gravity of tone around the underlying themes of cruelty and death, and the playful "children's story" language elsewhere makes for serious artistic difficulties because the grave message from the urgent private mythology sorts ill with the light tone and homiletics of the children's Christian story. This inevitably leads to some unfortunate lapses in manner. At one moment one may feel this is a solemn spectacle—but then suddenly Aslan is explaining to a child why she shouldn't eavesdrop on her school chum; or Aslan himself descends to frightening a nasty schoolmistress out of spite. Sometimes it is like switching from *Stories from the Bible* to *Billy Bunter*. Nor is this a matter merely of the difficulty of writing for children. Even in his expression of a Christian point of view, Lewis sometimes exhibits a callow inadequacy of tone. For instance, in his letter to Sister Penelope toward the end of his life:

> . . . when you die, and if "prison visiting" is allowed, come down and look me up in Purgatory. It *is* all rather fun—solemn fun—isn't it? (*Letters*, p. 307)

Can a man really be serious about his religion who writes like that? There is surely something childish about it (as in J. M. Barrie's words in the mouth of Peter Pan—"to die will be an awfully great adventure"—which Barrie more or less admits at the end to be an index of Peter's failure to grow up and find *life* as an adventure).

In the "Narnia" stories, there are serious difficulties of tone. At one moment it is "That old chap will let us do anything

we like," and at the next: "Oh, you're real, you're real! Oh Aslan!
. . ." (LWW, p. 147)
Then a lapse into the embarrassingly banal:

> "Oh, it's *too* bad,' sobbed Lucy, 'they might have left the body
> alone. . . ." (LWW, p. 146)

> She found him . . . not only healed of his wounds but looking better
> than she had seen him look—oh, for ages; in fact ever since his
> first term at that horrid school which was where he had begun
> to go wrong. (LWW, p. 163)

These problems of an appropriate language, and of balance
between different aspects of the tales, may be linked with the
wider question that others have raised of Lewis's sensibility.
Some have noted in his work a certain serious immaturity (see,
for instance, Robson 1966) and we have noted Barfield's doubts.
Critics have spoken of a certain "boyishness" about Lewis, and
of a certain trait in his character that made for an engaging
simplicity and a kind of awkwardness, not least in his dealings
with ethical issues.

Underlying this, I believe, we may find a deep weakness of
identity, and a consequent dread of the "regressed libidinal
ego," the intensely hungry infant self whose existence, buried
in the personality, threatens the adult's security. As W. R. D.
Fairbairn and others have found, this hungry infant self is feared
and hated because it threatens the prowess of the adult within
whom it lurks.

It is surely of this source of internal weakness of which Lewis
is writing here (of the *Psalms*):

> I can even use the horrible passage in 137 about dashing the Babylo-
> nian babies against the stones. *I know things in the inner world
> which are like babies*; the infantile beginnings of small indulgences,
> small resentment, which may one day become dipsomania or settled
> hatred, but which woo and wheedle us with special pleadings and
> seem so tiny, so helpless that in resisting them we feel we are
> being cruel to animals. They begin whimpering to us, "I don't ask
> much, but" or "I had at least hoped," or "you owe yourself *some*
> consideration." Against all such pretty infants (the dears have such
> winning ways) the advice of the Psalm is the best. *Knock the little
> bastards' brains out.* (*Reflections on the Psalms*, my italics)

The coarseness of tone suggests that Lewis had few emotional resources to deal with this problem of a seductive weak self that had a tendency to seek false solutions: he simply *hates* this aspect of the self. And I suggest this self-hate gives us a clue to the development of his need for a stern and even cruel authority. Because of the need to overcome this inward weakness, he could only conceive of such struggles in terms of hate: of forces in conflict—the conflict serving to disguise the deeper problem of weakness. And yet is is this false solution he offers us.

# 4

# The Torment behind the Fantasies

As will be clear, in order to understand the meaning of such fantasies as the "Narnia" books and C. S. Lewis's adult fantasies, I believe we have to go back to the very early days in the author's life. To understand what emerged, when he allowed his deeper creative impulses to operate, we need to examine, phenomenologically, the "positions" or patterns in his "psychic tissue" left by events in his infancy. The trouble is that there are seldom any records of this very early life of an author.

With George MacDonald, interestingly enough, there were a number of clues—for example, he kept in his desk for many decades a letter written by his mother about his sudden weaning as a baby. But even if there were particular features about an author's life as a baby, this would all be forgotten or suppressed by the mother and family, only months afterwards, because of the natural processes of forgetting and suppressing that make life tolerable.* We have to attend to meanings to be found in the work itself, especially in its symbolism.

When we do this, we find themes in the "Narnia" books that would seem to belong to a profound state of insecurity and dread. As I have said, the world of Lewis's fantasies and his view of the "real" world are paranoid-schizoid; and this suggests on "ontological insecurity," to borrow R. D. Laing's term. His fantasy worlds are full of entities which seem to be split-offs; that is, projections out of his inner world that menace and threaten to destroy the protagonists. There is a dread of these getting out of hand, as with "Tash" in The Last Battle, or the Witch in The Magician's Nephew. In the adult fantasies there

---

*The letters of Flora Lewis, which are in the Lewis Papers at Wheaton College and the Bodleian, may show her as a warm, witty, affectionate person; but this is still no evidence that she was capable of creative reflection as a mother. Biographical evidence here is difficult. Compare, for example, Sylvia Plath's Letters Home, edited by her mother, with her Journal, in which her hatred of her mother is painfully revealed.

is a suggestion that if we do not endorse the Christian solution and resist the demons who have tried to take over the world, then the world itself may be destroyed. He admits, in letters to Arthur Greeves, that though he is obsessed with his own cleverness, as when he is about to supervise a student, he often feels he is merely a posture before the mirror. In the end he seeks a relationship with God that is not a relationship, but a virtual forfeiture of the self in the absolute.

Of course, it is true that many of these characteristics, which I am detecting as schizoid, are to be found in fairy tales, folklore, and in such fantasies as those of Edmund Spenser. As Fairbairn (1952) points out, we are all schizoid, somewhere along the sliding scale of security and integration. These are universal problems; but at times we find in Lewis quite terrible fears of being injected with poison; or of being depersonalized, like his beetles; or being made into a mindless mechanism; or sucked into a void, that we may detect a pathological element, such as we find in the accounts of schizoid patients. And we also find throughout his work and his apologetics a rejection of being human, even at times a loathing, and a detestation of inner weakness, as in his remarks about "knocking the little bastards' brains out."

I have tried to restrain myself from making use of biographical material to "diagnose" Lewis because I want to try to make my phenomenological analysis of his symbolism the basis of my criticism of the fantasies.

But since I analyze these symbols on the basis of a theory that something went seriously wrong with the formative relationships between Lewis and his mother in the first years, I have to bring some biographical details up to justify such a hypothesis. It is clear, for instance, that Lewis did not make friends easily. His one long close relationship was with Arthur Greeves, who was a homosexual. There was a strange relationship with Mrs. Moore, an older Irish woman, who was like a mother to him. In later life Lewis married, in an oddly oblique way at first; but he later found a great deal of happiness. Yet his wife was already dying from cancer when they met, recovered for a period, and then fell into decline again: in being thus doomed, she seemed to have fitted into the image of woman he had from his terrible experience of his mother's death. Many of his earlier remarks are extremely hostile to woman, and his misogyny is legendary: he voted against admitting women to Oxford, as one might expect.

Perhaps the most remarkable admission is his remark: "You will remember that *I already learned to fear and hate emotion:* here was a fresh reason to do so." This is actually about the moment when his insane headmaster Capron beat the boys even harder *when he was grieving for his dead wife,* and the connection is significant (*Surprised by Joy,* p. 38). The whole history of Lewis's childhood is one in which, to survive, he cultivated what the psychotherapists call "diminution of affect." Interestingly enough, a schizoid personality with lack of warm feeling is no disqualification for academic life. As Guntrip points out, many successful people at universities are schizoid, and some live in their intellectual systems rather than in the real world. Only in crises does the inner weakness become evident. For the most part, intellectual energy and a tough shell of assertive confidence, hide the problem; and in Lewis his religious assertiveness almost seem to take on a *machismo* quality which seems to be rather a defense against love and the flow of feelings from one being to another. Only in his relationship to his brother, in the attempt to survive difficult circumstances, does he develop a deep loyalty to uphold against the world; and this kind of loyalty is one of his chief virtues in the "Narnia" chronicles.

The confusions over imagination, fantasy, reality, and truth that I detect in Lewis are, however, the main reason why I feel it is necessary to postulate some kind of failure in the maturational processes between Lewis and his mother as an infant. There is, actually, very little in *Surprised by Joy* about his mother in the early years. His parents, he tells us, were "bookish" people and "clever." His mother was a promising mathematician and a graduate who read a great deal; but, significantly, "cared for no poetry at all." She could well have been that kind of intellectual woman who finds it difficult to allow her consciousness to go over into "primary maternal preoccupation" in the first few months of her infant's life. Lewis gives a hint that his most natural relationship was with the nurse Lizzie, and it is interesting that when he found MacDonald he should have referred both to his mother's face and that of his nurse. It is true that he speaks of his mother's "cheerful and tranquil affection" in contrast to his father's "ups and downs," but it seems unlikely that a bad experience of the father could leave a child with such radical problems over finding reality. Of course, the father did not make things any easier by being emotionally confusing, or by giving him that "distrust or dislike of emotion as something uncomfortable and embar-

rassing and even dangerous." (p. 12) It is perhaps more significant when he says that "neither had ever listened for the horns
of elfland." And I believe that we must postulate an infancy
which was seriously deficient in play and the formative imaginative interchange between mother and child, on which the reality
sense is founded. Of course, Lizzie and the brother made up
for this to some extent. However, we may suppose a somewhat
lonely infancy with the child insufficiently responded to, an
upbringing deficient in body-contact, emotional warmth, play,
and imagination, with a serious weakness of identity at the
core.

Here perhaps a further excursion into Winnicott's account
of the dynamics of "being for" between mother and infant will
prove helpful. We take our own integration for granted, and
the sense of a whole continuous self in a world felt to be real.
But this sense of identity and world is, actually, an *achievement*;
and the need for this achievement is symbolized in many
fairytales (much of *Alice in Wonderland* is about this whole
problem of integration). Winnicott says

> There long stretches of time in a normal infant's life in which
> a baby does not mind whether he is many bits or one whole being,
> or whether he lives in his mother's face or his own body, provided
> that from time to time he comes together and feels something.
> (Winnicott 1958, p. 150)

The state of unintegration has a natural place in a baby's life.
All important is the mother's intuitive capacity to bring fantasy
and reality together, so that the infant may come to find himself
as one and real; and the mother as one and real: " . . . bits
of nursing technique and faces seen and sounds heard and
smells smelt are only gradually pieced together into one being
called mother." In the stories of George MacDonald and C. S.
Lewis, as in the poetry of Sylvia Plath, one often finds odd
experiences which clearly relate to early infant experiences,
of old smells and feelings—the odor of roses, sensations of being
cold, feelings of fur or hair, arms extended—offered, as it were,
towards the discovery of the mother, but remaining fragmentary,
in a state of unintegration. A great yearning is manifest in these
works to bring things together with integration.

The reference in Winnicott to the mother's face is important,
too, as we have seen. And again, in the writers under discussion,
one finds, as it were, pieces of the mother, or her detached

*eyes*, which appear as if not yet integrated. There are often symbols of *parts* of the mother. In Lewis, these are attributes of the mother, like the magic rings in the *Magician's Nephew*, which, it is clearly hoped, will give a magic power to bring the individual closer to reality. *Till We Have Faces* is a highly significant title.

In such writers, too, there is often a dread of disintegration. As Winnicott points out, a fear of the failure of integration is with us all.

> It is sometimes assumed that in health the individual is always integrated, as well as living in his own body, and able to feel that the world is real. There is, however, much sanity that has a symptomatic quality, being charged with fear and denial of madness, fear and denial of the innate capacity of every human being to become unintegrated, depersonalised, and to feel that the world is unreal. Sufficient lack of sleep produces these conditions in anyone. (Winnicott 1958, p. 150)

Winnicott adds a footnote: "Through artistic expression we can hope to keep in touch with our primitive selves whence the most intense feelings and even fearfully acute sensations derive, and we are poor indeed if we are only sane." (Ibid., p. 150 n.)

Fantasy, then, may be an important cultural way of keeping in touch with the primitive self. Fantasies may also be a way of engaging with dynamics within the consciousness which perplex and puzzle us—many of our dreams are surely of this kind? In George MacDonald's fantasies, there is one about a protagonist who, wandering about in a wild part of Scotland, encounters a girl who is also, at night and in certain other circumstances, a wolf. It is titled *The Gray Wolf.* In this story, like *Little Red Riding Hood*, what the reader encounters, surely, is the voracious impulse in his own unconscious: the hungry need for the mother that was once so powerful in infancy that it seemed to threaten to eat up the whole world? The question then arises whether such a symbolic representation of something in one's inner world contributes to a greater degree of understanding, of accepting aspects of oneself, or not. Does it help us to say, of the wolf, "this thing of darkness I acknowledge mine?" Winnicott seems to suggest here that some fantasy creations simply by-pass, magically, the problems we have in the inner life:

> A problem related to personalization is that of the imaginary com-
> panions of childhood. These are not simple fantasy constructions.
> Study of the future of these imaginary companions (in analysis)
> shows that they are sometimes other selves of a highly primitive
> type . . . this very primitive and magical creation of imaginative
> companions is easily used as a defence, as it magically by-passes
> all the anxieties associated with incorporation, digestion, retenion
> and expulsion. (Winnicott 1958, p. 151)

One important thing for us to consider is the nature of magic
and its meaning in imaginative literature.

The question is whether there is any progress in the reconciliation of conflict, as when the princess kisses the beast, or when
the making of shirts from nettles dissipates a spell. I am taking
it for granted, of course, that the entities in a fantasy, as in
a dream, represent dynamics in the psyche—aspects of ourselves
in the inner world. One important consideration here, I believe,
is the degree to which the entities of fantasy are believed to
be "real." We all know the experience, when, after awakening
from a nightmare, we cannot get back to reality and dismiss
it as a dream. The psychotic must feel like this when he cannot
distinguish fantasy from reality, and we read of cases in which
fantasy seriously disturbs an individual's capacity to deal with
life. If we believe that Winnicott is right, to argue that play
and imaginative culture are the way in which we come to find
self and other, and the reality of the world, then fantasy must
always belong to the "space between," the sphere of interaction
between self and world. An important part of all our efforts
in bringing up children is to lead them to become capable of
distinguishing between fantasy and reality, by "disillusioning"
them. What this may mean in a positive way is clear from
Len Chaloner's (1963) splendid book, Feeling and Perception
in Young Children. Her chapter on children and death seems
especially relevant.

Here we enter into complex processes that deal with the way
in which an infant develops, within the context of the mother's
responses, his capacity to find the real world, and to use symbolic creativity to deepen his awareness of others and the world.
I have dealt with these matters in my study of Sylvia Plath.
In a study of her poetry it becomes clear that some forms of
fantasy are not positive, that they represent modes of "magic"
by which the reality of self and world may be denied. Here,
too, another feature of the formative processes may be noted—
that of "impingement": whereas in normal circumstances the

mother's response is the foundation of the sense of self and world, through "creative reflection" and the mother's dynamics of play and imagination, it is sometimes possible for the mother's responses to become threatening. A mother who attends to her baby mechanically to compensate for a lack of genuine responsiveness may generate in her infant a "reaction to impingement." The female focus of attention then becomes "experienced as hate," and the impingement of the mother may seem to be a threat of annihilation (see Winnicott 1958, p. 303). A child may in consequence withdraw into an inner world, and "the first move towards the creation of the schizoid position had been made": to ward off threatening dangers, a world of internal objects has to be set up. Something of this kind seems to me to lie behind those experiences of the mother who made this such a grave preoccupation, both in the symbolism of George MacDonald and C. S. Lewis, and the defensive power one senses in their fairy stories. In this context H. Guntrip quotes a patient:

> I don't know that I want to come to terms with this blasted world of daily life. It's better to keep one's own fairy story going. Better not see people or things as they really are. Retire into your fairy story of wicked witches and bad dragons. . . . But my troubled dream-world is my real fairy-story world. (Guntrip 1961, p. 431)

This kind of fairy story becomes a retreat from reality. So we can have an enigma: a need to use fantasy to overcome a life problem, but with the danger inherent in it of the fantasy becoming a confusion between reality and fantasy. This, I believe, gives us a clue to some of Lewis's problems, and we may relate it to what has been said above, about the way he lived "in" his fantasies.

As a child he withdrew a great deal: "My real life—or what memory reports as my real life—was increasingly one of solitude." He wrote stories, combining two literary pleasures: "dressed animals" and "knights-in-armour"—elements that come into their own in the Narnia books. When his brother was home from school they played in Lewis's imaginary Animal-land, of which they drew maps and into which they introduced characters. Lewis says:

> It will be clear that at this time—at the age of six, seven, and eight—I was living almost entirely in my imagination . . . the imaginative experience of those years now seems to me more important than anything else. (Surprised by Joy, p. 21)

However, Lewis makes a distinction here which seems to help us to understand his strange literalness in some areas of thought:

> . . . imagination is a vague word and I must make some distinction. It may mean the world of reverie, daydream, wish-fulfilling fantasy. Of that I knew more than enough. I often pictured myself cutting a fine figure. . . . In my day dreams I was training myself to be a fool. (p. 21)

This seems a strange attitude: it is as if Lewis thought mere fantasying led to pride, or some kind of un-realism. He seems to regard as superior the invention of Animal-land because it was "invention," and was a world one stood outside:

> [T]his was a totally different activity from the invention of Animal-land. Animal-land was not (in that sense) a fantasy at all. I was not one of the characters it contained. I was its creator, not a candidate for admission to it. Invention is essentially different from reverie. . . . In mapping and chronicling Animal-land I was training myself to be a novelist. Note well, a novelist; not a poet. (pp. 21–22)

His invented world had no poetry in it, no romance: it was almost astonishingly prosaic. Animal-land had nothing whatever in common with Narnia. It excluded the least hint of wonder: "This invented world was not imaginative" (p. 22). The mother's lack of interest in poetry seems part of a whole deficiency of "fancy and imagination," and aesthesis. The home lacked beauty: "we never saw a beautiful building nor imagined that a building could be beautiful" (p. 14).

Lewis's aesthetic experiences in infancy are confined to a few strange items, the distant green Castlereagh hills, and a little moss garden his brother made on a biscuit tin lid: "As long as I live my imagination of Paradise will retain something of my brother's toy garden" (p. 14). It could be said, I believe, that the "Narnia" books were an attempt to "give" the world the wonder, beauty, and the imaginative endowment that the mother should have given it in the first place (cf. the moment when Aslan sings the world into being); that is they were an attempt to turn the fantasy of retreat or regression into a creative engagement with the world, the "living principle." They were an attempt to do this in middle age, picking up the hints and hopes which the child glimpsed at the age of ten when he began the process of mourning.

We may detect, in Lewis's account of his early preoccupations with fantasy, a strange confusion as to what was real, what was to be taken literally, and what was imaginative—due to some failure of play and intersubjectivity with the mother. This became, later in his creative life, a confusion between the symbolic and the literal,* which seems a feature of his religion.

The actual sight of his mother's dead body seems to have been a traumatic experience for Lewis that made all of these problems worse. It made grieving itself more complicated. As 'it' the mother had suffered the depersonalization, the dehumanization, he dreaded, as in his nightmares. There was no disfigurement "except for that total disfigurement which is death itself. Grief was overwhelmed in terror." The effect was universal: the world became fragmented, deprived of its wholeness and security; and as we have seen, the great continent had sunk like "Atlantis." The "Narnia" books are an attempt in middle age to restore the relationship between self and the world, which is also a relationship between body and world, and to solve the problems of reality and fantasy; that is, of fantasy getting out of hand, with the "brakes" off, in Winnicott's phrase. The dread was of becoming or being a "thing," a mere machine (a fear expressed by some schizoid patients).

This explains the force and power of Lewis's nightmares. Lewis as a child (he himself says) was generally happy except for the terror of certain dreams: "It still seems to me odd that a petted and guarded childhood should so often have in it a window opening on what is hardly less than Hell" (*Surprised by Joy*, p. 15).

His dreams were of two sorts—*spectres* and *insects*. The latter were the worst, and then Lewis makes the odd remark: "to this day I could almost find it in my heart to rationalise and justify my phobia. . . ." (p. 15). We may read this as, "I cannot even now give up my paranoia."**

Here we may find some evidence of a schizoid component in Lewis's sensibility before the later terrible experiences of his childhood. He seems to have had even as a child a dread of depersonalization—a dread of being, or of being made into, an automaton as if put together by extraneous and mechanical

---

*Again, Frances Tustin's work is relevant. See *Autistic States in Children* (Tustin 1981). There are moments when I detect an autistic quality in Lewis's feelings about reality.

**A character in Narnia says, "If there's a wasp in the room, I like to be able to see it" (VDT, p. 85).

"impingement." Beneath these feelings we may detect again a fear of annihilation: that fear of "implosion."

Of insects, he says,

> Their angular limbs, their jerky movements, their dry metallic noises, all suggest either machines that have come to life or *life degenerating into mechanism*. You may add that in the hive and the ant-hill we see fully realized the two things that some of us most dread for our own species—the *dominance of the female* and the dominance of the collective. (p. 16; my italics)

The latter phrase which I have put in italics is very revealing. Can anyone seriously "dread" the "dominance of the female" in our "species"? And what has the "dominance of the female" to do with the "mechanism?" The remark reveals the roots of Lewis' misogyny in a fear of the *impinging* mother whose handling is experienced as hate and a threat of annihilation; and who herself has betrayed him by going into the other world of death, so depriving him of the chance of completing his being.

Lewis links such fears with his powerful memory of an action book that terrified him (a "detestable" picture he calls it):

> In it a midget child, a sort of Tom Thumb, stood on a toadstool and was threatened from below by a stag-beetle much larger than himself. This was bad enough; but there is worse to come. The horns of the beetle were strips of cardboard separate from the plate and working on a pivot. By moving a devilish contraption on the verso you could make them open and shut like pincers: snip-snap–snip-snap–I can see it while I write. (p. 16)

How a woman ordinarily so wise as his mother could have allowed this "abomination" into the nursery, Lewis cannot understand.

> Unless, indeed (for now a doubt assails me) unless that picture itself is a product of nightmare. But I think not. (p. 16)

The toadstool and "Tom Thumb" make it plain that the image is one of castration: it is strongly paranoid (and called "devilish"), and associated with the mother. These phobic obsessions surely have their origins in the infant experience of impingement—experienced as hate—with the associated dread of the "bad breast" or "witch" aspect of the mother, who threatens depersonalization and annihiliation? In *The Voyage of the*

*Dawn Treader* one hears the castrating shears in a cloud of nothing. As I have suggested, there are other images of castration throughout his works. In all this, the White Witch is evidently in the same tradition as the women who are revived in Mac-Donald's fairy stories, and who turn malignant and become the Castrating Mother.

How dreadful Lewis's nightmares were is clear from a passage quoted in his biography from a letter to his father (30 March 1972).

> I dreamed that I was walking among the valleys of the moon—a world of pure white rock, all deep chasms and spidery crags, with a perfectly black sky overhead. Of course, there was nothing living there, not even a bit of moss: pure mineral solitude. Then I saw, very far off, coming to meet me down a narrow ravine, a straight, tall figure, draped in black, face and all covered. One knew it would be nicer not to meet that person: but one never has any choice in a dream, and for what seemed about an hour I went on till this stranger was right beside me. Then he held out an arm as if to shake hands, and of course I have to give him my hand; when suddenly I saw that instead of a hand he had a sort of metal ring which he closed round my wrist. It was sharp on the inside and hurt abominably. Then, without a word, drawing this thing together till it cut right to the bone, he turned and began to lead me off down the same long valley he had come from. It was the sense of being on the Moon you know, the complete desolateness, which gave the extra-ordinary effect. (Green and Hooper 1974, p. 18)

The moon here (as in Sylvia Plath) is the mother, or, rather, the moon is where the dead mother has gone—the world of death: the landscape is all deep chasms and valleys, which is the dead mother's body. The "spidery crags" are the places where perhaps threatening insects live. But the "he," with face all covered in black, is surely not really a he at all but She: or, rather, the cruel man who takes over from Mother. The painful image seems an evident and vivid image of castration: the symbol of a strangling, castrating "ring" will appear very significantly in *The Voyage of the Dawn Treader*.

The "monopods," the predatory monsters in the space fiction books, and the ordeals that characters undergo in Lewis's books, often seem to derive from infant fantasy of a castratory kind. This may be associated with his need to fantasy cruelty, as in *Till We Have Faces*, from people being shot through the throat to actual scenes of men being castrated. In the face of the dread of nothingness, strong, hate-filled thinking seems one way to survive.

The sexual meaning of the word "castrate," however, may lead us to another aspect of Lewis's predicament that must be mentioned here because of the kind of dark infant fantasies of which I have written. As I have said, it would well seem, in a child's logic, that it was sexual intercourse that has killed the mother. As we shall see, it is virtually a vision of the Combined Parents, which brings about the end of the world, in the last of the "Narnia" books. Some complexity of fantasies of this kind certainly lie behind some of the incidents in Lewis's works, such as this, from one of the adult fantasies:

> The picture which Orfieu and Scudamour show Ransom, Lewis and MacPhee is of a Dark Tower in which they are presently able to see the interior where a man sits like a graven image, filling them with horror, partly by his very unhumanness, but mainly by a poisoned sting like a miniature unicorn's horn which sticks out from his forehead and with which he stabs or inoculates in the spine of a series of normal human beings who come in one by one as into the presence of a god—and submit themselves to his agonizing process: "they entered the room as men, or (more rarely) women; they left it automata." (Green and Hooper 1974, p. 161)

This is an intense paranoid-schizoid fantasy, on the same theme of "implosion" and "impingement," of having some kind of hate injected into one, which turns one into a depersonalized machine. The unicorn's horn is clearly a phallic symbol, and so this process has a sexual connotation: again we have a sexual act bringing about the depersonalization Lewis so terribly dreads.

This unicorn with the poisoned horn seems a characteristic image in Lewis's fantasy; and I believe, possibly expresses an unconscious belief that some kind of poisonous coition gave his mother cancer and so destroyed his world.

Such paranoid fears would have been intensified by the death of the mother. In the poignant passages in Surprised by Joy, he relates how

> For us boys the real bereavement had happened before our mother died. We lost her gradually as she was withdrawn from our life into the hands of nurses and delirium and morphia . . . (her death) divided us from our father as well as our mother . . . we were coming, my brother and I, to rely more and more on each other for all that made life bearable. (pp. 24–25)

It is at this moment that he records the confrontation with his mother's corpse—"I do not know what they mean when they call dead bodies beautiful." But soon after these deeply traumatic disturbances, he encountered another experience central to his work. His mother had died, and his father proved unreliable. " . . . Everything that made the house a home had failed us" (p. 25). Now Lewis was sent away to a preparatory school that was so terrible he later called it "Belsen", and heads his chapter on it "Concentration Camp." The headmaster, the Reverend Capron, was actually certified insane a short while after Lewis left and the school was closed. Capron

> was a big, bearded man with full lips like an Assyrian king on a monument, immensely strong, physically dirty. Everyone talks of sadism nowadays but I question whether his cruelty had any erotic element in it.* (p. 33.)

Lewis believed there was a social snobbish element in Capron's choice of victims. One boy suffered because he was the son of a dentist:

> I have seen [Capron] make that child bend down at the end of the schoolroom, and then take a run of the room's length at each stroke. (p. 33)

Capron's selection of boys who were socially inferior suggests that in his violence he may have been punishing the weak infant in himself, whom he despised: surely a form of hatred for the "regressed libidinal ego" such as Guntrip discusses?

Imagine a child in the throes of grief, then, living in the hell of a school run by this psychopathological bully (who was actually vested in the priesthood of the church). While Capron's cruelty might not have what Lewis calls an "erotic" element, it obviously gave him perverted satisfactions; and these must have included a monstrous indifference to the suffering of weak creatures, as well as an excitement of attacking in others the weakness the man hated in himself. This, I believe, taught Lewis a certain kind of solution because this man's mad hate was cloaked in the authority of headship and priesthood.

Lewis's first bereavement was followed by the experience of a schoolmaster who was himself made mad by bereavement:

---

*"The smiling-lipped Assyrian, cruel-bearded King," Sonnet, Poems, p. 120, which is about mice destroying Sennacherib; that is, little creatures (like the little boys) overthrowing their mad tyrannical headmaster, surely?

Oldie's [Capron's] school presently repeated my home experience. Oldie's wife died and in term time. He reacted to bereavement by becoming more violent than before. (p. 38)

Lewis was evidently a sensitive and intelligent boy. He was very bookish and spent much of his time in solitude, reading and writing, writing about "Animal-land," and daydreaming a great deal. His already odd relationship with reality became even more distressed as his mother became fatally ill with cancer, and he lost her attentions:

> We lost her gradually as she was gradually withdrawn from our life into the hands of nurses and delirium and morphia, and as our *whole existence changed into something alien and menacing,* as the house became full of strange smells and midnight noises and sinister whispered conversations. (p. 24; my italics)*

Reality itself was thus already taking on a menacing nature for him before his mother's death. As Lewis makes plain, the effect of the death on the father in his relationship to the boys was *evil:* "It divided us from our father as well as our mother." Rejecting the idea that suffering draws people together, Lewis said, "The sight of *adult misery and adult terror* has an effect on children which is merely *paralysing and alienating.*" (p. 25; my italics) We may suppose from this that Lewis felt as a boy of ten that adult misery and terror were too much to be borne, while he also felt guilty about being so unable to help his father. He felt emotionally paralyzed; and the father became difficult, indeed hopeless.

> His nerves had never been of the steadiest and his emotions had always been uncontrolled. Under the pressure of anxiety his temper became incalculable: he spoke wildly and acted unjustly. (p. 25)

The episode brought the brothers closer together: they relied on one another.

> Everything that had made the house a home had failed us; everything except one another. We drew daily closer together (that was the good result)—two frightened urchins *huddled for warmth in a bleak world.* (p. 25; my italics)

---

*To the child, this may well have seemed to be a monstrous and deathly *confinement.* See my remarks above on the name "Tumnus": pregnancy and cancer.

This was a positive experience of love, and much that is benign in the writings stems from it. It also explains much of the intensity of certain themes in the "Narnia" books such as the loyalty between the horse and his boy: the qualities demanded of the children crossing the desert to Narnia in that book; the feeling throughout of the need for loyalty between the children against "them" and against menace and danger. It explains why Lewis is so angry with any character who is treacherous to such sibling loyalty—such as the silly Lasaraline in The Horse and His Boy; or Edmund when he betrays people; or Eustace when is is alienated from the rest in The Dawn Treader. It also explains more of Aslan, who in one sense embodies male sibling love.

After such terrible experiences, it is surely hardly surprising that Lewis seems often not to have been able to have appropriate feelings in certain areas of experience. Lewis describes the cruelties of his prep school in his biographical account in strangely cool language. For instance, speaking of the close relationships formed between the boys at "Oldie's" School, Lewis says, "That, I think, is why Belsen did me, in the long run, so little harm" (Surprised by Joy, p. 27).

I believe, on the contrary, that his experience of this cruel (and also inefficient) school did C. S. Lewis a great deal of harm and that one of the most catastrophic effects was to make it impossible for him to discriminate in certain important moral spheres. We now realize that a child has few standards of comparison; and if he is brought up by a bad or wicked character, he may come to admire that badness or wickedness, as "strength" since this is the only guidance he has had. These are the only characters with whom he could identify as he needs to identify. He may, in psychoanalytical terms, "identify with the aggressor," "imprinting," as it were, on hate. Lewis was in a sense an abused child.

A child finds it almost impossible to blame his parents, and this is one of the most terrible things about human existence. The child cannot judge, of its own experience, that it may be totally different from everybody's else's, or that there are other criterion. Capron served in loco parentis: the mother had gone, and the father was weak. One consequence of this was a distorted kind of learning; and I believe that Lewis learnt from the cruel and mad Capron in this way the need for submission to a kind of stern authority, the nature of which authority lies somewhere in a confusion between fantasy and actuality. (Into his magical figure who is to hold his world together—the "big dog"—merges the cruel father figure of "Oldie" Capron, as Aslan.)

Here I believe we can learn much from a case history from Winnicott. This is the case of a child who came to devise an "hallucinated internalised authority standing in the place of an adequate true conscience": a wizard. This is especially relevant because Winnicott discusses it in relation to religion. Winnicott suggests that religious solutions can be a form of *splitting*:

> All sorts of feelings and ideas of goodness that belong to the child and his or her inner experiences can be put out there and labelled 'God.' In the same way, nastiness in the child can be called 'the devil and all his works'. *The labelling socialises the otherwise personal phenomena.* (Winnicott 1966, p. 93; my italics)

These insights enable us to look at the relationship between religious belief and culture, in relation to morality or "ethical living."

The case in question is one of a boy who was "ordered about" by the voice of a "wizard"—a split-off entity of this kind, a "hallucinated authority" (Winnicott 1958, pp. 101ff, discussed by me in *Human Hope and the Death Instinct* [Holbrook 1971], pp. 204–12).

What brought the case to the clinic was the discovery that the boy at the age of nine had begun stealing. Winnicott found that there was a disturbance in the child's emotional development from the age of two. There were various contributory factors, including the disruption of his family life by the war at the age of two, and his separation from his mother when he went into hospital for a tonsillectomy, just after his sister's birth. His mother didn't die but he felt he had "lost" her, and he suffered terribly during some of the separations, so that he found it hard to keep his world together. From the age of six he had started a degeneration of personality. As Winnicott says in another discussion of the case, "*If he had been thrashed or if his headmaster had told him that he ought to feel wicked, he would have hardened up and organized a fuller identification with the voice of the wizard; he would then have become a domineering and defiant and eventually an anti-social person*" (Winnicott 1966, p. 28; my italics).

A moral system, with punishment, can, then, harden such a sinner in his attitudes that have their own perverse morality.

But at nine, or later, such a child as that in the case history would simply not be aware of the circumstances that caused his personality to degenerate, but which happened to him at age two, and age six. This in itself raises the question of what "wickedness" is. Winnicott is well aware of the need to penetrate beneath culpability.

The child's stealing had a *meaning*: "in stealing he was in the direction of finding the mother he had lost" (Winnicott 1958, p. 112). When he was staying away at his aunt's he would hallucinate his lost mother. "I would see my mother cooking in her blue dress and I would run up to her but when I got there she would suddenly change and it would be my aunt in a different coloured dress" (Winnicott 1958, p. 111). He often hallucinated his mother, employing magic, but constantly suffered from the shock of disillusionment. Winnicott talked to him about the awfulness of finding things you thought were real were not real. They talked of mirages: "you see lovely blue trees when there are really no trees at all" (Winnicott 1985, p. 111).

This case is illuminating when we are considering the fantasies of writers like MacDonald and Lewis who have "lost" their mothers. It helps us see how catastrophic was Lewis's loss by death of his mother, with whom it would seem he had not experienced sufficient *play*. It explains the intensity of the vision, the yearnings, the urgent hope. Winnicott says of his boy patient:

> I pointed out to him that the beauty of the mirage has a link with his feelings about his mother, a fact which I deduced from the blue colour of the mirage and of the mother's frock. (Winnicott 1958, p. 111)

When Philip, the boy in Winnicott's case history, suffered deprivation of the mother, his situation was really grim. He suffered depressions which he called "dreary times" and "*only just managed to keep the thread of experience unbroken*" (p. 111). Though Winnicott puts this in a clinical way, it refers to a very terrible experience indeed—a fear of total loss of existence, a fear of disintegration. The "blue" hallucinations were an attempt to counteract this depression, with the dread of total breakdown behind it. We may detect similar impulses both behind Lewis's fantastic inventions and his moral authoritarianism.

The uncle, to help the child, adopted a firm, disciplinary

attitude—Winnicott calls it "a sergant-major attitude"—and by dominating the boy's life he counteracted the emptiness which resulted from the loss of the mother.

Philip later heard a *wizard* with this uncle's voice, urging him to steal.

The boy yearned for his "good" mother (cooking in a blue frock). The alternative, says Winnicott, was "the witch, the cauldron, and the magic spells of the woman of early infancy, who is terrible to think of in retrospect, because of the infant's absolute dependence" (Winnicott 1958, p. 113).

Parallels between cases should not perhaps be pushed too hard. Yet, as I have been writing this book, Winnicott's remarks on this case history have been ringing in my head. There are parallels between the distress of the small boy who had to fantasize his lost mother; and the experiences recorded by Lewis, of his visions of other worlds like the intense landscape of Perelandra, and his fantasy quest for the mother: note the color Digory's apple brings to his mother. There are parallels between the uncle turned "wizard" and the experience of the cruel prep-school master who reappear as the authoritarian figures who dominate Lewis's stories, like Aslan, to whom he (and his reader, he suggests) must submit to as "real." There are parallels with what the small boy Philip might have become if he had "hardened up and organised a further identification with the Wizard." (Winnicott 1965, p. 28). He would, says Winnciott, have become "domineering and defiant" and "eventually an anti-social person" (Ibid.). There are places, which many critics have noted, where Lewis is domineering and defiant and where his tone becomes arrogant and cruel. And while he was by no means antisocial in his personal life, his fictional writing is dominated by a central need to fantasize cruelty, and to condemn or destroy those who are enemies to his cause. In Lewis cruelty is often exercised with intense self-righteousness, as we shall see; and this suggests something like the brave inverted morality of the boy who was stealing because "something was due to him." Lewis, too, feels something was due to him: a fullness of life denied him because of the loss of his mother, and his "fight" is an attempt to bring this about, often by ruthless and unremitting means. The most disturbing aspect of the case is that so many take this ruthless determination to be "Christian," just as Winnicott's patient felt he must be brave and obey his "voices," although in this his morality had become inverted.

C. S. Lewis wrote his books as homeletic treatises. He wants to make us better people. For us to become "better" requires greater integration, if psychoanalysis is to be believed: we need to accept our ambivalence. But if someone like Lewis persuades us to go in for "splitting," magic, putting our goodness into God and our badness into the Devil, and seeing the problem as "external" in that way, he could be (in Winnicott's language) "depleting" our capacities for ethical living (see the essay "Morals and Education" in Winnicott 1965). It could be worse if we simply hand over our responsibility to some entity projected away outside ourselves, to be made into an authority that is allowed to order us about, while we continue to fail to become whole, integrated and responsible, taking no existential responsibility for our choices and acts.*

I have mentioned that this study originated with the feeling that the principal solutions to problems of action, relationship, and ethics in the "Narnia" books seem to be based on hate. Here I should explain that I am using hate in a psychoanalytical sense. Hate is not the opposite of love, which is indifference. On the contrary hate is a product of frustrated love; and when it is turned outwards, it is an attempt to coerce "the other" into loving. With the schizoid person, as I have explained in a number of previous works, it is necessary for them to resort to hate, because love is not available. In consequence with the schizoid individual, that is, the individual who has not experienced good mothering at the very beginning, there is a very complex logic, as indicated by W. R. D. Fairbairn, based on the substitution of hate for love.**

Where the mother has failed to "be" for her infant, he may feel that "the reason for his mother's apparent lack of love towards him is that he has destroyed her affection and made it disappear." With the *depressive* person, by contrast, he feels it is his *hate* that has destroyed his mother's love; his love can therefore remain good in his eyes. For the schizoid individual, the reason why his mother has refused to accept his love is that his *love* is destructive and bad, a much more terrible problem.

It is a very tragic situation, and provides (as Fairbairn points out) some of the great themes in literature. Individuals with

*In extremes, of course, this following of moral exhortations from external authorities can be psychotic: viz., the Yorkshire Ripper (sentenced in 1981) who heard voices from God ordering him to kill prostitutes.

**"Schizoid factors in the personality" in *Psychoanalytical Studies of the Personality*, 1952.

any considerable schizoid tendency have great difficulty in showing love because they have the deep anxiety that "each man kills the thing he loves." (The phrase is from Oscar Wilde's *Ballad of Reading Gaol*.) They experience difficulty in emotional giving, for they can never entirely escape the fear that *their gifts are deadly*.**

> Hence the remark of a patient of mine, who, after bringing me a present of some fruit, opened the next day's session with the question, "Have you been poisoned?" (Fairbairn 1952, p. 25)

I believe what happened at "Belsen" was that Capron taught Lewis, at a crucial point in his emotional life, that existential security lay in the solutions of hate. He offered himself, as it were, as a father substitute while the child could not communicate to his father the pain and horror of his school (the father was, after all, responsible):

> My brother and I certainly did not succeed in impressing the truth on our father's mind. For one thing . . . he was a man not easily informed. . . . What he thought he had heard was never exactly what you had said. We did not even try very hard. (*Surprised by Joy*, p. 36)

In his few pages about his terrible school, C. S. Lewis makes clear that the origins of the strange moral system with its attachment to other realities than this which dominates the "Narnia" books originates in this need to get the truth about reality through to someone who doubts it. Lewis develops this impulse into the attempt to make others believe in a spiritual reality, if not by homily, then by threats.

At the same time, the truth about Capron was too mad to be told. So, Lewis even says "My father must not bear the blame for our wasted and terrible years at Oldies; and now, in Dante's words, 'to treat of the good that I found there. . . .'" (*Surprised by Joy*, p. 36). A child in such a situation has nothing with which to compare his terrible life: "we had no standard of comparison; we supposed the miseries of Belsen to be the common and unavoidable miseries of all schools" (p. 36). A boy

> would hate to be thought a coward and a cry-baby, and he cannot paint the true picture of his concentration camp without admitting

---

*See the image of a unicorn's horn poisoning human beings with its injections.

himself to have been for the last thirteen weeks a pale, quivering tear-stained, obsequious slave. (p. 36)

Despite this admission of the pathetic truth, Lewis defends himself against the pain of the reality by making such submissiveness a virtue. For instance, he makes it a primary virtue for the child in Narnia to have the capacity to be strong in courage, and above all (if one is a girl) not to "wet one's bowstring." The other virtue is never to let others down, and this I believe he insists on because of the comfort he had gained from his close tie with his brother:

At home, the bad times had drawn my brother and me closer together: here, where the times were always bad, the fear and hatred of Oldie had something of the same effect upon us all. (p. 38)

The school "contained no informer":

We stood foursquare against the common enemy. I suspect that this pattern, *occurring twice and so early in my life, has unduly biased my whole outlook.* To this day the vision of the world which comes most naturally to me is one in which "we two" or "we few" (and in a sense *"we happy few"*) stand together something stronger and larger. . . . (p. 38, my italics)

Lewis came to feel that it was natural for human existence to be like this, and this is the basis of his paranoid devotion.

This close cohesion between boys suffering appalling injustice and cruelty turned with Lewis's into "belonging" to an authoritative religion. It explained the seductive energy by which he seeks to establish a self-righteous cohesion among Christians. This verges itself on the paranoia; he thrives on cohesion against danger. The unusual "battle" situation of World War II seemed to him natural: "England's position in 1940 was to me no surprise; it was the sort of thing I always expect" (p. 38). This means surely that it felt natural to him to live in a world that was paranoically conceived? Black-and-white was natural to him, and in consequence he deals with the world by splitting and projection.

It is interesting that after delineating the dreadful situation at Oldie's, he should discuss a decline in taste: "There was also a great decline in my imaginative life" (p. 40). He read "twaddling school stories," "more wish fulfilment and fantasy: one enjoyed vicariously the triumph of the hero" (p. 40). He read *Ben Hur* and *Quo Vadis,* and says that the attraction was "erotic in rather a morbid way." They were mostly, as literature, rather bad books. Yet out of these bad books came the material from which, in relation to the same suffering, he later exercised his fantasy over Narnia. The need was to establish *another world* that would be in a special relationship with this in terms of a *real* fantasy.

As Lewis himself admits, his passion for other worlds demands psychoanalytical explanations; his idea of "other planets" was not just a romantic spell, while his motive was "exorcism":

> This was something coarser and stronger. The interest, when the fit was upon me, was ravenous, like a lust.* This particular coarse strength I have come to accept as a mark that the interest which has it is psychological not spiritual behind such a fierce thing there lurks, I suspect, a psycho-analytical explanation. I may perhaps add that my own planetary romances have been not so much the gratification of that fierce curiosity as its exorcism. The exorcism worked by reconciling it with, of subjecting it to, the other the more elusive, and genuinely imaginative, impulse. (*Surprised by Joy,* p. 41)

The "Narnia" books are the product of the same compulsive need. Lewis goes through world after world in search for one in which one might have a benign relationship with reality, not menaced by malevolent forces—worlds in which one could assert one's personal value, courage, and self-reliance, but not (as at "Belsen") in hopeless dread, however much strength one might summon in oneself.

The trouble was that the explored worlds are so paranoically conceived that what emerges as the highest survival value are the vengeful mental rages as of a small distressed boy, with some degree of schizoid weakness in his personality, trying desperately to survive.

There seems to be some confirmation in some of Lewis's poems of my view of his personality and its schizoid elements.

The editor of C. S. Lewis's Poems warns us against the "personal heresy." Yet surely one poem, *The Naked Seed,* is a statement of a feeling of schizoid emptiness in Lewis himself:

---

*The word "ravenous" indicates the intense *oral* need in Lewis's impulse to find the other world where the mother was.

> My heart is empty. All the fountains that should run
> > With longing, are in me
> Dried up. In all my countryside there is not one
> > That drips to find the sea.

The poem addresses Christ, who was able to "care for Lazarus in the careless tomb . . ." implying a deadness in himself by comparison. He asks Christ to "watch for me till I wake" (p. 117), in which surely we have expressed the desire to *begin living* in some new kind of existence.

In the same section of poems, there is one that even seems to show an awareness of his conditions. It is titled *Poem for Psychoanalysts and/or Theologians*. It is clearly about the breast, and the feeling of being deprived of it, of being cast out of Eden.

> Naked apples, woolly-coated peaches
> Swelled on the garden's wall. Unbounded
> Odour of windless, and spice-bearing trees
> Surrounded my lying in sacred turf. . . .
>
> > > (*Poems*, p. 113)

As in some of the passages in *Perelandra*, there seems to be an intense vision of being at the breast. "I was the pearl, / Mother-of-pearl my bower." The sky is egg-shell blue, streaked with "Milk-white cirrus."

The protagonist of the poem hears the gates shut behind him: "I wander still. But the world is bound." The world is a breast, and the relationship to it is parallel to that with the Mother, in the way Karl Stern makes clear.*

Another strange element in Lewis is the sexual undercurrent associated with fantasies of cruelty and aggression. I have already referred to Lewis's strange obsession with wiping one's sword after a murder; and while I believe this to be a symbol of unconscious guilt (and the need to renounce it), I also suspect that there is something in it of guilt *about masturbation*. There is one poem which seems to me to suggest that this problem was one that tormented Lewis. The poem has some of the guilt-ridden quality that haunts a boy's poem about the same subject that came into my mind while I was contemplating the meaning of Eustace's suffering in *The Voyage of the Dawn Treader*. This

---

*See *The Flight from Woman* (Stern 1960).

poem was published in *The Keen Edge*, by Jack Beckett (1965), an analysis of poems by adolescents:

> Today a menace roves our earth
> It lay in the deep, the mist of evil
> No one can master this menace today
> But this menace can master you.
>
> The evil binds and strikes to kill
> Letting you make your death
> You cannot control yourself again
> But are left helpless to evil.
>
> Once you are struck by this killing evil
> It clings to burn and kill
> And gradually crushes innocence
> And sinks in until your death.

(p. 142)

Masturbation can seem as terrible as this to a child; and I felt, coming across a poem by Lewis, that he felt this, too:

### Forbidden Pleasure

> Quick! The black sulphurous, never-quenched,
> Old festering fire begins to play
> Once more within. Look! By brute force I have wrenched
> Unmercifully my hands the other way.
>
> Quick, Lord! On the rack thus, stretched tight
> Nerves clamouring as at nature's wrong.
> Scorched to the quick, whipp'd raw—Lord, in this plight
> You see, you see no man can suffer long.
>
> Quick, Lord! Before new scorpions bring
> New venom—ere fiends blow the fire
> A second time—quick, show me that sweet thing
> Which, 'spite of all, more deeply I desire.

(*Poems*, p. 116)

I can't think what else this poem is about if not masturbation: "nature's wrong" seems to suggest something like "abuse," and the reference to wrenching his hands the other way seems to make it plain. Notable is the intense sadistic undercurrent ("rack . . . stretched tight . . . whipp'd raw . . ."). These preoccupations we shall find much illuminated by the letters to Arthur Greeves.

The anxious child masturbates as a manifestation of liveliness to counter depression, and identifies, in doing so, with parents in their sexuality. If a child is in difficulties with his "bad" mother imago after her death, masturbation would involve him in talion fears—fears that the "Revengeful Bad Mother" would castrate him, in retaliation for his Oedipal interference in the parental sexuality. To this we may add that where the boy Lewis is concerned, there is dread that the father killed the mother by sexual acts. It could be that Eustace's dragon's smoke and its menacing appearance could symbolize these predatory aspects of parental sexuality. I believe that masturbation plays a greater part in Lewis's cosmology than we realize. His spiritual feelings of ecstasy often seem sublimations of masturbation excitement, and (as the humiliation of Aslan suggests) the crucifixion is, as it were, a focus for the sublimation of those sadistic fantasies that accompanied or stimulated masturbation. I have tried to suggest that behind Lewis's sadism we may find the excitements of the thrashings Lewis experienced at the hands of the Reverend Capron. But behind this too we may find another source: Lilith. Lewis was fascinated by George MacDonald's books because in them, as in *Lilith*, he found the phantom of the dead mother. In the poem accompanying this letter we find a clue to the possibility that Lewis masturbated (like "Rudolph") *in order to bring the dead mother to life*. The White Witch who blights Narnia is thus the dead mother who, as Lilith, tempts him to masturbation and whose effect is only to make the world seem drab again when the excited vision is dissipated. In its place is left a feeling that the world is without promise or meaning, such as could be found by a better relationship with a woman who was not a witch: the poem virtually says "the bad (internalized) mother seduces me":

### Lilith

When Lilith means to draw me
Within her hungry bower
She does not overawe me
With beauty's pomp and power,
Nor with angelic grace
Of courtesy and the pace
Of gliding ship comes veil'd at evening hour.

Eager, unmasked, she lingers,

Heart shaken and heartsore—
With hot, dry, jewelled fingers
Outstretched, beside her door.
Offers, with gnawing haste,
Her cup, whereof who taste
(She promises no better) thirst far more.

What moves, you ask, to drink it?
Her charms, that all around
So change the world, we think it
A great waste, where a sound
Of wind like tales twice-told
Blusters, and cloud is rolled
Always above, yet no rain falls to ground.

Across drab iteration
Of gaunt hills line on line
The dull road's sinuation
Creeps: and the witch's wine,
Tho' promising nothing, seems,
In that land of no streams
To promise best—the unrelished anodyne.

(*Poems*, p. 95)

What is the answer he gives to the question "Why masturbate?"?
The answer is equivocal; and there is a great deal of anger
beneath the meaning of stanza three. He seems to be expressing
a bitter resentment that woman has the power to imbue reality:
"Her charms that all around so change the world." Because
of this, we think it "a great waste" when there is a great storm
in the world; and there is a sound of wind "like tales twice-told"
that "blusters": that is, he is weary of the old tale in his psychic
life, about the way in which the bad mother and loss of the
mother have devastated his life. There are clouds up there always. They are always sterile—yet this hullaballoo, in which
woman seems a kind of catastrophic empty blast, is taken as
a great pother, which seems a waste—and so we are obliged
to respond to her charms in the vain hope that this will restore
the waste and bring the fertile rain. (It is indicative that we
have to put so much into stanza three to complete the sense.)
The world looks even duller after the seduction, and the road
of one's life looks like a winding serpent of *sinuation* (and like
the serpent sin of which Lewis speaks elsewhere of plucking
away from one's body). All that can be said at the end is that
the "witch's wine" at least promises an "anodyne." Now, retro-

spectively, we can see that when Eustace's flesh is torn from his body, we experience something of Lewis's deep sense of loathing of his own body because of the *sin* into which the phantom woman lured him. The intensity of the conflict is clear from the next letter (1 June 1930):

> I have "fallen" twice since you left after a long period of untroubled peace in that respect. Serves me right, for I was beginning to pat myself on the back and even (idiotically) beginning to fancy that I had really escaped, if not for good at any rate for an indefinite time. The interesting thing was that on both occasions the temptation arose when I was almost asleep, quite suddenly, and carried me by storm before I had my waking mind fully about me. I don't mean to disclaim any responsibility on this account: but I feel grateful that the enemy has been driven to resort to *stratgem* (not by me but by God) whereas he used to walk boldly up to me for a frontal attack in the face of all my guns. . . . (*They Stand Together,* p. 355)

This reveals that masturbation was at the center of Lewis's religious life ('It' was a glorious alternative to 'That' in the language of the letters), and his paranoia was bound up with it. Therefore, we can read much of the "Narnia" stories and the space fiction fantasies as being symbolizations of a struggle against masturbatory temptation. It is this that he wants to communicate to children, and to "arm" them against.

If I am right, this guilt about masturbation might explain other things about Lewis. It would illuminate the strange image of sin being a green lizard which one needed to pluck from oneself. But it also suggests a deep division within the self, and the loathing of being human that pervades Lewis's work. In another poem, *Pan's Purge*, we have a vision like that in *That Hideous Strength*, of the animals "correcting" man in the name of Pan:

> The scorpions and the mantichores and corpulent tarantulas
> Were closing in around me, hissing, *Long Live Pan!*
> And forth with rage unlimited the Northwind drew his scimitar,
> In wrath with ringing scimitar
> He came, with sleet and shipwreck for the doom of Man.

Perhaps the *scorpions* link this with masturbation, if I am right about the previous poem? An avalanche is unleashed upon man:

> Towering and cloven-hoofed, the power of Pan came over us,
> Stamped, bit, tore, broke. It was the end of Man. . . .

And man is reborn anew, as "corrected" man:

> . . . hear on the huge pasture, the young voice of Man.
>
> (Poems, pp. 5–6)

This impulse to annihiliate man so that he may be reborn seems to me analogous to that found in schizoid suicide. That is, it belongs to a desire to leave behind the old self with its cravings and its evil qualities (which, in Lewis, included masturbation), so that one may become pure of sin at last. It is this which lies beyond the flaying of Eustace, as we shall see. Eustace had become a dragon who enjoys eating another dragon. What he suffers is Aslan's cure for sin and self-loathing.*

Another insight is relevant here, concerning sexual fantasy. According to psychoanalytical insights, the child often fantasies, in masturbation, an involvement in parental sex; and these fantasies may be intensely oral, because the child conceives of sex as a dangerous form of eating (lovers say "I could eat you" and at the time of writing a man in Paris has actually eaten his girlfriend). As we have seen, it is Lilith who tempts to masturbation. Here, I believe, we may have a clue to C. S. Lewis's need for mental rage and his fear of depersonalization. Strangely, his need to work, by fantasy, in mourning as a child, seems to have become linked, through sadistic punishment, to the need to imagine intense oral-sadistic hate such as we experience at the end of That Hideous Strength—one of the space fiction fantasies. Yet to him such cruel fantasies even seem to be a glimpse of heaven, even as they are also the deepest dehumanization. I believe that what we find behind Lewis's fantasies is a deep psychic confusion. Yet he seems outwardly sane and clear-headed: certainly single-minded. How could this be sustained? The Reverend Capron is quoted as saying on one occasion, "always stick to the truth." It seems to me that what he taught the unfortunate Lewis was "always stick to false solutions." He taught Lewis to hate with consistent purity: with all the conviction of a self-righteous minatory attitude towards others.**

---

*Incidentally, if (as here) Pan is to scourge man, what do we make of the moments in the "Narnia" books when a Pan-like impulse to the orgiastic is urged on children in the name of Christ?

**Throughout writing this book I confess I have felt a brooding, rather threatening personality, embodied in the works, rather angrily forbidding my penetration to the weaknesses I was seeking to understand.

Yet the consistent hate is so idolized that nobody notices. The Reverend Capron, after all, was a clergyman. There was a facade of "learning" (though the children did hardly any work) and his bestial tyranny was cloaked as "education":

> ... Oldie [Capron] did not teach at all. He called his class up and asked questions. When the replies were unsatisfactory he said in a low, calm voice, "Bring me my cane. I see I shall need it." If a boy became confused Oldie flogged the desk, shouting in a crescendo, "Think—think—THINK!!" Then to execution, he muttered, "Come out, come out, come out." When really angry he proceeded to antics: worming for wax in his ears with his little finger and babbling, "Aye, aye, aye, aye. . . ." I have seen him leap up and down round and round like a performing bear. . . . (*Surprised by Joy*, p. 34)

In these few sentences we have revealed the origins of the apocalyptic last battle in *The Last Battle*. The boy Lewis needed, at that moment of bereavement, to reinforce the super-ego; and so he took this beastliness and insanity into himself as an educational lesson. It is significant that there is always much *learning* in it all, in the stories, as we shall see; but it is always learning of the projection and splitting kind: not to "know yourself," but learning to endure and fight.

Throughout the "Narnia" books there is one central value: prowess. Only in the excitement of battle, of being strong in battle, is there is a real feeling of existential assurance. This is also a feature of the adult fantasies. In *That Hideous Strength*, the adult fairy tale, the Christian "side" feel, in preparing for battle, that they are actually *entering into the harmony of the universe* in being willing to die. If we apply the Little-Red-Riding-Hood analysis, however, the wolf is a manifestation of the (oral) need for the mother. So, the pride is in fighting off the need for dependence which menaces one. One may recall Lewis's admission, "A boy home from school likes to cut a dash. . . . He would hate to be thought a coward." Aslan, as super-ego, encourages most strongly the denial of one's weak needs; and in this way, again, the creative effort moves towards a false path, since what is needed is an embracement of "the bad," not a defiance of it. Lewis's feelings seems to be that the deepest spiritual satisfaction is to be found in mental rage and hostility, directed in hate against those weaknesses which threaten to reveal one's deepest needs, projected over others and hated in them, as "split-offs" from one's inner problem of ambivalence and being human.

# 5

## Surprised by Joy

We have to try to distinguish between what the explicit knowing self tells us, and the message man's unconscious mind sends through the fantasies. In Lewis's work the complex between imagination and the reality-sense, belief and apprehension is really very strange when examined.

As Lewis records in *Surprised by Joy*, he lost his faith in youth, and was for a time an atheist. He then regained his faith; and this is recorded in detail, with a great deal of thought about the implications. However, we may, I believe, find in this record a number of significant elements, which play around the question of *what is real*. Behind the problems of sincerity I have referred to above, I believe there was a serious problem for Lewis about what is real. There are asides in *Surprised by Joy* which indicate strange difficulties here. Lewis's father was continually impressing upon his children that life was a poor thing, and Lewis records that he conveyed to him the impression that "adult life was to be an unremitting struggle in which the best I could hope for was to avoid the workhouse by extreme exertion" (p. 56). This goes with his feeling, taken in from such writers as Wells and Sir Robert Ball, about "the vastness and coldness of space, the littleness of Man": "it is not strange that I should feel the universe to be a menacing and unfriendly place" (p. 67). Life at a vile boarding school, he said, "teaches us to live by hope"—and at this point he said that this was in a perverse kind of way a preparation for the Christian life.

Because of his problems over reality and the way in which he expected so little of life, and found it so unpromising, he devised a rich and powerful fantasy world. We could even say that he almost *lived in* his fantasy life. At the same time, as he records often, he distrusted the emotional life. So, he seems to have almost lived in two worlds, and speaks of this in terms of a divided personality:

I am telling the story of two lives. They had nothing to do with each other: oil and vinegar, a river running beside a canal, Jekyll and Hyde. Fix your eye on either and it claims to be the sole truth. When I remember my outer life I see clearly that the other is but momentary flashes, seconds of gold scattered in months of dross, each instantly swallowed up in the old familiar, sordid, hopeless weariness. When I remember my inner life I see that everything mentioned in the last two chapters was merely a coarse curtain which at any moment might be drawn aside to reveal all the heavens I knew there. The same duality perplexes my home life. (*Surprised by Joy*, p. 115–16)

From this kind of account, and from other sources in Lewis, I deduce serious underlying problems, not only to do with reality, but with apperception—that is, the capacity to perceive the world in such a way as to find it imbued with emotional significance, problems of fantasy and imagination in relation to reality.

And this I would like to relate to the way in which, now and then, one has a feeling of his fantasy life getting out of hand. His pages about Boxen seem to me to be strangely disconnected with anything, though he admits that there is a certain resemblance between "the life of the two kings under Lord Big and our own life under our father" (*Surprised by Joy*, p. 81). They even seem to me slightly deranged ("Lord Big's most consistent opponent, the gadfly that always got inside his armour, was a certain small brown bear, a lieutenant in the Navy. . .") (p. 81). Yet both this Boxen fantasy and his Animal Land of childhood he attributes to the "outer"; that is, to the world of everyday life, and not the world in which he pursues what he calls "joy" through the imagination. Yet there is a strange sense with him that the imaginative life does not engage with the world, in the sense of imbuing it with meaning. Lewis is oddly ambivalent about the status of his life of imagination:

[M]y secret, imaginative life began to be so important and so distinct from my outer life that I almost have to tell two separate stories. *The two lives do not seem to influence each other at all.* Where there are hungry wastes, starving for joy, in the one, the other may be full of bustle and success; or again, where the outer life is miserable, the other may be brimming over with ecstasy. By the imaginative life I here mean only my life as concerned with Joy—including in the outer life much that would ordinarily be called imagination, as, for example, much of my reading, and all my erotic or ambitious fantasies; for these are self-regarding. Even Animal-Land and India belong to the "Outer." (*Surprised by Joy*, pp. 79; my italics)

The dissociation is perplexing. At the end of the chapter he goes on:

> I have been describing a life in which, plainly, imagination of one sort or another played the dominant part. Remember that it never involved the least grain of belief; I never mistook imagination for reality. . . . Boxen we never could believe in, for we had made it. No novelist (in that sense) believes in his own characters. . . . (p. 82–83)

A novelist does, surely, believe in his own characters to the extent that he or she will feel that Anna Karenina's suffering is of the kind that a human being inevitably suffers, over authenticity, or as when an Elizabeth Bennett is seeking to realize what her true self requires if she is to be fulfilled? Creative symbolism does relate to a reality of the subjective world; and we may take it in Lewis's work that (for example) Aslan represents Christ with us.

But the passages above do surely indicate an odd literalness in Lewis, combined with a strange failure to relate the one world with the other—a feeling that because "imagination" is so separate from "reality" that "the two lives do not influence one another." And perhaps this may be linked with his occasional moments in which one wonders whether he is being serious—because if the imagination, even when seeking "Joy," is so little able to impinge on the "other" life, then it doesn't *matter*. Yet at the same time, he adhered to a strong literalness over belief itself.

Lewis was making heroic attempts to solve his problems of existence. He speaks of his desire to do this in appropriate terms. Of his fascination with magic (later discarded), he writes:

> This ravenous desire to break the bounds, to tear the curtain, to be in the secret revealed itself, more and more clearly the longer I indulged it, to be quite different from the longing that is Joy. Its coarse strength betrayed it. Slowly and with many relapses I came to see that the magical conclusion was just as irrelevant to Joy as the erotic conclusion had been. . . . (*Surprised by Joy*, p. 167)

The "erotic conclusion," like the fascination with the occult, we can see from this to have been impelled by the search for

"Joy," the apprehension of a sense of meaning. At last Lewis found a mode and topography by which he could pursue his quest—only this time it was to be real and true.

The breakthrough came through his discovery of MacDonald. The reader who is a Christian will take this to mean that through MacDonald Lewis found the path to Christian love. I want to see it rather as the discovery of the poetic *mode* by which the personal mythology of the search for the dead mother and the source of meaningful existence might be pursued. All those torments which Lewis records as troubling his life up to then were suddenly given the hint of a possible solution. It is worth quoting the whole passage from *Surprised by Joy*:

> The woodland journeying in that story, the ghostly enemies, the ladies both good and evil, were close enough to my habitual imagery to lure me on without the perception of a change. It is as if I were carried sleeping across the frontier, or as if I had died in the old country and could never remember how I came alive in the new. For in one sense the new country was exactly like the old. I met there all that had already charmed me in Malory, Spenser, Morris and Yeats. But in another sense all was changed. I did not yet know (and I was long in learning) the name of the new quality, the bright shadow, that rested on the travels of Anodos. I do now. It was Holiness. (pp. 169–70)

The modes of MacDonald's fantasies exactly suited Lewis's taste, for that kind of literature that belonged to a faery world. But there was a difference which the slightly genteel word "ladies" indicates: the symbolic content, to do with the Phantom Woman of the Unconscious, exactly fitted the hungry need in Lewis, and pointed to a way in which the quest could be pursued with a hope of a positive outcome to an engagement between the imagination and the reality of his inner world. The way he goes on to talk about it reveals clearly that what he found in MacDonald was the glimpse of the mother's face, or the distant sound of her voice:

> For the first time the song of the sirens sounded like the voice of my mother or my nurse. Here were old wives' tales: there was nothing to be proud of in enjoying them. It was as if the voice which had called to me from the world's end were now speaking at my side. It was with me in the room, or in my own body, or behind me. If it had once eluded me by its distance, it now eluded me by proximity—something too near to see, too plain to be understood, on this side of knowledge. It seemed to have been always

with me; if I could ever have turned my head quickly enough I
should have seized it. Now for the first time I felt that it was out
of reach not because of something I could not do but because of
something I could not stop doing. If I could only leave off, let
go, unmake myself, it would be there. (pp. 169–70)

The Christian will see this as the light on the Road to Damas-
cus. The student of psychoanalysis will see it as an experience
of the discovery of a mode by which Lewis felt able to communicate, as a patient does under therapy, with the very structure
of the being and psyche, having found the mode by which to
engage by "dream work" and creative-symbolic effort, with the
deepest problems. The very way in which Lewis recounts the
experience suggests a healing of the gulfs between fantasy and
reality, a new "reality principle" in the employment of the imagination:

> . . . gradually, with a swelling continuity (like the sun at mid-
> morning breaking through a fog) I found the light shining on those
> woods and cottages, and then on my own past life, and on the
> quiet room where I sat. . . . (p. 170)

Up to now, every visitation of joy had increased the gulf between
reality out there and the visionary life.

> I saw the bright shadow coming out of the book into the real world
> and resting there, transforming all common things and yet itself
> unchanged. Or, more accurately, I saw the common things drawn
> into the bright shadow.

Previously, each visitation had left the common world momentarily a desert: that "Joy" had reminded him of another world,
and he did not like the return to ours. But now "That night
my imagination was, in a sense, baptised" (p. 171).

What Lewis had found, the Christian will believe to be God's
love, that "Holiness." I take it to mean that he had found mother's love; that is, the feminine element modes by which he
could explore and come to terms with the internalized mother
in himself. As with MacDonald, the trouble is that the mother
who did not prove adequate in infancy, and who then died,
is also, besides being the life-giver, possibily the ultimate re-
jector. In MacDonald, time after time, when this woman is approached with love, she turns malignant. In Lewis, we have
at least one glimpse of her as the creature who tempts him

to those erotic yearnings which, in masturbation, seem to be a way to find her, only to prove to be a false dynamic that merely exacerbates the problem of the dreary and meaningless aspect of a meaningless world and makes the problem of reality worse. She can thus be the "Woman" become a "Mother Earth" who is alien from man, and is "apart" and bleak in its lack of those qualities of at-one-ness, such as can be given by the positive experience of the mother's love (see Stern 1966). And here I believe we begin to penetrate to the very core of Lewis's problems. As I read it, his religion and his philosophy of existence end up in a rejection of this world, which is the unreal phantom of Plato's cave, and the old world which shall disappear as Narnia does. It also involved a rejection of this human self, not least his body, which seems only fit for (guilty) jettisoning. I am not sure that this is good Christianity: that is something for the Christians to decide.

What I am concerned about is what his fantasies teach as literature, both to his child readers and the adult reader, at the unconscious level. I believe that in the end Lewis's use of MacDonald's modes brought him to false conclusions. He comes to the conclusion, through his art, that the universe is the paranoid-schizoid universe that he felt it to be in his early youth. He records feeling in childhood "a deep (and, of course, inarticulate) sense of resistance or opposition on the part of inanimate things" (p. 56). His dreams and nightmares indicate a deep fear of depersonalization; and this seemed to be confirmed by much life experience, such as his time in the trenches. One can see an analogy between his phobias as of insects, his fantasies in his space fiction, and his accounts of war ("horribly smashed men moving like half-crushed beetles as if it were happening to somebody else"). His yearnings continually come to seem to him false, in that they do not satisfy the hunger for "Joy": for instance, talking about sexual experience, he says that it is like offering "a mutton chop to a man who is dying of thirst." The spiritual yearning is not at all a "disguise of sexual desire" (Ibid, p. 161).

What I suppose he is resisting here is a postulated Freudian view that spiritual yearnings are but sexuality sublimated. More recent schools of psychoanalytic thought would by no means see matters like that. To an existentialist therapist like Victor Frankl, our spiritual yearnings are what make us human; but Frankl would certainly have something to say about a man who called sexual experience a mere "mutton chop." It is important to consider Lewis and sex, because his rejection of sex, as we shall see, is a part of his whole rejection of this body and this world. His thinking about sex is largely conditioned by an obsession with masturbation, however much he plays down the part sexuality plays in life. What else can he mean but masturbation when he writes of sublimation:

> [I]t is not a disguise of sexual desire. Those who think that if adolescents were all provided with suitable mistresses we should hear no more of "immortal longings" are certainly wrong. I learned this mistake to be a mistake by the simple, if discreditable, process of repeatedly making it. From the Northerness one could not easily have slid into erotic fantasies without noticing the difference; but when the world of Morris became the frequent medium of Joy, this transition became possible. It was quite easy to think that one desired those forests for the sake of their female inhabitants, the garden of Hesperus for the sake of the daughters, Hylas' river for the river nymphs. I repeatedly followed that path—to the end. At the end one found pleasure; which immediately resulted in the discovery that pleasure (whether that pleasure or any other) was not what you had been looking for. . . . One had caught the wrong quarry. . . . It was the irrelevance of the conclusion that marred it. . . ? (Surprised by Joy, p. 160–61)

It wasn't a moral sense of chaste horror that made him recoil from the "erotic conclusion" he says, but a feeling: "Quite. I see. But haven't we wandered from the real point?" He concludes:

> Joy is not a substitute for sex: sex is very often a substitute for Joy. I sometimes wonder whether all pleasures are not substitutes for Joy. (p. 101)

In none of these discussions does Lewis offer any sense of finding another person through sexual meeting, and the letters to Arthur Greeves seem to make it quite clear that when he says he followed the nymphs into pleasure that he is talking of masturbatory sex, on which subject they held long discussions, calling it "That." We shall see later what other forms of sexual excitement Lewis indulged in, but nothing he says on this subject should be read as having anything to do with love. He goes on, by the way, after the above passages, to discuss the parallel problem in his imagination. He felt that without an object even religious imaginations would become a "self-caressing luxury" turning love into autoeroticism.

Incidentally, it is worth noting here Lewis's remarks in *Surprised by Joy* on sodomy at his public school, where there was an entrenched system of perversion between the prefectoral elite, the "Bloods," and the small boys who were "Tarts." Lewis himself declares he was "bored" by sodomy. One man's perversion is, of course, another man's poison: Lewis's excitement was "the rod" as we shall see. In his discussion of this system, he makes the most extraordinary apology for a state of affairs that seems to have been associated with a good deal of misery, humiliation, sadism, and viciousness in which children were systematically corrupted by domineering adolescents. He even seens this pattern of perversion as "the only chink left": it was

> . . . in that time and place, the only foothold or cranny left for certain good things: the one oasis (though green only with weeds and moist only with foetid water) in the burning desert of competitive ambition. . . . A perversion was the only chink left through which something spontaneous and uncalculating could creep in . . . Eros, turned upside down, blackened, distorted, and filthy, still bore traces of his divinity (p. 108)

There seem to be strange rationalizations behind Lewis's arguments here. It may be true that over a place like Wyvern it would be strange to consider carnal sins as the worst kind of lapse. Yet in the light of what the psychotherapists tell us, the exposure of immature children to homosexual practices could manifest against the child's discovery of the self and other, and inhibit or even cripple his emotional development. As we shall see, Lewis's own fantasy life about sex was itself oddly perverted, and so his rationalizations may be seen as a defense of these inclinations in himself. The obsessional preoccupation with wiping one's sword makes it likely that Lewis's masturbation fantasies were accompanied by sadistic imagery.

To return to Lewis's sense of relationship with reality: towards the end of *Surprised by Joy* he recounts his final conversion back to Christianity. When he traces this path, it leads to a submission to an absolute authority; he interprets "en la sua voluntade" as "His compulsion is our liberation," and the liberation seems to be from all volition. It is as if he yearned to leave all the problems behind, of engagement with the self and the world, through which most of us suppose we shall find fulfilment and meaning. Lewis is often taken to be an expert on "love," but, up to *Till We Have Faces*, this seems an experience on which he is profoundly unreliable, while, in his yearning for the forfeiture of the self in total submission, he seems as far from the quest for existential freedom and authenticity as one can get, as will appear.

Lewis has considerable difficulty with the question of love: it requires an object. To concentrate on your own love is "to cease thinking about the loved object."

> In introspection we try to "look inside" ourselves and see what is going on. But nearly everything that is going on a moment before is stopped by our very act of our turning to look at it. Unfortunately this does not mean that introspection finds nothing. On the contrary, it finds precisely what is left behind by the suspension of all our normal activities; and what is left behind is mainly mental images and physical sensations. The great error is to mistake this mere sediment or track or by-product for the activities themselves. . . .
> (Surprised by Joy, p. 206)

This seems to be extraordinarily sceptical, and what is missing seems to be consciousness—consciousness, at the level of being, which can be examined, and is not mere "sensations." The experiencing "I" seems not to be "there."

Lewis says that his waitings and watchings for "Joy" had all been mistaken. They had been a futile attempt to find some mental content, and to contemplate the enjoyed: all he could find would be a mental image or a quiver in the diaphragm. They were but the mark in the sand.

Desire is turned not to itself but the object. So, he found he was wrong to desire the "Joy" itself. Joy was of no value; it was that of which joy was the desiring. But who was the desired? This must be what he calls the "naked Other."

> This brought me already into the region of awe, for I thus understood that in the deepest solitude there is a right road out of the self, a commerce with something which, by refusing to identify itself with any object of the sense, or anything whereof we have any biological or social need, or anything imagined, or any state of our own minds, proclaims itself sheerly objective. Far more objective than bodies, for it is not, like them, clothed in the senses; the naked Other, imageless (though our imagination salutes it with a hundred images), unknown, undefined, desired. (p. 209)

The next stage was a "cetripetal" one: a movement towards the utter absolute, which is the utter reality. He enters into a theistic idealism, something like Berkleyism. He now had a philosophical God who could never allow a personal relationship to Him, any more than Hamlet could know Shakespeare. Finally, he became aware that he was shutting something out that was forcing itself upon him. He speaks of choosing, but felt more like "a man of snow who was beginning to melt" (*Surprised by Joy*, p. 212). He speaks of how, throughout his life, he had had the feeling that he did not want to be interfered with, but wanted to call his soul his own. He had always, in this spirit, rebelled against authority; but now he finally put himself under an absolute authority:

> Total surrender the absolute leap in the dark, were demanded. The reality with which no treaty can be made was upon me. The demand was not even "All or nothing". . . , the demand was simply "All." (p. 215)

It is clear from Lewis's last paragraph that he found relief and meaning in *an ultimate surrender to a dominating authority*:

> who can duly adore that love which will open the high gates to a prodigal who is brought in kicking, struggling, resentful, and darting his eyes in every direction for a chance of escape. The words *compelle intrare*, compel them to come in; but, properly understood, they plumb the depths of the Divine mystery. The hardness of God is kinder than the softness of men, and His compulsion is our liberation. (p. 215)

I do not have the qualifications to offer criticism of this position from alternative Christian points of view. But what I find doubtful about it is that we end *Surprised by Joy* with a sense of rejection of every source of understanding, insight, and meaning, such as living in this world offers. There is a profound distrust of the world, of the body, and the self: all are rejected, including the imagination. Everything is surrendered, in favor of an absolute, ideal, ineffable and intangible essence, whose authority is harsh and total. I suppose this is Christianity in one of its modes; but it seems to me to mark a failure, in terms of the problem of life.

# 6

## Sin, Guilt, and Masturbation
## —The Revelations in the Greeves Letters

When I first began to try to puzzle out the meanings of Lewis's fantasies, I began to find under the surface certain strange elements which seemed to me to have unconscious significance. These led me towards suspicions of the sadistic excitements, and guilt about masturbation. I hesitated to plunge into so complex and embarrassing a subject—but when I came to the Greeves letters these topics immediately became of foremost importance.

They came together in the strange pervading obsession with wiping one's sword. Often the children who are given swords and urged to use them on the enemies of faith are counseled that it is most important not to put the sword back in the scabbard still wet. It is important to keep the sword clean, so it can be used with despatch again. This, of course, applies to the males. The female parallel is that they must keep their bowstrings dry, a preoccupation which I interpret in terms of not losing effectiveness by breaking down into pity. The readiness to fight and kill must be sustained in some "pure" way—even (I felt) some *inhuman* way, to deny one's vulnerability.

It is possible that the small boy Lewis, excited by Capron's sadism, masturbated, and then felt a terrible sense of guilt. The flesh which felt the retributive anger became embroiled in the toils of self-indulgence (Turkish Delight); the sword became messily and stickily in danger of being caught in its scabbard, meaning that when he needed to feel strong and assertive, he would be undermined by self-loathing because he had given way to fleshly indulgence. From the strange poems Lewis wrote about masturbation (to which he was tempted by Lilith) it would seem that the underlying yearning was for comfort, for the mother's response, the breast. But as we know from psychoanalysis, such impulses often have a rapacious fantasy behind them—a hunger to empty the breast, accompanied by a dread of the

118

consequences. So, as in pornography, there may be an element of "violence and rage" as Masud Khan has pointed out directed against the "self-body or other body"; that is, there is a sadistic element in the masturbatory fantasy. This is so because "the instinctual sexual drive is dissociated from natural bodily expression, sharing and gratification" (Khan 1979, p. 225). So Lewis's sadism has a fetishistic, obsessional, perverted element that goes with the fantasy of bloody swords.

I found myself bewildered upon this path at first without any biographical evidence. Now, however, we have the letters from Lewis to Arthur Greeves (1914–1963) edited by Walter Hooper.* In those Greeves had deleted certain passages and these have been uncovered by infrared and ultraviolet fluorescence. I doubt whether it is really ethical to so uncover words the original participants wished to be concealed; but, since they are revealed, I feel I must discuss them, and I find they confirm the insights I had labored for by phenomenological disciplines.

What the letters in general reveal is a close man-to-man relationship, with emotional ties of a platonic kind:

> At hour of man, when, with our limbs outspread
> Lazily in the whispering grass, we lie . . .
> > friend with friend
> To talk the old, old talk that has no end,
> Roaming—without a name—without a chart
> The unknown garden of another's heart. . . .
> > (They Stand Together, p. 5)

In this homosexual friendship, he reveals a critical attitude to women. In one letter Lewis writes with characteristic misogyny: "Of course, like all the rest of her sex she is incapable of seeing anything fair . . ." (p. 66).

In an early letter to Greeves he begins to write of the "sensuality of cruelty" (a phrase expunged by Greeves). And then surprisingly (28 January 1917) comes this:

> "Across my knee" of course makes one think of positions for whipping: or rather not for whipping (you couldn't get any swing) but for that torture with brushes. This position, with its childish, nursery associations would have something beautifully intimate and also very humiliating for the victim. (p. 159)

---

*They Stand Together, The Letters of C. S. Lewis to Arthur Greeves, 1914–1963, ed. Walter Hooper. London: Collins, 1979.

Notice that "very humiliating" here is part of the excitement and note, too, the reference to "childish, nursery associations." That this occasional discussion with Greeves has its roots in child experiences at "Belsen" is perhaps indicated by the next letter.

> I am given to understand that the idea of suffering yourself appeals to you more than that of inflicting. It used to be so with me, and perhaps the experienced victim does get a more vivid voluptuous sensation than the operator—at first. But of course once you are really in pain you can't think of anything else while the operator grows keener all the time. (p. 160)

A few weeks before Lewis had written "it is only a few days ago that we were ragging about together in your bedroom" (18 September 1916): is one to suppose these two were practicing some of their sexual fascinations?

Lewis betrays a clearly perverted excitement at times. Of Maurice Maeterlink he writes (31 January 1917) "I often think he must have been a special devotee of the rod." Lewis quotes from a book about slave girls: "we need care nothing for their ill humours so long as the twigs smart and the whips sting. . . . That sentence is dragged in quite unnecessarily and is exquisitely worded." (1.161) Then, he writes,

> The only other member of your family whom I am interested in could be punished in another way—to the general enjoyment of the operator and to the great good of her soul. (*They Stand Together*, p. 161)

Lewis is, of course, still a young man, and with a young man's extravagance; but it is significant that he and Greeves exchange fantasies about *whipping women*.

At this point Greeves tells Lewis he has come to a certain conclusion that he will not commit to paper:

> You say you have come to a conclusion which will disappoint me, but you don't want to put it onto paper. What tawdry nonsense! If any person did read our letter, he would be an ill-bred cad and therefore we shouldn't mind what he saw. . . . My own Philomastix is only a harmless piece of Greek affectation . . . "philo" . . . means "fond of" while "mastix" is the ordinary word for a whip. (p. 165)

Apparently Greeves had come to the conclusion that "he didn't

love the Rod as I do." (It is himself that Lewis calls
ΦΙΛΟΜΑΣΤΙΞ.)

> Very, very few are affected in this strange way and I am only sur-
> prised that you can enter into my feelings even as much as you
> do. As a matter of fact, just as the other—the normal desire has
> a poignant sensual side and a vague sentimental side, so that has
> too. . . . Yes, that business about stepping on Zoe appeals strongly
> to the sentimental or theoretical side of this feeling. . . . (p. 166)

Again, we may pick up the association between the sadism
and the desire to triumph over woman. These exchanges are,
I surmise (and Hooper seems to think this) about *masturbation
fantasies* rather than actual acts. The words Lewis uses have
a special perverted mode that is recognizably the same mode
he uses elsewhere, including Narnia, for this sadistic enthusiasm
(and it is the playful note we meet elsewhere): "[T]here's no
special virtue in a whip—hundreds of other methods of world
torture are just as good" (p. 169). Here Lewis refers to his own
poem *Dymer.*
In the next letter (28 February 1917), Lewis writes of a lady.
She is "a suitable subject for the lash":

> Is she not absolutely perfect from head to heel . . . and moreover
> the necessary part of her body—one of the most beautiful parts
> anyway—shaped with an almost intolerable grace? The gods—whom
> I'm always abusing—certainly produced a masterpiece in her. . . .
> Ah me! If she had suffered indeed half the stripes that have fallen
> upon her in imagination she would be disciplined. . . . (p. 171)

The meeting point between Lewis and Greeves appears to
have been this tendency to sadistic fantasy. Greeves seems to
have been homosexual ("I mean, you are interested in a brand
of *that* which doesn't appeal to me, and I in one that doesn't
appeal to you," 6 March 1917, p. 174). Greeves is more interested
in masochism, while Lewis writes "imagine yourself the slave
of some Eastern queen who whips you . . ." (p.162) and again
signs himself "Philomastix."
According to Lewis, the infliction of suffering is a male pro-
clivity: to enjoy suffering is female:

> His taste is altogether for suffering rather than inflicting: which
> I can feel too, but *it is a feeling more proper to the other sex.*

VERGERS POUR LES VIERGES. (p. 170; my italics)

In the next letter written a week later, he writes as quoted above about "that lady": "her as a suitable subject for the lash."

What does Lewis mean by *"That"*? In general, I suppose, sex; but more specifically masturbation:

> We must be careful never to talk of *"That"* in the precincts of the sacred wood—as well, our vegetable loves, the hazels and brambles, might be jealous. . . . (p. 176)

If the "vegetables" can be "jealous" perhaps this implies there was something between them—possibly mutual masturbation? Certainly they are on a plane of intimacy at which one can inquire of the other whether he has masturbated lately. Immediately after a voluptuous description of the statue of Shelley in University College ('I pass it every morning on the way to my bath'), Lewis writes coyly: "He is lovely. (No—not since I came back. Somehow I haven't even thought of it.)" (p. 180). Of another associate he writes: "Wish I was sharing them (tea and biscuits) with you instead of that six feet of spectacled priggery. . . ." This follows a remark that he wishes Greeves is having "some nice afternoons (in that way?) in the garden" (p. 182). "That way" presumably means in masturbation. The slightly jocose tone may be compared with that in which Lewis ridicules the constraint imposed on schoolgirls and wishes them responsive to the Pan-cry. The essence of it all is that these orgies are wished on girl children by an Oxford don who thinks of masturbation when he passes the statue of Shelley swooning on his way to his bath:

Sadistic sex is now "my subject":

> Butler tells me that the person to read on my subject is a Frenchman of the seventeenth century called the Visconte de Sade: his books, however, are very hard to come by. (p. 188)

In June Lewis got drunk when two students were given firsts: "I am afraid I must have given myself away rather as I went round imploring everyone to let me whip them for the sum of 1s. a lash!" He goes on having had his first experience of being "royally drunk": "The story that you have a headache after being drunk is apparently quite a lie (like the other one about going mad from THAT). . . ." Butler, having witnessed Lewis's "desire to whip" challenged him and told him more about de Sade (p. 191).

The reference to the "going mad" story makes it plain that

"THAT" is masturbation. In a letter from France he speaks of his old times with Greeves as "love":

> Perhaps you don't believe that I want all that again, because other things more important have come in: but after all there is room for other things besides love in a man's life. (p. 206)

Greeves has had to part with one "Tommy" and Lewis asks "were you bound to him by the chains of desire as well as by 'pure' friendship?" (p. 208). Putting two and two together it seems possible that Lewis and Greeves had some kind of sexual relationship. Greeves was clealy a homosexual:

> I admit the associations of the word paederasty are unfortunate but you should rise above that. As well what does "Uranian" mean— it ought to mean "Heavenly" as far as my knowledge goes. . . . (p. 217).

As the years go by, Lewis begins obviously to become more "moral." He gives Greeves a lecture on promiscuity:

> If you have alone established "Uranianism" in your own mind as something virtuous and natural, I must remind you that for men in ordinary sexual arrangements, a promiscuous desire for every beautiful person you meet is usually disapproved of. Your talk about continually meeting people and having to conceal your feelings suggests that you have no intention of confining yourself to one love: but perhaps I have misunderstood you. (p. 224; 17 June 1918)

Some twelve years later, after Lewis had regained his faith, there is a great deal of self-examination. One could say Lewis wallows in it: "Things are going very well with me spiritually" (p. 338). There is one extraordinary letter about his vanity, self-satisfaction, and spiritual endeavor; and in this there are passages relevant to a consideration of the "Narnia" stories. In these there are supposed to be references to Plato's *Republic*. When the Queen of the Underworld tries to persuade the childen in *The Silver Chair* that the real world and the sun are not real, or when a new world is glimpsed through the gateway in *The Last Battle* and a new world is entered as the old one is destroyed—these ideas are taken from Plato's figure of the Cave. If the prisoners were released out of the cave, they could see the shadows of real objects and the sun; and they would not assume that their shadows were the only reality (Biggs 1985). Again, Lewis picks up a mythology of "another world."

In his letter to Greeves of 30 January 1930, Lewis uses Plato to suggest that sex is "the central feature of the material life" and must be "a copy of something in the spirit" (*They Stand Together*, p. 338). He uses the word *It*, meaning spiritual joy, in opposition to *That*, meaning masturbation:

> I seem to have been supported in respect to chastity and anger more continuously, and with less struggle, for the last ten days or so than I often remember to have been: and have had the most delicious moments of *It*. (p. 338)

This feeling is "so very like sex" that he debates whether it isn't sublimation:

> One knows what a psychoanalyst would say—it is sublimated lust, a kind of defecated masturbation which fancy gives one to compensate for external chasity. . . . If he can say that *It* is sublimated sex, why is it not open to me to say that sex is undeveloped *It*?—as Plato would have said. And if as Plato thought, the material world is a copy or mirror of the spiritual, the central feature of the material life (=sex), must be a copy of something in the spirit. (p. 338)

One might (says Lewis) have a myth about the psychoanalyst— he is a man who is "always insisting that real people are only fanciful substitutions for the *real* things (as he thought them) in the mirror" (p. 339). One gets from the debate a strange sense of *dissociation*, as if Lewis is trying himself to escape into another world, while seeing those who try to understand the human consciousness as watchers in a mirror. He speaks of his own intense self-admiration and says, "I catch myself posturing before the mirror, so to speak, all day long" (p. 339).* With students, he thinks what to say to the next pupil ("for *his* good of course") and "then suddenly realise I am really thinking how frightfully clever I'm going to be and how he will admire me . . ." (p. 339). Later he goes on:

---

*Cf. Because of endless pride
      Reborn with endless error
      Each hour I look aside
      Upon my secret mirror
      Trying all postures there
      To make my image fair
            (Quoted in *The Inklings*, p. 244)
The need for reflection has become the adult's posturing before a mirror in which he seeks to glimpse "God's shadow."

There seems to be no end to it. Depth under depth of self-love and self-admiration. Closely, connected with this is the difficulty I find in making even the faintest approach to giving up my own will . . . (p. 339)

No wonder his work is suffused with guilt. Yet (as here) there is something indulgent in the confession, and there is no real insight or humility, while he is clearly proud of being, knowingly, so vain.

About this time Lewis sends the poem about Lilith to Greeves that I have discussed, about masturbation:

> . . . I enclose my latest: I think you understand the experience—when we fall not because That is so attractive but because it makes everything else seem so drab. (29 April 1930)

In a much later letter (12 September 1933), he says that in lust the "search for rapture was good and even divine" but the way to it is wrong: it is dull, cold and abstract. When we are tempted,

> We must remember that *just because* God wants for us what we really want and knows the only way to get it, therefore must, in a sense, be quite ruthless about sin. He is not a human authority. . . .
> (*They Stand Together*, p. 464)

Here he quotes MacDonald twice: "The *all-punishing, all-pardoning* Father" and "*Only God understands evil and hates it.*" Perhaps Lewis felt that this "sin" was one which threatened to make the world dead and without meaning. For this reason he must have a God who is ruthlessly determined to punish it. (Did the Reverend Capron beat boys because they masturbated?) His own inclination towards an authoritarian solution has behind it a dread of indulging in a phantasy that seems to lead to spiritual elevation (It) but leave him exposed to annihilation and nonmeaning (by "That"). "Evil," as he says (p. 465) "is simply good spoiled"—that is, bad breast, or breast destroyed by infant need; and behind this lurks the fear of hate:

> You know what the biologists mean by a parasite—an animal which lives on another animal. It is there only because good is there for it to spoil and confuse. (p. 465)

The opposition between good and evil in Lewis's world is not imagined in terms of symbolism: it is literal and thus embodied in everything. It is not only that he believes (as most Christians do) that Christ was a real man, and was the son of God. It is that pagan stories are God expressing Himself through the minds of poets, while Christianity is "God expressing himself through what we call real things'" (p. 427). The mythopoeia of Christianity is not symbolism, but literal truth. Lewis admits the ineffable quality of myths:

> [I]n Pagan stories I was prepared to feel the myth as profound and suggestive of meanings beyond my grasp even tho' I could say in cold prose "what it meant." (p. 427)

But he goes on,

> Now the story of Christ is simply a true myth: a myth working on us in the same way as the others, but with this tremendous difference that *it really happened:* and one must be content to accept it in the same way, remembering that it is God's myth where the others are men's myths. (p. 427)

That Lewis needs literalism suggests a terror about reality itself and how it may be reliably "found"; and about the threats that reality may at any time be blighted, by "That," by sin. He yearns for a kind of "It" that is a new world in which these dangers do not exist. He must believe literally in this other world (and Plato's model of the cave gives this yearning endorsement):

> God will invade . . . when that happens it is the end of the world . . . when you see the whole natural universe melting away like a dream and something else—something, it never entered your head to conceive—comes crashing in; something so beautiful to some of us and so terrible to others that none of us will have any choice left . . . it will be the time when we discover which side we really have chosen. (Sammons 1980, p. 11)

A concomitant of this yearning for another world to which one must show absolute loyalty is Lewis's paranoid feeling that the earth is in danger, being fought over by demons; and his feeling (symbolized in the story of Eustace and the dragon) that one's flesh is sinful and is best peeled away from one. A long way behind these feelings I detect a failure of play with the mother—that play which benignly establishes one in one's body as a being-in-the-world, creatively engaged, through the "living principle" with reality, from one's inner capacities for "ethical living" and the existential pursuit of meaning.

As we shall see from the fantasies, Lewis's self in the world is not like that at all, not a free soul at all.

# Part 2
## The Children's Stories

# 7

## Prince Caspian

I have examined with some thoroughness the first "Narnia" fable. I propose now to make a critical analysis of each of this series of tales.

In *Prince Caspian*, the second book of the sequence, we are, when we get to Narnia, some hundreds of years after the time when the children reigned there—although, when they were back on earth, only a year or so had passed since their first expedition. In my terms, whenever we move into Narnia, we move into the timeless world of the unconscious mind. So the "history" relates to psychic history. Lewis is exploring the kind of thing Melanie Klein called a "position," that is, a structure or dynamic in the mind that embodies a development experienced at a certain stage in growth and which lasts throughout a person's life. So, entering Narnia, Lewis is entering the dateless halls of memory, as embodied now in the "psychic tissue."

At the beginning of Chapter Five, Prince Caspian is learning from his old tutor about Old Narnia: "thinking and dreaming about the old days, and longing that they might come back, filled nearly all his spare hours" (PC, p. 54). Here we have a glimpse of the boy Lewis, wishing he were back in the days before his mother died.

Here and there, once more, there are hints of the unconscious meaning behind the "Narnia" books. For one thing, there is a significant moment when Aslan appears to Lucy: rather, surely, visions of that "play" with the mother that is so desperately sought.

> . . . the next thing she knew was that she was kissing him and putting her arms as far around his neck as she could and burying her face in the beautiful rich silkiness of his mane. (PC, p. 124)

We remember that Lucy loved the feel and smell of fur when she first crawled through the wardrobe.

131

> "Aslan, Aslan. Dear Aslan," sobbed Lucy. "At last."
> The great beast rolled over on his side so that Lucy fell, half sitting and half lying between his front paws. He bent forward and just touched her nose with his tongue. His warm breath came all around her. She gazed up into the large wise face. . . . (p. 124)

—all of which are gestures of the kind made between mother and infant

> "Welcome, child," he said.
> "Aslan," said Lucy. "You're bigger."
> "That is because you are older, little one."
> "Not because you are?"
> "I am not. But every year you grow, you will find me bigger."
> For a time she was so happy that she did not want to speak. (p. 124)

Whatever "Christian" significance Lewis may have felt this to have, it is perhaps more easily understood in terms of body play—with an element that derives from the fact that Aslan's mane is Capron's beard, which gives a sexual element to the submission to a "wise" authority.

This second book, *Prince Caspian*, is an attempt to develop some of the philosophical themes in relation to the history and topography of Narnia. These themes include the need to believe in Aslan, the need to be brave and to kill, and the question of animals and their relationship to man. We find a dread of man being taken over by some wild force:

> "Such a horrible idea has come into my head, Sir."
> "What's that?"
> "Wouldn't it be dreadful if some day, in our own world, at home, men started going wild inside, like the animals here, and still looked like men, so that you'd never know which were which?" (PC, p. 107)

This may seem like a Christian remark about the possibility of men becoming possessed by evil; but it does also express a characteristic fear of depersonalization in Lewis, and his dread of being "taken over" by predatory "forces." The remark is made when Lucy and Susan draw away from the Dwarf Trumpkin and the boys who are about to skin a bear. The bear, declares Trumpkin who shot it, "only wanted a Little Girl for his breakfast." "There's good eating on a bear," and there follows a paragraph which, like the episode of the fish with the Beavers, is strangely obsessed with dead animal flesh:

> Raw meat is not a nice thing to fill one's pockets with, but they folded it up in fresh leaves and made the best of it. They were

all experienced enough to know that they would feel quite differ-
ently about those squashy and unpleasant parcels when they had
walked long enough to be really hungry. (PC, p. 108)

How can we explain what again seems to be an odd insensitivity
to children's feelings? I believe the answer is the intense *oral*
undercurrent in this work: the chunks of meat relate to Lewis's
recurrent need to fantasy the biting and crunching of flesh.
Behind such obsessions are very primitive oral-sadistic fantasies
in the unconscious.

The bad mother turns up at one point, in yet another form,
as a hag with a werewolf. These, with Nikabrik the Dwarf, suggest calling up the White Witch: but there is no failing to recognize the hag:

> Her nose and chin stuck out like a pair of nutcrackers, her dirty
> grey hair was flying about her face. (PC, p. 147)

> A dull, grey voice at which Peter's flesh crept replied, "I'm hunger,
> I'm thirst. Where I bite, I hold till I die, and even after death they
> must cut out my mouthful from my enemy's body and bury it with
> me.* I can fast a hundred years and not die. I can lie a hundred
> nights on the ice and not freeze. I can drink a river of blood and
> not burst. . . ." (PC, p. 143)

—here, indeed, is the Castrating Mother again in full oral spate:
"No one hates better than me," she declares, like a true Lilith.

With such predators in Narnia, it becomes again important
to be strong; and Narnia, we are told, has an air which improves
sword play:

> . . . the air of Narnia had been working upon him [Edmund] ever
> since they arrived on the island, and all his old battles came back
> to him, and his arms and fingers remembered their old skill. (PC,
> p. 93)

So:

> It was not like the silly fighting you see with broad swords on
> the stage. It was not even like the rapier fighting you sometimes
> see rather better done. This was real broad sword fighting. The
> great thing is to slash at your enemy's legs, and feet because they
> are the part that have no armour. And when he slashes at yours

---

*This comes from the vampire myth. See the ridiculous vampire story by
George MacDonald, *The Cruel Painter*, which is in *The Gifts of the Christ
Child*.

you jump with both feet off the ground so that his blow goes under them. (PC, p. 93)

The tone should be studied; it displays a zany kind of delight in combat, as do other passages in this story, in which there are exciting fights:

At one slash of Trumpkin's sword her head rolled on the floor. Then the light was knocked over and it was swords, teeth, claws, fists and boots for about sixty seconds. Then silence. (PC, p. 147)

"Now? Miraz," they yelled. "Now. Quick! Quick! Kill him!"
. . . he was on top of Peter already. Edmund bit his lips till the blood came, as the sword flashed down on Peter. It looked as if it would slash off his head. . . . Peter swung to face Sospesian, slashed his legs from under him, and, with the back-cut of the same stroke, walloped off his head. . . . (PC, p. 167)

It is all enthusiastic fun:

Many a Telmarine warrior that day felt his foot suddenly pierced as if by a dozen skewers, hopped on one leg cursing the pain, and fell as often as not. If he fell, the mice finished him off: if he did not, someone else did. (PC, p. 167)

This "jokey" tone is surely disturbing. It smacks of the enthusiast for the whip.

When Lewis says it is "good" to slash at someone's feet with a broadsword, he means it. He feels he can adopt such a tone because all the fighting advances his cause, which is Aslan's. But anyone who has read the Letters to Arthur Greeves in They Stand Together will have serious doubts.

Aslan is continually concerned to encourage the children to be brave:

"You have listened to fears, child," said Aslan. "Come let me breathe on you. Forget them. Are you brave again?"
"A little, Aslan," said Susan. (PC, p. 133)

But then Aslan turns to the dwarf:

"And now, where is this little Dwarf, this famous swordsman and archer, who doesn't believe in lions? Come here, son of Earth, come HERE!"—and the last word was no longer the hint of a roar but the real thing. . . .
Aslan pounced. Have you ever seen a very young kitten being

carried in the mother cat's mouth . . . the Dwarf flew up in the air.

He was safe as if he had been in bed, though he did not feel so. As he came down the huge velvety paws caught him as gently as a mother's arms and set him (right way up too) on the ground. . . . (PC, p. 134)

We have surely heard that roar before?

Then as the prelude to execution, he muttered, "Come out, come out, come out. . . ." . . . I have seen him leap up and dance round and round like a performing bear. . . . (Lewis on Capron in *Surprised by Joy*, p. 34)

The lion who frightens a dwarf so that the dwarf shall believe in Him, becomes for this moment a strange amalgam of the lost mother and an insane child-beating clergyman—a product of identifying with the aggressor, a cruel super-ego.

From my point of view, Aslan is the magic "Big Dog" who appears when he is needed to overcome some menacing situation. From Lewis's point of view, there is no question but that this "Big Dog" is real. The only question is whether or not a person *can believe in Christ-Aslan: not so to believe is a bad thing.* So, when the children are lost in the forest, Lucy suddenly sees Aslan:

"Look! Look! Look!" cried Lucy.
"Where? What?" asked everyone.
"The Lion," said Lucy. "Aslan himself. Didn't you see?" Her face had changed completely and her eyes shone. (PC, p. 110)

Obviously, at this level, Lewis is trying to *teach* children the importance of believing in Christ.

"Where did you think you saw him?" asked Susan.
"Don't talk like a grown-up," said Lucy, stamping her foot. "I didn't *think* I saw him. I saw him." (PC, p. 111)

The dwarf is doubtful and suggests that Aslan must be a pretty elderly lion by now, and might have gone wild and witless like so many others:*

Lucy turned crimson and I think she would have flown at Trumpkin, if Peter had not laid his hand on her arm. (p. 111)

---

*There is here almost a glimpse of the beaten child's perception that Capron was not really a good reliable father figure, but a cruel and deeply disturbed middle-aged man.

There follows a discussion referring to the original discussion as to whether Narnia existed.

Later Lucy has a discussion with Aslan himself about this:

> "Yes, wasn't it a shame," said Lucy. "I saw you all right. They wouldn't believe me. They're all so—."
>
> From somewhere deep inside Aslan's body there came the faintest suggestion of a growl.
>
> "I'm sorry," said Lucy, who understood some of his moods. "I didn't mean to start slanging the others. But it wasn't my fault anyway, was it?" The Lion looked straight into her eyes. "Oh, Aslan," said Lucy. "You don't mean it was? How could I—I couldn't have left the others and come up to you alone, how could I? Don't look at me like that . . . oh well, I suppose I *could.* Yes, and it wouldn't have been alone, I know, not if I was with you. But what would have been the good?"
>
> Aslan said nothing.
>
> "You mean," said Lucy rather faintly, "that it would have turned out all right—somehow? But how? Please, Aslan! Am I not to know?"
>
> "To know what *would* have happened, child?" said Aslan. "No. Nobody is ever told that." (PC, pp. 124–25)

The conversation goes on, and is homiletic—it seems intended to impress upon the child reader that she must "believe and have faith" and not waver, and that where others are concerned one's faith must be an example, whatever the outcome. So it is an attempt to *trap* the reader in Christian belief. If he doesn't accept it, Aslan will be cross: the minatory quality of Aslan will be turned on us—and if we don't believe in Christ we shall have nightmares.

Aslan, in this, is schoolmasterish; or, one might say, head-masterish, capronic. He seeks to make people believe by *frightening them*, and by his rather minatory pauses. Then, if they believe, they have access to his magic:

> Lucy buried her head in his mane to hide from his face. But there must have been magic in his mane. She could feel lion-strength going into her. Quite suddenly she sat up.
>
> "I'm sorry, Aslan," she said. "I'm ready now."
>
> "Now you are a Lioness," said Aslan. "And now all Narnia will be renewed." (PC, pp. 125–26)

I suppose in a way all this does represent the kind of feeling a child has towards Christ in his prayers, and the magic may be felt to be appropriate to a child's religious thinking. But we may also read it, I believe, as a child's wish-fulfilment dream in which the world is to be restored by the power of one magic over another. For this, one must become lion-hearted; but also have contemptuous devaluation for whatever is represented by the dwarf.

There is an urgent seriousness about the quest to restore the mother and the world. Some of this seriousness rubs off on to the Aslan-as-Christ theme, however embarrassing the foot-stamping, blushing, and doubt. Neither seriousness is reconcilable with the more ridiculous moments in *Prince Caspian*. Here Lewis displays serious lack of a sense of proportion—a feature we shall examine in more depth later.

We may accept mice and giants in a fairy story, but it surely stretches our credence, when Aslan, with all his might and power, restores Reepicheep's tail:

> "Ah!" roared Aslan. "You have conquered me. You have great hearts. Not for the sake of your dignity. Reepicheep, but for the love that is between you and your people, and still more for the kindness your people showed me long ago when you ate away the cords that bound me on the Stone Table . . . you shall have your tail again. . . ." (PC, p. 178)

It was hard enough for us to accept that Christ-as-Aslan must die for a grumpy little boy: much more difficult to find the agony of the crucifixion invoked, simply to restore a mouse's tail by magic. Whatever meaning can there be in this symbolism?

A more embarrassing theme is Lewis's attempt to reconcile Aslan and Dionysus. "Pale Birch-girls" and other tree spirits from the classical world are shouting "Aslan, Aslan!" and dancing round him, with certain other figures.

> One was a youth, dressed only in a faun skin with vine-leaves in his curly hair. His face would have been almost too pretty for a boy's, if it had not looked so extremely wild. You felt, as Edmund said when he saw him a few days later, "There's a chap who might do anything—absolutely anything." He seemed to have a great many names—Bromios, Bassereus, and the Ram were three of them.
>
> There were a lot of girls with him, as wild as he. There was even, unexpectedly, someone on a donkey. And everyone was laughing: and everybody was shouting out "Euan, euan, eu-oi-oi-oi-."
>
> "Is it a romp, Aslan?" cried the youth. . . . And apparently it was. . . . The man on the donkey, who was old and enormously fat, began calling out at once,
>
> "Refreshments! Time for refreshments." (PC, p. 137)

There is a feast. Everything is covered with grapes:

> Really good grapes, firm and tight on the outside, but bursting into
> cool sweetness when you put them into your mouth, were one of
> these things the girls had never had enough of before . . . one saw
> sticky and stained fingers everywhere . . . everyone flopped down
> breathless on the ground and turned their faces to Aslan to hear
> what he would say next. (p. 138)

The boy is Bacchus and the old man is Silenus. Say the girls:

> "I wouldn't have felt safe with Bacchus and all his wild girls
> if we'd met them without Aslan."
> "I should think not," said Lucy. (p. 138)

But it is surely impossible to contemplate Bacchus without taking into account abandoned, orgiastic imbibing and passionate
sex. How does Aslan make this all right? Lewis's portrayal of
Bacchus and his constant companion Silenus is donnish and,
since it must be confined to the sensibility of the latency period
because he is writing for children, really ridiculous. Yet beneath
the surface strains a masked sensuality, which makes our response one of acute embarrassment:

> . . . firm and light on the outside, but bursting . . . when you put
> them in your mouth . . . one of those things the girls had never
> had enough of before . . . sticky and stained fingers—. (p. 138)

The "breathlessness" and the "sticky and stained fingers" (which
the "girls had never had enough of before") sound like the
"romps" Lewis had with Arthus Greeves. Here they are made
"safe" by "Aslan" (Lucy's "I should think not" is like something
E. M. Forster's Harriet might have said, she representing English
middle-class inhibitedness). In what possible sense can the
image of Christ be reconciled with a Bacchanalian sacred indulgence in wine and "wild girls"—belonging in any case to a
civilization in which the sexual orgy would have a fertility
meaning? It can't be anything to do with Christian marriage.
It is all absurdly academic and inappropriate, not least in a
story for children. The cry "Euan, euan, eu-oi-oi-oi!" is taken
from classical learning, and comes from the Dionysian "Dithy-
ramb": Is Lewis really suggesting that it would be appropriate
for these children to give themselves over to some kind of ecstatic state, like that in which the worshippers of Dionysus
saw themselves as the god's goat-like attendants? Could he not

imagine the kind of elements there must have been in those ceremonies derived from fertility cults? In what sense can Lewis really have believed that children should give themselves up to such abandon?*

The other embarrassing episode in *Prince Caspian* comes only a few pages after the light-hearted account of how Peter "walloped off" the head of Sopespian. There is a whole procession of Aslan, Bacchus, and his Maenads, while a river-god is freed at the Ford of Berna. But then they come to a school:

> . . . a girl's school where a lot of Narnian girls, with their hair done very tight and ugly collars round their necks and thick tickly stockings on their legs, were having a history lesson. (PC, p. 170)

Their teacher is called Miss Prizzle.

We have just been dealing with matters of life and death, and with themes of "classical" mythological significance. Suddenly, with astonishing banality, Aslan is made an instrument for simply frightening the life out of the kind of schoolteacher C. S. Lewis dislikes. The classroom turns into a jungle: "Then she saw the lion, screamed, and flew, and with her fled her class, *who were mostly dumpy, prim little girls with fat legs*" (PC, p. 171; my italics). Here again we have a jokey lapse into "contemptuous devaluation," and the child reader is encouraged to enjoy the discomfort of the ugly little girls' fear, and that of their silly teacher, whose name sound faintly rude, echoing "bull's pizzle." But in fact what Aslan does to them is exactly parallel to the Reverend Capron's assault on the dentist's son; it is cruel and contemptible (not least because it is *contemptuous*). Lewis has turned his vengeful feelings against "Belsen" into a form of mysogyny.**

---

*The clue to the origins of this absurd recommendation of the orgiastic for schoolchildren is to be found in *Surprised by Joy*, p. 93, just after his apology for sodomy: "A new quality entered my imagination . . . the orgiastic drumbeat. Orgiastic, but not, or not strongly, erotic. It was perhaps unconsciously connected with my growing hatred of the public school orthodoxies and conventions, my desire to break and tear it all." The advocacy is thus a form of childish revenge, and is not to be confused with the orgiastic cults of modern sexual liberation—indeed, is extremely naive in this respect, hence the absurdity.

**Taking into account Lewis's secret inclinations towards woman as revealed in the Greaves letters, we may suspect behind the name "Prizzle" a fantasy of whipping a woman with a dried bull's penis—the excitement of which, to one like Lewis, would be obvious.

Note the word "prim" but Lucy and Susan are also prim enough not to dance naked and take part in libidinal activities with Bacchus's "wild girls." How far, in this donnish "liberation" may they do? One hardly dare think.

There is no doubt that when it comes to fighting, however, to Lewis maturity is the capacity for really exciting swordplay. In *The Horse and his Boy*, the hermit gives a running commentary on a battle: "King Edmund is dealing marvellous strokes. He's just slashed Corradin's head off. . . . I can't see what's happened to Rabadash. I think he's dead, leaning against the castle wall, but I don't know. . . ." (HB, p. 161). The tone of the language goes with a boyish excitement, and conveys approval for the skill of killing. But something, as throughout Lewis's fantasies, is wrong. It is perhaps too heavy to talk of compassion or even about the hurt to victims since we do not think of these over the old Witch whom Hansel and Gretel push in the oven, or the people the big dog throws into the air in *The Tinder Box*. Perhaps with Lewis the trouble is that excited delight in violence is combined with a tone of endorsing it as all jolly good fun, and then endorsed by his solemn didactic message, urging that this is the way to the Kingdom of Heaven.

From time to time one feels one wants to say to Lewis, "Do you know what you are saying?" This springs from a sense that, beneath the Christian disguise, he is revealing a strange inability to really know what happens when people fight, or weapons strike bodies; again, in his happy lust for fantasy killing, in some strange way, he has not yet reached the stage of concern, because it cannot, imaginatively, reach reality. The same lack of a sense of bodily reality affects his references to "liberated" or Bacchanalian behavior:

> "You'll stay with us, sweetheart?" said Aslan. "Oh, *may* I? Thank you, thank you," said Gwendolen. Instantly she joined hands with two of the Maenads, who whirled her round in a merry dance and *helped her take off some of the unnecessary and uncomfortable clothes that she was wearing.* (PC, p. 171; my italics)

How much may Gwendolen take off? In one sense it could be taken in some such terms as *The Water Babies*—we should cast off our clothes and become our naked spiritual selves. But it seems to indicate some extraordinary naivety to offer an approving fantasy of Maenads stripping children for a dance. Surely Lewis would have detested any "free" modern school which encouraged such behavior? So, there is a serious lack of realization, a *voulu* quality, in such incidents, as if he doesn't know whether he is serious or not.

This leads to serious kinds of disproportion, in which all the values that the books are supposed to establish are thrown away; and we are left simply not knowing whether this writer means what he says. A representative example comes at the end of *The Silver Chair*, parallel to the humiliation of Miss Prizzle. Prince Caspian asks to see something of the children protagonists' world. "You cannot want wrong things any more, now that you have died, my son," said Aslan. (SC, p. 204)

So they are to be allowed five minutes of earth time. This is all it will take to *set things right*. They are going to achieve this goal at Experiment House—the "progressive" school that Lewis hates so much. Aslan "seemed to know it quite as well as they did": Christ, it seems, is concerned about the wrongness of healthy "hygienic" education (based presumably on humanistic "Weston"* ideas). The assault on this school is endorsed by Aslan, who gives the children a special blessing by breathing upon them and touching their foreheads with his tongue. He puts his back to the wall "and turned . . . his lordly face towards his own lands" (SC, p. 204). It is all quite ritualistic, and Lewis brings out his most "noble" language ("lordly face . . . lands") to describe it.

But what does it all add up to? Would Christ wish to *punish* people who ran a rather bad school, by terrorizing them, sending children equipped with riding whips and swords to *beat* them, because they follow "scientific" ideas? The biblical language, "rushing down upon them," gives a religious sanction to this characteristic indulgence in attacking and discomforting those you hate. In the stories such creatures as Calormenes are delineated as *evil*; but here the victims are simply individuals of whose humanistic life-style (Bedales?) Lewis disapproves. Yet the children are inspired by the very Son of God to attack them!

In *Prince Caspian* there is, at the end, an even more cruel episode. Following the dance of Gwendolen with the Maenads, the dancers come to another school where a "tired-looking girl" was teaching arithmetic to a number of boys "who looked very like pigs." As we have seen, *a man is turned into a tree for beating a boy*; but the boys are turned into pigs *simply because*

---

*Weston is the hated scientist in the Perelandra fantasies.

*their faces looked mean.* Here, evidently Lewis draws on a deep fund of contempt for his fellow victims at "Belsen," as well as for the headmaster.

After the Bacchanalia, and the fantasy of the mother restored to life, *Prince Caspian* returns to the emphasis on punitive authority, in laying down the historical development of the "Emperor's magic."

> At the sight of Aslan the cheeks of the Telmarine soldiers became the colour of cold gravy, their knees knocked together, and many fell on their faces. (PC, p. 175)

The Telmarines (whose name presumably derived from "tell-it-to-the-marines") are sent back to their own country (p. 184).

> "Men of Telmar," said Aslan, "you who seek a new land, hear my words. I will send you all to your own country, which I know and you do not."
> "We don't remember Telmar. We don't know where it is. We don't know what it is like," grumbled the Telmarines.

Lewis presents them as weak and contemptible people who grumble, are weedy, or do not do what they are told. He loves scenes in which inadequate people of this kind are subjected to firm leadership and awesome rule:

> "You came into Narnia out of Telmar," said Aslan. "But you came in to Telmar from another place. You do not belong to this world at all. You came hither, certain generations ago, out of the same world to which the High King Peter belongs."
> At this, half the Telmarines began whispering. "There you are. Told you so. He's going to kill us all, send us right out of the world," and the other half began throwing out their chests and whispering. "There you are. Might have guessed we didn't belong to this place with its queer, nasty, unnatural creatures. We're of royal blood, you'll see." And even Caspian and Cornelius and the children turned to Aslan with looks of amazement on their faces. . . .
> "Peace," said Aslan in the low voice that was nearest to his growl, the earth seemed to shake a little and everything in the grove became as still as stone. . . . (PC, p. 184)

After this passage, there is a passage through a wooden arch into yet another world and another time. I have said that in fantasying such passages Lewis was seeking the world where his dead mother was in order to complete mourning. But he has a strange awareness that one can become too old to complete the processes of growth which should have been completed at a certain age. From time to time the children seem likely to have become "too old": "Not Sue and me. He says we're getting too old . . ." (PC, p. 188). The question of one's fulfilment and integration cannot be solved, because a certain kind of imagination is no longer available; and the child's access to the inner world is thus cut off. There is some truth in this: the child has an open route to the *unconscious* as the adult does not.

It is also true that no one after childhood could have Lewis's simple-minded belief in the kind of "strength" he cherishes of military-style preparedness: "The hour has struck. Our council on the Dancing Lawn must be a council of war. . . ." (PC, p. 72).

When we re-read some of his broadcasts we realize that our attitudes to soldierly "courage" have changed since Lewis's time. Today military solutions are felt to be no longer possible—and are certainly less respectable. As he tells a story, we are expected to give assent to a feeling that it is literally a matter of disgrace to be "no good" in war:

> "We're awfully fond of children and all that, but just at the moment, in the middle of a war—but I'm sure you understand."
> "You mean you think we're no good," said Edmund, getting red in the face.
> "Now pray don't be offended," interrupted the Dwarf. "I assure you my dear little friends. . . ."
> "*Little* from you is really a bit too much," said Edmund, jumping up. (PC, p. 91)

While this kind of passage may seem to be satirizing the child's concern about bigness and littleness, there is no doubt that when it comes to dealing with the world, Lewis believes that toughness is all. As we have seen: "The great thing is to slash at your enemy's legs and feet because they are the part that have no armour . . ." (p. 93).

Lewis's attitudes to prowess belong to the days when a public school prefect said, throwing out a small boy's hyacinth, "We don't want any of that effeminate stuff here!"* Moreover, the dangers of weakness are often found on one's own side: here a son is in danger from another son, and we may understand

---

*Quoted by Richard Carline in *Draw They Must* (London: Arnold, 1968), an excellent book on the history of art education.

that nothing could be worse in Lewis's "Belsen" ethic than traitors among the beaten children. Afterwards:

> You can't help feeling stronger when you look at a place where you won a glorious victory. . . . (p. 117)

Towards the beginning of the book, Prince Caspian sleeps out under the stars for the first time: "he began already to harden and his face wore a kinglier look" (p. 76). But, examined closely, the book is disturbing in the subtle way it tries to persuade children that the path to maturity is this kind of "hardening." There can be no doubt about this message, whether one takes the story to be a Christian allegory, or merely a fairy story. Aslan continually endorses those triumphs of aggression which end, as here, by Peter declaring, "Let the vermin be flung into a pile . . ." (p. 149).

# 8

## The Magician's Nephew

In *The Magician's Nephew* the theme again is the passage from *this world* into the *Other World*, where the dead mother is to be found. In this story, the "bad" mother, the Castrating Mother, is very much in evidence—as is evidence that we are correct in interpreting the "Witch" in such terms.

The way to the other world is by means of certain magic rings, which Uncle Andrew has discovered. These I have suggested are "transitional objects"—they symbolize the experience of the mother, and exist in that intermediate area between mother and infant: between self and world. They have the characteristics of the first plaything (the *nipple*) and the brightness of the *mother's eyes*. Certainly, they belong to the *oral* stage, as we have seen:

> What she noticed first was the bright red wooden tray with a number of rings on it. They were in pairs—a yellow one and a green one. . . . They were the most beautifully shiny little things you can image. *If Polly had been a very little younger, she would have wanted to put one in her mouth.* (MN, p. 17; my italics)

The last sentence takes us back to Winnicott's essay on playing and reality:

> Now at some point the baby takes a look round. Perhaps a baby at the breast does not look at the breast. Looking at the face is more likely to be a feature. . . . (Winnicott 1971, p. 112)

The rings come as symbols from Lewis's hope for a new beginning, a new birth, which is somewhere in the moment when the vision of the mother's eyes or breasts presents itself.

The mother's role in creating a benign world is a central theme in the attempt to accept the mother's death. When she died, Lewis's world was ruined; but was he right to pray for her recovery? Wasn't her death ordered by God, and so isn't the problem that of simply reconciling oneself to this death? To solve this problem, he must fantasy going right back to "the breast," to the origin of his life, to the Tree of Life in the Garden of Eden where the fruit of the knowledge of good and evil is to be found. But is such knowledge a good thing? Is *eating*, in the sense of taking in (psychic) sustenance, a good thing? There is a great deal about eating in this book; and as we get to the most significant areas of eating (or taking awareness and knowledge into oneself), there one finds the "bad" mother lurking. The book belongs very much to the "oral" stage and is full of the joys and dangers of that stage, and the dread that belongs to a failure to complete the stage of concern, to find the "other."

Lewis unconsciously knew that his exploration was very important to him. So he says

> It is a very important story because it shows how all the coming and going between our own world and the land of Narnia first began. (MN, p. 9)

It is in this book that we learn that the original wardrobe was made from timber from the tree, which grew from the core of the apple, that Digory brought back from the Tree of Life to restore his mother. The symbolism is clear: it tells us that the whole going-into-Narnia process has to do with giving life back to the mother, and the magic of it has to do with the mother's body. (Perhaps *Digory* is one who *digs* into the original problem in the unconscious?*)

I have said that Aslan is in one sense the good mother. One thing the good mother does is to create our world. In her play with us, and by her love, she enables us to find a benign and beautiful earth. As we have seen, when the boy Lewis's mother died, a whole continent fell out of his life—like Atlantis. When Uncle Andrew talks about the "rings," he says the box is "Atlantean." Here we have a clue to the meaning of the magic rings. They represent that magic by which meaning may be given to the world again, if there is enough rebirth, or going-through-into-other-worlds, to bring back those things that have been lost.

---

*Martha Sammons suggests he was "probably modelled after Lewis himself" but was named after his old tutor "Kirke," described as the person who wanted to know everything.

Unfortunately, one of the things that gets brought back is the "bad" mother. When I discussed *The Lion, the Witch and the Wardrobe*, I hazarded the interpretation that the lamp post symbolized the existence of the father in Narnia; that is, the phallus within the mother's body as well as the paternal illumination and guidance. I also hazarded (from her treatment of Tumnus) that Jadis was the Castrating Mother. In *The Magician's Nephew* both interpretations are confirmed in a comic, pantomime way.

Brought into London by a mistake in the magic use of the rings, the Witch breaks a bracket off a lamp post:

> A change came over her expression and she changed her knife to her left hand. Then, without warning, she did a thing that was dreadful to see. Lightly, easily, as if it were the most ordinary thing in the world, she stretched up her right arm and wrenched off one of the cross-bars of the lamp-post. (MN, p. 88)

The hushed and awesome language is like that used to describe the crucifixion—another castration—the primal scene episode in which Aslan is humiliated. This language comes to be used because Lewis is fantasying one of his worst fears of the dreaded strength of the vengeful "bad" mother:

> If she had lost some magical powers in our world, she had not lost her strength; she could break an iron bar as if it were a stick of barley-sugar. She tossed her new weapon up in the air, caught it again, brandished it, and urged the horse forward. (MN, p. 88)

There is a brutal struggle before Digory manages to counteract the Witch's power. "His lip was cut and his mouth was full of blood." There is a "trembling scream": Uncle Andrew is crying, "Oh, oh, is this delirium? Is it the end? I can't bear it" (p. 89). By the use of the rings Digory has managed to get the Witch back into the strange no man's-land between worlds where

> as soon as the Witch saw that she was once more in the woods she turned pale and bent down till her face touched the mane of the horse. (p. 90)

—but also with her in limbo are Uncle Andrew, Polly, the cabman, and his horse Strawberry. They try again, and find themselves in "Nothing."

"This is not Charn," came the Witch's voice. "This is an empty
world. This is Nothing."
    And really it was uncommonly like Nothing. There were no stars.
It was so dark that they couldn't see one another at all and it
made no difference whether you kept your eyes shut or opened.
(p. 91)

The situation is nightmarish; and it is as if one had tried to
over come some menace in a nightmare, only to annihilate everything. The question is if one tries to bring the "bad" phantom
woman from the fantasy world into this one, perhaps all you
will do is to annihilate this world into "Nothing." Since the
mother is the one who should create one's world, could she
not also be (in her bad form) one who destroys it? Here lurks
an infantile fear of oral fantasy ("with no brakes on") destroying
everything.
    In the subsequent pages, there are some conventional elements
from comic fiction—the cabby crying "Gawd!" and "Garn!" for
example. But what is happening in the serious myth is Aslan
creating a world—Narnia. What they hear is a voice, singing
a song; and this creates the world as it sings.

    And as he walked and sang the valley grew green with grass
    . . . when he burst into a rapid series of lighter notes she was not
    surprised to see primroses suddenly appearing in every direction.
    (MN, pp. 97 and 99)

In my terms, what Polly and Digory are witnessing is the mother,
by her singing and play, creating the world for her baby. Aslan
is at this moment the embodiment of "being for," and of "the
living principle," of those processes Winnicott (1971) discusses
in *Playing and Reality*.
    Uncle Andrew is hostile to this process: he wants to return
to the mundane everyday world of "male doing." But in his
attempts to seize the magic rings, he incurs the wrath of the
Witch: "if anyone goes with ten paces of either of the children
I will knock out his brains" (MN, p. 98).
    The witch, who is pure hate, understands the noise better:

    The Witch looked as if, in a way, she understood the music better
    than any of them. . . . She would have smashed the whole world,
    or all worlds, to pieces, if it would only stop the singing. . . . (p. 95)

The Bad Mother wants to stop the creation because she is envious of the creative consciousness: here again Kleinian theories

of Bad Breast and Envy are relevant. Polly recognizes that what she is witnessing is the creation of the world by imagination, that creature "female element" capacity by which the mother creates our world:

> She felt quite certain that all the things were coming (as she said) "out of the lion's head." When you listen to his song you heard the things he was making up: when you looked round, you saw them. This was so exciting that she had no time to be afraid. (p. 99)

But now the Phantom Bad Mother displays her hatred of creativity.

> Suddenly the Witch stepped boldly out towards the Lion. It was coming on, always singing, with a slow heavy pace. It was only twelve yards away. She raised her arm and flung the iron bar straight at its head. . . .
> . . . The bar struck the Lion fair between the eyes. It glanced off and fell with a thud in the grass. The Lion came on. . . . (pp. 99–100)

As nearly always in Lewis's "Narnia" books, the spiritual conflict is between externalized agents; and here Aslan proves magically unassailable. In my terms we have the Castrating Mother attacking the Good Mother with the father's penis. Yet the magic is so strong that at once this grows into a young lamp-post:

> It was a perfect little model of a lamp-post, about three feet high but lengthening, and thickening in proportion, as they watched it, in fact growing just as the trees had grown. (p. 102)

To underline the unconscious point, Uncle Andrew is made to say (to the amusement of anyone who understands the unconscious symbolism): ". . . Now I wonder what sort of seed a lamp-post grows from. . . ." while Digory comments:

> "This is where the bar fell—the bar she tore off the lamp-post at home. It sank into the ground and now it's coming up as a young lamp-post." (But not so very young now; it was as tall as Digory while he said this.) (p. 103)

Uncle Andrew sees this growth process as a way of making money out of old engines, while "the first thing is to get that brute shot."

> "You're just like the Witch," said Polly. "All you think of is killing things." (p. 103)

Consciously, obviously, Lewis saw Uncle Andrew as a scientist—one of those godless (or demon-possessed) scientists who simply want to manipulate the world. He is "false male doing" in this sense (and mine). But he is also the inadequate father, who threatens one with annihilation, by his poisonous penis, which kills in intercourse. Yet at the same time, there is in the male principle a powerful fertility, which the mother took with her into the other world.

Uncle Andrew is also a Nietzschean figure, who floats above normal morality (in schizoid superiority). He did not destroy the magic box given to him by old Mrs. Lefay* who had "got to dislike ordinary ignorant people. . . ." "I do myself" adds Uncle Andrew. Digory, the boy protagonist, considers this "rotten": the man should have kept his promise.

> "Rotten?" said Uncle Andrew with a puzzled look. "Oh, I see. You mean that little boys ought to keep their promises. Very true: most right and proper, I'm sure, and I'm very glad you have been taught to do it. But of course you must understand that rules of that sort, however excellent they may be for little boys—and servants—and women—and even people in general, can't possibly be expected to apply to profound students and great thinkers and sages. No, Digory, those like me, who possess hidden wisdom, are freed from common rules just as we are cut off from common pleasures. Ours, my boy, is a high and lonely destiny." (MN, p. 23)

Digory thinks this is rather fine . . . until he "remembers the ugly look he had last seen on uncle's face, the moment before Polly had vanished." "'All it means,' he said to himself, 'is that he thinks he can do anything he likes to get anything he wants'" (p. 24). I have tried to show how Lewis had been seduced into feeling that cruelty like that shown to him at school had been a form of "care." But in Uncle Andrew at least he presents a thoughtless cruelty as bad: he is like the hubristic scientists in Lewis's adult fairy tales. As a scientist, Uncle Andrew lacks all imaginative sense of the suffering of others, not least of animals. He has tried some of the powder on his guinea pigs and "some exploded like little bombs" (p. 26). He first of all tricks Polly into the other world; then he blackmails Digory, who is concerned for her safety, into going after her. Behind the disturbing caricature of Uncle Andrew, I believe

---

*Mrs. Lefay is presumably Morgan le Fay, though I am not sure what this makes Uncle Andrew.

we can find a healthy resentment in Lewis, at his own father's unreliability and his callousness in sending him to a dreadful school; and a healthy resentment at the cruel Capron. But, as we shall see, his answer, as elsewhere, tends towards a fantasy of enjoyable revenge.*

The next chapter is *The Wood Between the Worlds*,** and in this wood reptation takes place again. We have another fantasy of birth:

> ... everything became muddled ... there was a soft green light coming down on him from above, and darkness below. He didn't seem to be standing on anything, or sitting, or lying. Nothing appeared to be touching him. "I believe I'm in water," said Digory, "or *under* water." That frightened him for a second, but almost at once he could feel that he was rushing upwards. Then his head suddenly came out into the air and he found himself scrambling ashore, on to smooth grassy ground at the edge of a pool. (MN, p. 31)

Afterwards, he described it as "a *rich* place: as rich as plumcake" (p. 32). And there is the little girl lying as if asleep—also just born.

The place is, however, an "in between" place. As I have said above, one of the fears of the individual who yearns for a rebirth is the dread of becoming stuck in the womb. We have looked at the "Nothing" place.*** Earlier there is another "Nothing" place. There is much perplexity in this book about the *topography* of rebirth:

> "Nothing ever happens here. Like at home. It's in the houses that people talk, and do things, and have meals. Nothing goes on in the in-between places, behind the walls and above the ceilings and under the floor or in our own tunnel. But when you come out of our tunnel you may find yourself in my house. I think we can get out of this place into jolly well Anywhere! we don't need to jump back into the same pool we came up by. Or not just yet." (MN, p. 37)

---

*In the light of *That Hideous Strength* I suppose Lewis may have conceived of Uncle Andrew as being literally possessed, diabolically, like Weston, his hubristic scientist.

**If the (mother's) genital is the gateway to this world, then the wood between the worlds is the pubic hair or bush, which is also the fur coat in the wardrobe.

***I detect behind this long discussion an infant suspicion that parental intercourse, because it causes death (by mutual eating) can cause Nothingness, since when something is eaten it disappears, which puzzles the infant.

It is as if Lewis is fantasying the possibility of returning to a suspended state of regression, out of which one could later be born into the new life.

Taking hold of a green ring, and jumping into a different pool, the children find themselves in a ruined city: "It led into a vast shadowy hall which appeared to be empty. . . ." (p. 44).

In *The Voyage of the Dawn Treader*, the ship approaches a vortex of nonbeing: "the place where dreams come true" (VDT, p. 156). Here, the dreadful possibility is explored that in seeking a new world beyond a new birth, one might simply enter a dead world that was finished; that is, the world of death where the mother is may be a dead end world. The great ruined mansion in *The Magician's Nephew* is the mansion of the unconscious—but also the mansion of a dead identity. It is peopled with people in rich clothes transfixed by magic (a common image in Lewis, as in many fairy stories). There are dead identities.* The people are sitting in rows; and as the children go back to the end of the room, the faces become crueller and crueller, and some become less and less *humanized*. Among these is one big female figure, "with a look of such fierceness and pride that it took your breath away" (MN, p. 88): here is Jadis again, the White Witch.

The children quarrel, and Digory strikes the bell. There is a nightmarish consequence—a rising sound that, as in some nightmares, grows and grows—bringing the building crashing down, and the White Witch to life. The next chapter is called *The Deplorable Word*. This draws our attention to the intense oral nature of the symbolism. As we have seen, Aslan creates Narnia by song. So, the word, which expresses from the mouth, could also destroy. Terrible sounds are destructive in the halls of Charn, while a certain ("deplorable") word can end the whole world. In this we find the schizoid fear of love, for the richest oral expression is love, and here it is devastating.**

The Queen speaks of her "high and lonely destiny," and how she has exterminated thousands.

> "Was it the Deplorable Word that made the sun like that?" asked Digory.
> "Like what?" said Jadis.
> "So big, so red, and so cold." (MN, p. 61)

---

*This place resembles the hall of the dead in MacDonald's *Lilith*.
**Here again we have Lewis's *concrete* sense of the direct power of the word to have an aggressive effect in the world.

Ours, the Queen realizes, is a younger world; and she wants to get into it, greedily. We have reached a point at which the Bad Phantom Mother who belongs to the World of Death, having been found, threatens to get out of hand! She is "not the kind of person one would like to take home!" (p. 62). Now it seems likely she will destroy this world!

The children escape Charn—but the Queen has been holding on to Polly's hair, and so comes with them. She is not at home in the World in Between, and there is a look of terror in her eyes. But as they reach London, "She looked ten times more alive than most of the people one meets in London" (MN, p. 67). This is a strange remark: in it one glimpses in C. S. Lewis an underlying *admiration* for the strength of the false solutions of hate, for the phantom herself.**

A problem for the child, of course, is what would be the "Bad" mother's relationship to the father? In fact, she turns the mother's "reflecting" power into a chastening exposure of Uncle Andrew's unreliability and weakness (which are the qualities Lewis must have regretted most in his father):

> Then, in one stride, she crossed the room, seized a great handful of Uncle Andrew's grey hair and pulled his head back so that his face looked up into hers. Then she studied his face just as she had studied Digory's face in the palace at Charn. . . . At last she let him go: so suddenly that he reeled back against the wall. . . . (MN, p. 60)

"I see," she says scornfully, "you are a Magician, of a sort." In normal life there is "no art to find the mind's construction in the face," as Duncan puts it in *Macbeth* (I iv.12). The Witch is capable of detecting unworthiness in the face she cruelly scans: "My eyes can see through walls and into the minds of men" (MN, p. 70). And she threatens him with the miseries Lewis experienced at Wyvern:

> At the first sign of disobedience I will lay such spells on you that anything you sit down on will feel like red hot iron, and whenever you lie in bed there will be invisible blocks of ice at your feet. (p. 70)

She seems to threaten to castrate him (he is "looking like a dog with its tail between its legs"). Digory is obviously worried she may turn on him; but

---

*A Jungian might say he was deeply attracted by his own destructive anima.

Now that she had Uncle Andrew, she took no notice of Digory.
I expect most witches are like that. They are not interested in things
or people unless they can use them; they are terribly practical. . . .
(p. 71)

Uncle Andrew has to have a drink: "most upsetting! And
at my time of life!" and he puts on clothes of the kind he
would wear at a wedding or funeral. In this Lewis is giving
us the view of the child, of the grotesque behavior of adults,
as seen from the point of view of the child in the latency period.*
Here is this monstrous witch woman; yet Uncle Andrew is actually attracted to her, sexually, gazing at his dressed-up self in
the mirror and saying to himself, "A dem fine woman, sir, a
dem fine woman. A superb creature."

"Andrew, my boy," he said to himself as he looked in the glass,
"You're a devilish well preserved fellow for your age. . . ." You see,
the foolish old man was actually beginning to imagine the Witch
would fall in love with him. (p. 74)

In Chapter Seven the Queen tries to reduce Aunt Letty to
dust by words—but her destructive powers, so effective in her
world, do not work on earth so she merely hurls Aunt Letty
across the room. Later, Digory hears Aunt Letty talking about
his own mother who is dying: "I'm afraid it would need fruit
from the Land of Youth to help her now. Nothing in this world
will do much . . ." (p. 81). Digory has already been in another
world, so such a way of talking has another meaning for him.
"There might be a real land of youth somewhere. There might
be almost anything. There might be fruit in some other world
that would really cure his mother" (p. 81).

There must be worlds you could get to through every pool in the
wood. He could hunt through them all. And then—*Mother well
again.* Everything right again. (p. 82)

"Well, you know how it feels," says Lewis. "If you begin hoping for something that you want desperately badly; you almost
fight against the hope because it is too good to be true" (p. 81).
So, the author reveals once more the origins of the "Narnia"
books and their motive, which is the perplexity of what is real

---

*This perspective, of course, is the basis of the profound and serious comedy
of Henry James's *What Maisie Knew.*

and what is not; what one may hope for, and what it is futile to hope for, in the urge to go through into the other world to find the Dead Mother. "You've been disappointed so often before."

But it was no good trying to throttle this hope. It might really, really, it might just be true. (p. 81)

Strangely, the best effect of the "Narnia" books, reading between the lines, is the impression that is given of the anguish and misery of that bereaved boy of ten.

Aslan creates a very special world—of talking beasts and walking trees—joined by fauns, satyrs, dwarfs and naiads. As we have seen, it seems doubtful if this classical world can really be reconciled with the Christian myth, while Lewis's rewriting of Christian myths to amuse children produces some fascinating convolutions of theology. Five hours after Narnia was born "an evil" has entered it—brought by Digory, who is, after all, only seeking first to save Polly, and secondly to cure his mother! It is an odd way of explaining the arrival of sin in the world (or any world for that matter). Aslan is already preparing himself, however, to be a sacrifice to redeem this evil: "Evil will come of that evil, but it is still a long way off, and I will see to it that the worst falls upon myself" (MN, p. 126). Some of the rewriting of Genesis is also a little embarrassing—as for instance, when the honest cabby and his wife are made Adam and Eve, the first King and Queen of Narnia, as the honest worker and his wife: "Can you use a spade and a plough and raise food out of the earth?" (p. 129).

The myth again becomes much more convincing if we take it as the quest for mother. Obviously, in this myth, it is necessary to penetrate all corners of the earth, and all other possible worlds, and all times, past and future, to find and redeem her. So we must even go back to the creation of the world in order to solve the problem, and even remake the original parents. The ordinary animals must also be transformed—so, in Chapter Twelve, the cabman's horse is transformed into a flying Pegasus.

All the magic in the books is in the service of the search for the mother, not least the invention of Aslan himself:

"But, please, please—won't you—can't you give me something that will cure Mother?" . . . now, in despair, he looked up at its face. What he saw surprised him as much as anything in his whole life. For the tawny face was bent down near his own and (wonder of wonders) great shining tears stood in the lion's eyes. They were such big, bright tears compared with Digory's own that for a moment he felt as if the Lion must really be sorrier about his Mother than he was himself. (MN, pp. 131–32)

Digory's flight is a flight into memories of the experience of the mother's body. He seeks the (good) breast, as we can see in the illustration:

> . . . a heavenly smell, warm and golden, as if from all the most delicious fruits and flowers of the world, was coming up to them from somewhere ahead. . . . (p. 144)

This is the feel and smell of the mother's body in infancy: "The air came up warmer and sweeter every moment" (p. 144). There is a rhyme, set up on this Eden, which says that "those who steal" or those who climb the wall "shall find their heart's desire and final despair" (p. 146).

In terms of the Christian myth, this can mean that man must not take what is forbidden to him by God: the apple. In my terms, however, it refers to the problem of ambivalence, the mixture in us of love and hate.

Digory's perplexity here enacts a genuine existential problem. All the cunning arguments are given to the Bad Mother, who tried to corrupt him by blackmail.

The Witch tells Digory that the apple he has taken for Aslan is the apple of youth, the apple of life. But Digory has no use for immortality:

> "I'd rather live an ordinary time and die and go to heaven."
> "But what about this Mother of yours who you pretend to love so. . . . Do you not see that one bite of that apple would heal her?" (p. 150)

She tempts him to make his way back quickly and directly to his mother without attending to Aslan's will or keeping his promise to the lion.

> "All will be well again. Your home will be happy again. *You will be like other boys.*"
> "Oh!" gasped Digory, as if he had been hurt, and put his hand to his head. For he now knew that the most terrible choice lay before him. (p. 150; my italics)

This is the powerful persuasion—for to bring back the mother "so that he can be like other boys" is the whole motive behind C. S. Lewis's writing life!

The Witch's temptations are strong blackmail: what is service to Aslan to stand in the way of the restoration of the Mother?

> "And what would your Mother think if she knew that you *could* have taken her pain away and given her back her life and saved your Father's heart from being broken, and that you *wouldn't* . . . ." (p. 151)

The Witch speaks with all the seductive force of a desire to believe in instant (manic) magic ("Five minutes later you will see the colour coming back into her face" [p. 150]). "Cruel, pitiless boy" she calls him, and she denies the bonds of concern. When Digory protests his Mother would want him to keep his promise, her reply is sly:

> "But she need never know," said the Witch, speaking more sweetly than you would have thought anyone with so fierce a face could speak.
>
> "You wouldn't tell her how you'd got the apple. Your Father need never know. No one in your world need know anything about this whole story. You needn't take the little girl back with you, you know."
>
> That was where the Witch made her fatal mistake. . . . (MN, p. 151)

The Bad Mother has no real imaginative concern so she reveals herself to have a mean, cold heart like Uncle Andrew. She suggests leaving "the little girl" forever in the world of fantasy, too. Digory knows now what choice to make; he has found the hate at the heart of the Witch's seductive logic, and a denial of the value of individuals, such as is implicit in love: he has found concern.

Yet there is also a sense in which Digory's choice is not free choice. Like all the ethical choices in the "Narnia" books, it is made under strict magical control. "'Well done,' said Aslan in a voice that made the earth shake" (p. 154).

As we shall see, the dealings with Uncle Andrew are vengeance fantasies simply disguised by that "Christian" gloss. Uncle Andrew is very excited about the bar off the lamp post growing into a lamp post tree and thinks he will turn it into a new form of scientific manipulation of this new world. His is that "false male doing" Lewis satirized in scientists:

> "He thinks great folly child," said Aslan.
> "This world is bursting with life for these few days because the song with which I called it into life is still hanging in the air and rumbles in the ground. . . . I cannot tell that to the old sinner, and I cannot comfort him either; he has made himself unable to hear my voice. If I spoke to him, he would only hear growlings and roarings. Oh Adam's sons, how cleverly you defend yourselves against all that might do good!" (MN, p. 158)

This is common Christian sermonizing: that man in his pride is deaf to Christ's voice. But in the "Narnia" books, it is the *threats*, the growlings and roarings that bring the promptings of conscience and promote ethical living. To be convincing, such promptings would have to come, as do some of Digory's, from within. With these, for once, Lewis allows a genuine moral dynamic.

Not all Digory's, however, do come from within; and again Lewis relies upon authoritarian, external morality. What exactly is the difference between taking the apple direct to his mother, and taking it to Aslan?

> "Understanding, then, that it would have healed her: but not to your joy or hers. The day would have come when both you and she would have looked back and said it would have been better to die in that illness."
> And Digory could say nothing, for tears choked him and he gave up all hope of saving his Mother's life; but at the same time he knew that the Lion knew what would have happened, and that there might be things more terrible even than losing someone you love in death. . . . (MN, p. 163)

Aslan repeatedly refuses elsewhere to reveal what would have happened; that is not given us, he says. But here he does just that: "That is what *would* have happened, child, with a stolen apple. . . ." (p. 163) He gives Digory an apple from the Tree of Life that *will* bring joy. The difference is simply that Digory has now deferred to God's will. In this, I suppose, we have an echo of the small boy's dismay that his prayers were not answered. But, if the mother had recovered without deference to God's will, why should she later look back and think it would have been better to die? Lewis is perhaps still trying to convince himself that there could have been a "bad" kind of survival: this is the confused argument here.

There is, however, a more acceptable explanation in terms of what you do with the dead mother in memory. There—in the inner world—it is true that it would not work to restore the mother without reaching the point of reconciling oneself to her death. One must reach a real sense that there *are* perhaps things more terrible even than losing someone you love in death—and that is *not* completing the process of mourning, or of completing it in a false way so that the world remains disintegrated. The pain of completing mourning must really be accepted, and the mother as a human being who died "out there" must be found. Manic denial will not do: there has to be real grief. This episode is, however, the closest Lewis gets to a genuine "whole" engagement with the existential problem.

The children now pass through an aura of golden goodness— "they felt they had never really been happy or wise or good, or even alive and awake, before" (MN, p. 165). This is the sense of goodness and substantiality that comes from reparative effort. They experience also (again) the smell and feel of the mother's body.

The apple of the Tree of Life transcends normal perception as we have seen, in the passage above the apple, which symbolizes the power love can given to the world (p. 7–8).

With Uncle Andrew we return to the problems of hate—and the solutions of hate. Uncle Andrew is in one sense the kind of scientist who believes he is entitled to the "do anything he likes to get anything he wants" hubristic. He has never liked animals and has done "cruel experiments" on them, so that he hates and fears them even more.

It isn't surely inevitable that a scientist who does cruel experiments would hate animals? We may look beneath his offered excuse for the vengeance directed at Uncle Andrew, and see in him the characteristics of the Bad Father, who let Lewis down as a boy, and of the Headmaster *in loco parentis* who was so cruel to the little creatures in his charge.

In any event, Uncle Andrew is simply subjected to oral hate:

> What struck him most was the number of open mouths. The animals had really opened their mouths to pant; he thought they had opened their mouths to eat him. (p. 119)

There follows a long sequence in which Uncle Andrew is subjected to humiliation, and the reader is invited to enjoy this.

The animals are shown as not knowing what they are doing. They don't understand what Uncle Andrew is: ". . . It isn't an animal at all. It's not alive . . .". They push him about, bury him, squirt him with water, and so on.

> The sagacious animals went on doing this till gallons of water had been squirted over him, and water was running out of the skirts of his frock-coat as if he had been for a bathe with all his clothes on. In the end it revived him. He awoke from his faint. What a wakening it was! But we must leave him to think over his wicked deeds (if he was likely to do anything so sensible) and turn to more important things. (p. 123–24)

It is characteristic of Lewis to invite the reader's enjoyment of pain and discomfiture inflicted on a bad character. This again is capronic. He seems really to believe that people must be shocked into recognizing a spiritual reality, and into feeling good spiritual feelings. If not, they must be brutally punished. He seems to have no capacity to see that spiritual or ethical feelings generated by such means would be false, like those inspired by the beatings of Headmaster Keate who is reputed to have told a boy who did not believe in the Holy Ghost that he would beat him until he did. Again, we have a manifestation of the lesson Lewis learnt at "Belsen": to be good you must be hurt and humiliated. At a deeper level, what Uncle Andrew is subjected to is an infantile fantasy of what Melanie Klein would call a "urinary attack."

Later, Uncle Andrew is put in a kind of cage of brambles, pelted with nuts and worms by animals, and has a wild bees' nest lobbed over his enclosure, "slap in the face (not all the bees were dead)" (MN, p. 157). Aslan takes the view that he brought all these punishments on himself, and as usual endorses the cruelties: his view is "serve him right." Again, this is a fantasy of a primitive excretory assault, such as an infant directs against those he hates and fears—the basis of psychopathological behavior in an adult rather than an appropriate response.

> "Bring out that creature," said Aslan. One of the Elephants lifted Uncle Andrew in its trunk and laid him at the lion's feet. He was to frightened to move. (p. 157)

Aslan likes his enemies to be too frightened to move—a characteristic hardly to be imagined in Christ, though no doubt one of Robert Capron's.

One interesting theme in this story is that of visions of color. There is a moment in the autobiography where Lewis speaks of color; and there seems to be a kind of blue he associated with the child vision and the mother, especially her eyes, as we have seen. (See also the autobiography, *Surprised by Joy*.) As the children approach what we might call the Place of the Good Breast, lovely colors and scents are experienced.

> The valleys, far beneath them, were so green, and all the streams which tumbled down from the glaciers into the main rivers were so blue, that it was like flying over gigantic pieces of jewellry . . . a heavenly smell, warm and golden. . . . (MN, p. 144)

I have said these are the colors and scents of the mother's body.

There is the same effect at the moment when Digory takes out the Apple of Life for his mother ". . . as if there was a window in that room that opened on Heaven" (p. 167). As Digory waits to hear whether she is recovered: "whenever he looked at the things around him, and saw how ordinary and un-magical they were, he hardly dared to hope . . ." (p. 168). We are taken, I believe, right back to the moments when young Lewis struggled with the dread of his mother's death, when the only color in the world seemed to be his hope; but, in the end, the ordinary things become nonmagical, and "not worth looking at" (while she became an "it"). Yet, of course, such problems are not solved by magic, any more than the hearts of men are improved by ill treatment or the growls of Aslan.

Yet Aslan is sent to warn us. He speaks of

> . . . the world where a dying sun shone over the ruins of Charn . . . that world is ended, as if it had never been. Let the world of Adam and Eve take warning. (p. 164)

What shall we do to be saved?—we might ask. Humiliate our scientists? Punish those whose attitudes to life we reject? Lewis's answer, I suppose, would be to believe and have faith:

> Both the children were looking up into the Lion's face as he spoke these words. And all at once (they never knew how it happened) the face seemed to be a sea of tossing gold in which they were floating, and such a sweetness and power rolled about them and over them and entered into them that they felt they had never really been happy or wise or good, or even alive and awake, before. And the memory of that moment stayed with them always, so that as

long as they both lived, if ever they were sad or afraid or angry, the thought of all that golden goodness, and the feeling that it was still there, quite close, just around some corner or just behind some door, would come back and made them sure, deep down, inside, that all was well. (MN, p. 165)

There are two things to say about this: first, for most children, such a feeling comes from relationship with the mother—looking into the mother's eyes:

The mother in her good aspects—loving, helping, and feeding the child—is the first good object that the infant makes part of his inner world. (Klein 1963, p. 6)

The second is that through Aslan (=Good Mother), Lewis is trying to mother himself, seeking to feel alive as he has never felt before. The solution in the end is too manic, too external (as it is not for Digory), too much a matter of wishful thinking, that everything will be managed, controlled, and manipulated by the magic of the big dog. There is a reference to "Witch Jadis," even in the mother's sick chamber; and she and Uncle Andrew are too much "out there": split-offs. They are not embraced as aspects of the self, of human nature. The punitive, controlling minatory and magically directing Aslan is an instrument of this manic denial. What is so attractive about him is that he is omnipotent; and like the dog in Bowlby's patient's dreams, is ready to fulfil all one's wishes. Whatever the implications vis-à-vis Christianity, I don't believe man will be saved from his worst possible fate by believing in magic and omnipotent mentors, of such a punitive kind.

# 9

## *The Voyage of the Dawn Treader*

The third book in the "Narnia" series is *The Voyage of the Dawn Treader;* and at first glance or in a casual reading, this has many benign elements in it. There are, for example, the lilies blooming all over the Silver Sea or Lily Lake. Yet this voyage also represents the deepest penetration into the other world of death, and so brings out the most dreadful dreads* from Lewis's unconscious.

The book is full of episodes in which the protagonists are threatened with going out of existence altogether. One character, a nasty cousin of the Pevensie children, is turned into a dragon, eats another dragon, and is restored to human form only by being virtually flayed alive by Aslan. The air is full of menace— there are invisible creatures, the invisible and hostile monopods, creatures with only one big foot, under which they can hide as if under a mushroom. There is a powerful hostile magic that threatens Susan as she tried to find a magic which will counteract influences directed against the children.

It might seem that, at the level of Christian parable, some of these incidents might have an obvious explanation.** Take the incident of Eustace and the dragon.

Greedy and aggressive people perhaps become "dragonish" because they are selfish (Eustace tries to steal the water rations on board ship). But we surely feel that Lewis's wrath falls on Eustace because he is a pacifist and has been to a school where they have no corporal punishment (in response to his ill treatment of Reepicheep, the mouse gives him six of the best with his sword, to the author's evident satisfaction.) Eustace is only a child, and his faults are those of minor delinquency. They

---

*I take this phrase from a Winnicott case history. A little girl spoke of her "dreadful dreads" as the worst thing that could happen to her.

**The idea of *The Voyage of the Dawn Treader* may have come from the eighth century work *The Voyage of St. Brendan, Navigatio Sancti Brendani,* a *peregrinatio amore Dei.*

hardly deserve having his flesh torn from his body. Of course, the Christian apologist will say that is what Christ does for us: takes away our Old Adam and gives us a new being. But the event has a symbolism which conveys guilt about the body and its hunger, and so a sexual connotation.

Other images defy interpretation unless we make an interpretation of that kind. What does it mean when the phallic monopods say, "We want something that little girl can do for us"? (VDT, p. 119). What does it mean when Susan sees her face in a mirror which gives it a *beard*? Why should it happen, as they approach the "island where dreams come true," that there should be a dreadful vortex, even where it is promised that they will find someone "alive again"?

To solve these questions, we have to go back into a state of infantile fantasy in which, for example, the air can be full of detached weapons from the "bad" mother, or combined parents, consisting of part-objects: projectiles of hate sent in talion revenge. In Sylvia Plath's poetry such part-objects are to be found, stolen penises, or detached phalluses, "flying about like clubs." The monopods seem to be projectiles of this kind. Helped by the illustrations (see pp. 142–43), we can see that their feet are a displacement for penises, as in foot fetishism. Lucy is perplexed by them:

> In fact the longer she gazed at them the less like mushrooms they appeared. The umbrella part was not really round as she thought at first. It was longer than broad, and it widened at one end. (VDT, p. 142)

There are other moments in Lewis's book in which, in the latency period, boys and girls seem to be looking at aspects of adult sexuality, while at the same time remaining in the state of seeing sex as eating. Jill has a parallel shock in *The Silver Chair* faced with a Harfang King, who is likely (though she does not know it) to eat her: "His tongue was so very large and red, and came out so unexpectedly, that it gave Jill quite a shock." That sex is eating is perhaps clear from the remark made by Hwin the horse in *The Horse and His Boy* to Aslan: "Please . . . you're so beautiful. You may eat me if you like. I'd sooner be eaten by you than fed by anyone else" (p. 169).

We have seen in *The Magician's Nephew* that the protagonists pass through a "Nothing" place. In *The Voyage of the Dawn Treader* another Nothing place is encountered, in the sea. In this vortex, there is heard the noise of the threat of castration:

"Do you hear a noise like . . . like a huge pair of scissors opening and shutting . . . over there?" Eustace asked himself. (p. 157)

In this terrible place one may face ultimate dehumanization:

> Suddenly, from somewhere—no one's sense of direction was very clear by now—there came a cry, either of some inhuman voice or else a voice of one in such extremity of terror that he had almost lost his humanity. (p. 155)

Here, "There are some things no man can face" (p. 156). It is a very nightmarish episode, and the essential dread is expressed by the stranger:

> The stranger, who had been lying in a huddled heap on the deck, sat up and burst out into a horrible screaming laugh:
> "Never get out!" he yelled. "That's it. Of Course. We shall never get out." (p. 158)

Here again we have the schizoid fear that to regress may lead to being trapped in the womb. The dead mother has been sought in that world of death. As one comes near her the "bad" mother has sometimes menaced: now, as in some of MacDonald's stories, perhaps the place where she is is a "vortex of nonbeing"? Lucy prays to Aslan, but why should Christ help them to escape this black void? A bird comes to perch on the gilded dragon at the prow—presumably the Holy Spirit—though it is also perhaps the albatross from *The Ancient Mariner*. Soon "there is nothing to be afraid of." The darkness vanishes forever: they have destroyed it. But what kind of "enemy" was it?

I think it is the area of knowing what one should not know, and willing what one should not will. We may relate the incident to Digory's problem. It was wrong for Digory to dream of restoring his dying mother to life by himself. He must defer to the will of Aslan. It could be that it was *right for her to die*. Aslan tells Digory that if he had simply gone straight to mother: ". . . The day would have come when both you and she would have looked back and said it would have been *better to die in that illness*" (MN, p. 163; my italics). There are, reflects Digory, "things more terrible even than losing someone you love by death."

In these passages, we see the grieving boy Lewis debating with himself in his anguish. We have seen how he prayed, but his prayers had not been answered. To wish his mother alive by magic seems a mortal sin: the black cloud is the center of his dread of the vortex of nothingness into which his mother has been drawn. The most dreadful thing about it is to believe that in that vortex one may find the dead mother; and yet fear that if one goes into it, one may never get out. To put it into different terms, if, in one's need, one seeks to go back to the womb, and the mother is dead, one may enter into a regression from which one never can escape. Perhaps once one finds the secret at last, it may be so terrible that that would be the end of everything.* Then, of course, all hope of finding and redeeming her would be lost, as would all chance of a new life.

The hunger for the mother's existence is dealt with in another way with Eustace. Aslan saves the children from the black hole by sending the albatross (symbol of reparation from The Ancient Mariner). He saves Eustace from his transformation into a dragon (because of his dragonish thoughts) by tearing his flesh off, and "undressing" him of his corruption. In both episodes, the dread is of the need for the (dead) mother—the need seeming so terrible that it threatens one's existence in the world and one's relationship to reality, so that if one persists in it one may literally be torn to pieces. These episodes are extremely frightening at the unconscious level.

Certainly the passage in The Voyage of the Dawn Treader, in which Eustace becomes a dragon, is the weirdest episode in all the "Narnia" books. The writer succeeds in giving up the physical feeling of becoming a dragon—as Kafka succeeds in his Metamorphosis in giving us the feeling of a man becoming a beetle.

> He moved his right arm in order to feel his left, but stopped before he had moved it an inch and bit his lips in terror. For just in front of him, and a little to his right, where the moonlight fell clear on the floor of the cave, he saw a hideous shape moving. He knew that shape: it was a dragon's claw. It had moved as he moved his hand and became still when he stopped moving his hand. (VDT, p. 80)

---

*See Karl Stern (1966) on woman as the mysterium tremendum. Some like Tolstoy, have felt that no one could tell the truth about woman and live. As Dr. Rosemary Gordon argues, the third and last phase of woman is as Mother Earth, and then her womb becomes the grave. Several writers— Baudelaire, Tolstoy, Lawrence among them—have seen a menacing landscape as a predatory woman's body.

This is another nightmare, and belongs to the dread of being "taken over," the schizoid fear of coming to be imploded by an alien force. As we have seen, Lewis was often tormented by such fears. What does it mean to think of oneself as a dragon with claws? In this episode there is a deep feeling of being in a corrupted body. There is terrible pain, and the dragon weeps dreadfully.

I believe the dreadful episode may be understood in relation to a complexity of unconscious preoccupations. We may link it to the strange symbolism of the swords and the guilt the boys feel about leaving them bloody—the fear of contamination by sin. Lewis disguises the real subject by his suggestions that Eustace is greedy, and is being punished for this. The truth seems rather to be that Eustace observes the death of the father, when the old dragon dies, and his thoughts are Oedipal. He takes the father-dragon's place; and later, to make the replacement clear, he eats the old dragon. This symbolizes the way in which the child takes the father into himself, by identification; and, of course, Eustace, insofar as Lewis identifies with him, takes into himself the unreliable Lewis-father, and the bestial Capron-father-figure. The problem is taking into one's very fabric the "bad" father. When Eustace wakes up next morning and looks into a pool to confirm his identity, he finds that he has become a dragon:

> . . . in an instant he realised the truth. That dragon face in the pool was his own reflection. There was no doubt of it. It moved as he moved, it opened and shut its mouth as he opened and shut his.
>
> He had turned into a dragon while he was asleep. Sleeping on a dragon's hoard with greedy, dragonish thoughts in his head, he had become a dragon himself. (VDT, p. 81)

The dragon's hoard is the legacy of the introjected father figures.

As with the question of the contaminated swords, there is another aspect of this episode that seems relevant. One of the problems of taking on the father's identity, besides the Oedipal problem, is that of taking on the father's kind of sexuality; and this seems clearly here from the oral overtones. An aspect of chid sexuality is masturbation: the child identifies with parental sexuality and masturbates, perhaps out of anxiety. Guilt about masturbation can make a child, like Eustace, feel that he is a monster: "He realised that he was a monster cut off from the whole human race" (p. 81). Such anxieties and fears would be exacerbated by Oedipal feelings and the (infantile) theory that sex = death. The dragon's claw is the masturbating hand.

In his autobiography Lewis declares that he was bored by the homosexual practices at school and college (though he is strangely explicit about the "bloods" and "tarts" and their practices); but he says nothing about masturbation, though later he was obsessed with it. We have looked above at the symbolism of dread and guilt he uses to discuss this "sin" in his poems.

One of the most disturbing aspects of the dragon episode is that Eustace suffers terrible pain from a ring, a bracelet which he slips on his own wrist from the dragon's hoard. It is "'Too big, but not if I push it right up here above my elbow'" (VDT, p. 78). When he wakes up and has become a dragon, this bracelet is the first thing he feels.

> He was puzzled by the pain in his arm at first, but presently it occurred to him that the bracelet which he had shoved up above his elbow had become strangely tight. His arm must have swollen while he was asleep (it was his left arm). (p. 80)

The unconscious meaning is, I believe, something like this: by masturbating, Eustace had done two things—invited retribution from the White Witch and turned himself into a monster apart. The ring or bracelet, which was in the old Dragon's hoard, is the mother's genital; and he has, as it were, thrust a limb into this ring by identifying with parental coition (it is also of course a wedding ring). Now he must suffer terrible pain—a kind of castration. (The parallel with the castration nightmare on p. 89 should be obvious.)

The word in which the limb is described ("thick stumpy foreleg . . .") and later the description of the whole dragon body seem to me to suggest repugnant feelings about one's male genitals, while at the end of the chapter the ring is left hanging on a rock projection that the artist draws like loins, and looks quite like an erection. Dragons, thinks Eustace, are "snaky things" and the whole episode is full of genital feeling.

The punishment is a mortification of the flesh. Yet strangely the experience of the pain of being trapped in the ring itself brings relief—at least now nothing can be worse. Because of this Eustace reaches the immoral schizoid conclusion: that one may as well give oneself up to hatred and get what satisfaction one can out of that. He becomes dragonish: but then yearns to be human and feels sure he can make people understand who he was:

> As for the pain in his left arm (or what had been his left arm) he could now see what had happened by squinting with his left eye. The bracelet which had fitted very nicely on the upper arm of a boy was far too small *for the thick, stumpy foreleg of a dragon.* It had sunk deeply into his scaly flesh and there was a throbbing bulge on each side of it. He tore at the place with his dragon's teeth but could, not get it off. . . . In spite of the pain, his first feeling was one of the pain, his first feeling was one of relief. *There was nothing to be afraid of any more. He was a terror himself now and nothing in the world but a knight . . . would dare to attack him. He could get even with Caspian and Edmund now. . . .*
>
> But the moment he thought this he realised that he didn't want to. He wanted to be friends. He wanted to get back among humans and talk and laugh and share things. . . . (VDT, pp. 82–83; my italics)

Again, we have a contemplation of dehumanization; but now, strangely, Eustace, in yearning to be human again, begins to experience truth: "When he thought of this the poor dragon that had been Eustace lifted its voice and wept" (p. 83).

But being dehumanized, he pays the dragon the ultimate tribute by eating it (and the child does, in fact, eat the father by identifying with him and taking him into himself). As Winnicott might put it, there is only room for one to be King of the Castle.

> He took a long drink and then (I know this sounds shocking, but it isn't if you think it over), he ate nearly all the dead dragon. He was half-way through it before he realised what he was doing; for, you see, though his mind was the mind of Eustace, his tastes and his digestion were dragonish. And there is nothing a dragon likes so well as fresh dragon. That is why you so seldom find more than one dragon in the same country. (p. 83)

The next few pages are intensely paranoid. Edmund says: "'If there's a wasp in the room I like to be able to see it. . . .'" (p. 85). And then there is new excitement in preparing to deal with the threat of the dragon. In C. S. Lewis's "Narnia" books nothing makes the protagonists happier than preparation for conflict: "It was nicer than waiting about and everyone felt fonder of everyone else than at ordinary times. . . ." (p. 84). Much as some old soldiers still feel that their service days were the best times of their life: at least, in the intensity of false solution behavior, they felt real.

It is clear from the account of the purgation of Eustace that Lewis gave a great deal of thought to it, and supposed it enacts certain Christian beliefs: "I looked up and saw . . . a huge lion coming towards me. I was just afraid of it. . . ." (p. 94).

Aslan shows Eustace a pool that sounds like the source of life in the Garden of Eden. This is perhaps the true source of creative reflection. Before he can experience this, Eustace must go through a severe process of self-abnegation.

I believe this process of self-disgust and self-rejection is deeply disturbing, and it is one of those episodes in Lewis's fantasies which seems most unpalatable. In it, I believe, we experience Lewis's strange dislike of being in a human body, and sense his disparagement of humanness, his misanthropy. By taking the father into himself, Lewis-Eustace has taken in the "bad" father; and all the contamination he believes, unconsciously, to be in the father's body.

Lewis's unconscious problem is now how to rid his body of all those hideous qualities that he had taken in from the bad father, and from the menacing parental sexuality. The answer is that Aslan, who represents "good" parental force, must strip these away. Just as he became the father by eating him, Aslan must, by a similar process of tearing up the body and "unpeeling" it, rid it of its poisonous and dangerous properties. Whether or not the grisly episode is suitable for children depends on how much one supposes they may be subjected to psychotic fantasy without being harmed:

> . . . the lion told me I must undress first, I was just going to say that I couldn't undress because I hadn't any clothes on when I suddenly thought that dragons can cast their skins. . . . So I started scratching myself and my scales began coming off all over the place. And then I scratched a little deeper and instead of just scales coming off here and there, like it does after an illness or as if I was a banana. In a minute or two I just stepped out of it. I could see it lying there beside me, looking rather nasty. . . . (VDT, p. 95)

The process of purgation goes on, in detail, and is disturbingly morbid. And then, despite Eustace's efforts at self-purification, Aslan joins in:

> . . . Then the lion said . . . you will have to let me undress you. . . . So I just lay flat down on my back to let him do it.
> . . . the very first tear he made was so deep that I thought it had gone right into my heart. And when he began pulling the skin

off, it hurt worse than anything I've ever felt. The only thing that made me able to bear it was just the pleasure of feeling the stuff peel off. You know—if you've ever picked the scab off a sore place. It hurts like billy—oh but it is such fun to see it coming away. . . . (p. 97)

The "beastly stuff" lies on the grass "ever so much thicker and darker and more knobbly looking than the others has been."

And there was I as smooth and soft as a peeled switch. . . . I'd turned into a boy again. . . . (p. 97)

It is worth noting that the imagery is very phallic ("peeled switch" . . . "banana" . . . "knobbly" . . . "snaky sorts of things"). It seems possible that one of Lewis's problems was a dread of (adult) bodily lust (as he is said to have deliberately avoided food that was supposed to stimulate sexual desire).* This may be associated with his feeling (which I postulate) that sexual intercourse created the cancer that killed his mother. The discomfort we feel in this episode is that of a thrashed child.

Another related image in *The Dawn Treader* is the Goldwater Pool, which turns everything to gold. In this pool lies dead nobles and there is here another threat from one's greed, except that it is also clear here that what is really being sought is *reflection* and the underlying fear is that the hunger for the mother will destroy one.

Elsewhere, there are mirrors that have their own strange symbolism too. In the Monopod chapters we were in a territory of invisible paranoid threats from disembodied male objects. We recall that these creatures demand "something the little girl can do for us." So, Lucy has to undertake a quest—searching for the magician, and for the clue to undoing the spell on the monopods, in a magic book. Aslan, as we have seen, is the "Big Dog," who will do everything for the searching protagonist by his magic: the magician is the "Good Father" who will do the same for Lucy. Thus the question of sexuality, male or female, comes up; and so we have almost thrown away a genital image.

---

*In the *Screwtape Letters* sin is spoken of as a kind of green lizard one plucks off oneself. Characteristically, sin is an external entity, with a sexual connotation, a split off. It seems also likely that Capron's assaults on the bodies of boys, which was exciting to the child Lewis, also conveyed a sense that the body was sinful and needed punishing, a form of rejection.

Seeking the father has to be done under threat of talion revenge from the castrating mother, so Lucy sees malignant eyes everywhere.

It would have been nicer still if there weren't those masks hanging on the wall . . . the empty eyeholes, did look queer, and if you let yourself you would soon start imagining that the masks were doing things as soon as your back was turned. . . .
For one second she felt almost certain that a wicked little bearded face had popped out of the wall and made a grimace at her. She forced herself to stop and look at it. And it was not a face at all. It was a little mirror just the size and shape of her own face, with hair on the top of it and a beard hanging down from it, so that when you looked in the mirror your own face fitted into the hair and beard and it looked as if they belonged to you. . . . (VDT, p. 128)

Lewis writes strangely about this vision:

"I just caught my own reflection with the tail of my eye as I went past," said Lucy to herself. "That was all it was. It's quite harmless." But she didn't like the look of her own face with that hair and beard, and went on. (I don't know what the Bearded Glass was for because I am not a magician.) (p. 129*)

Again, we have the odd self-conscious remark, as over Eustace eating the dragon, showing that Lewis himself was touched by doubt as to what all this meant. What Lucy sees with "The tail of her eye" is a female genital that is also a face. The comparison is made in surrealist paintings and Ted Hughes's *Fragment From An Ancient Tablet* (in Crow):

Above—the well-known lips, delicately downed.
Below—beard between thighs.

Above—the face, shaped like a perfect heart,
Below—the heart's torn face. . . .

(Crow, p. 85)

I suppose that with Eustace, Lewis is exploring his male sexuality; with Lucy, female genitality. In both episodes, the atmo-

---

*There is a complex symbolism here that may be illuminated by referring the reader to the case of "Rudolph" discussed above. The mother's face and eyes are sought after as the clue to being reborn and the "mirror" is thus a gateway to being, and so also the female genital a birth passage, just as there is a mirror in the wardrobe.

sphere is heavy with dread. Perhaps we are moving from the oral to the genital phase with all its dangers?

When she finds the magician's book, Lucy has to be saved from indulging in vanity by Aslan growling. The passage is very much like one in Alice, with the child passing through various moods, tears splashing on the fantasies she sees. But then Aslan appears and all is well. The Dufflepuds are made benign: ". . . even the bearded mirror now seemed funny rather than frightening . . ." (VDT, p. 188). Aslan is necessary here, I believe, because Lewis is pursuing the problem of how a world filled with malignant male genital elements like the Monopods could be made benign. Her female element must be confronted with genital sex as Lucy is by the mirror. Helped by potent magic—Aslan—she may come to find it "funny rather than frightening," which means perhaps she can accept her feminity and unleash it on Aslan:

> Her face lit up till, for a moment (but of course she didn't know it), she looked almost beautiful as that other Lucy in the picture, and she ran forward with a little cry of delight and with her arms stretched out. . . . Aslan was solid and real and warm and he let her kiss him and bury herself in his shining mane. And from the low, earthquake-like sound that came from inside him, Lucy even dared to think that he was purring. . . . (VDT, p. 136)

As will be obvious, there is a great deal here of what the analysts call unconscious material. One problem with C. S. Lewis is that he often seems to have insufficient maturity to handle the deeply disturbing material his unconscious mind unleashes. In the next chapter, three enchanted lords are lying asleep at the eternal banquet, their grey hair growing all over the table like a huge bird's nest. Into this room comes an extremely beautiful girl, with silver candlesticks: the scene is full of complex unconscious themes—yet these are never engaged with while the language reverts to the level of prep-school jargon ("So that before the half-hour was nearly several people were positively sucking up to Drinian and Rhine (at least that was what they called it at my school) to get a good report"). From the country of the unconscious we are brought back to Belsen School with a jolt, and back to prep-school immaturity.

The same is true of the sea of lilies at the end, which is evidently meant to be a symbolic rebirth into purity. In places the topography is deeply poetic, but a certain banality undoes the conclusion. After the high vision of the lily-covered sea:

They came on and saw it was a lamb.

"Come and have breakfast," said the Lamb in its sweet milky voice. (p. 208)

This cosy lamb turns into Aslan, "towering above them and scattering light from his mane."

"I am the great Bridge builder. . . ."

"You are too old, children . . . and you must begin to come close to your own world now." (p. 209)

In their world, says Aslan "I have another name. . . ." So it is made clear that Lewis intends Aslan as Christ.

Here again we must raise the question of proportion, and the ethical and artistic meaning. The ordeals Eustace goes through can hardly be justified in terms of suffering made necessary by his sins for they are childish and petty. He suffers, it seems clear, because C. S. Lewis doesn't like him; because the author hates him—perhaps because he is a boy moving from the latency period into the Oedipal phase.

Does the dragon experience redeem Eustace?

It would be nice, and fairly nearly true, to say that "from that time forth Eustace was a different boy." To be strictly accurate, he began to be a different boy. He had relapses. There were still many days when he could be very tiresome. But most of that I shall not notice. The cure had begun. . . . (p. 95)

Again, I believe, we have to remember the suffering of Lewis at prep school. Of Eustace, Lewis says:

. . . deep down inside himself he liked bossing and bullying: and, though he was a puny little person who couldn't have stood up to Lucy, let alone Edmund, in a fight, he knew that there were dozens of ways to give people a bad time if you are in your own home and they are only visitors. . . . (p. 9)

The book, we remember, opens with this tirade of hate:

There was a boy called Eustace Clarence Scrubb and he almost deserved it . . . [his parents] were very up-to-date and advanced people. They were vegetarians, non-smokers and teetotallers and wore a special kind of underclothes. In their house there was very little furniture and very few clothes on the beds and the windows were always open.

Eustace Clarence liked animals, especially beetles, if they were dead and pinned on a card. He liked books . . . if they had pictures of . . . fat foreign children doing exercises in model schools. (p. 9)

Eustace eats Plumptre's Vitamized Nerve Food (p. 18), is a *pacifist*, and goes to a school where they don't have corporal punishment, but where "experiment" is encouraged. When beaten by Reepicheep he goes to his bunk and is "careful to lie on his side." Lewis gloats on others receiving the kind of pain he suffered as a boy at school: "It might have been red-hot by the feel" (p. 35). To Lewis, not being "toughened" to "fight" and suffer is obviously the greatest sin because it leaves one vulnerable. One gets a sense that the boy in Lewis despises children at school who did not suffer as he did.

Where people become decadent—as in Lone Islands in *The Voyage of the Dawn Treader*—they leave themselves open to the possibility of being overcome by the White Witch, and ensnared in her spells. The worst lapses are to have one's "armour in a disgraceful condition" (p. 52) or to fail to wipe one's sword.

Thus the real message of *The Voyage of the Dawn Treader*, again, is that one should make oneself strong to deal with the world. Aslan declares he had "another name," but we may suspect it is "Robert Capron," despite the endorsement of the Holy Spirit as albatross (the ship is lit up by a beam of light):

Lucy looked along the beam and presently saw something in it. At first it looked like a cross, then it looked like an aeroplane, then it looked like a kite, and at last with a whirring of wings it was right overhead and was an albatross. . . . It called out into a strong sweet voice. . . . (pp. 158–59)

Albatrosses do not "whirr": the whirr comes from Coleridge's "the whizz of my cross-bow." In Coleridge there is a reparative pity which is not found in Lewis: Coleridge's Mariner finds concern as Lewis does not.

Lewis's Christ, his Holy Ghost, even his "Emperor Beyond the Seas," do not elucidate from his protagonists' deep outward-giving generosities ("I blessed them unawares"). They are, as to a small boy on his knees praying in distress, agents there to serve us by their potent magic, demanding absolute obedience.

# 10

## The Silver Chair

The Silver Chair is about rescuing a prince (whom we may take to represent an aspect of the self) from imprisonment in a silver chair. Careful examination of the symbolism (including the artist's drawings*) reveals that this chair is a female genital: the bad mother's vulva. Like the mirrors, the wardrobes and pools, it is an aspect of the mother's body.** I bring to bear here in phenomenological interpretation the illustrations from Dr. Von Naevestad's The Colours of Rage and Love (1979). Many of the patient's drawings there show the "bad mother" as a big menacing genital that dominates the patient's life. In The Silver Chair the central symbol is that of an imprisoning female genital that will not let the protagonist go.

Again, the story begins at school. The children are at a progressive school that Lewis denounces because (like Eustace's) it denies the recognition of the spiritual life. ("Bibles were not encouraged at Experiment House" [SC, p. 14]).

The unconscious theme here is the Narnia theme. A worm, green as poison, has killed the mother; the son seeks to exorcise it. The worm is the Jadis Witch in another color. She is the malignant anima and contains, or is combined with, the father's penis with which he killed the mother, the sin-phallus.

Here, the action largely takes place in the "deep realm," underground—the territory of the womb and of the subconscious. "Many sink down into the underworld and few return to the sunlit lands" (SC, p. 123 and passim). Here again we have explored the schizoid fear of "going back inside" and then becoming trapped.

---

*Lewis, of course, is not responsible for the illustrations; but illustrators often pick up unconscious themes in a work, and in the "Narnia" books, I believe, exceptionally so.
**The word chair means flesh in French.

So, there are many paranoid-schizoid elements—winds that could take your skin off, Harfang people (that is, Harm-fang, oral-sadistic people) who eat babies, and are hoping to eat the children. The children in the Harfang castle discover first that they are served "talking stag"; that is, an animal symbol of aspects of humanness. They they discover a recipe for cooking people: "MAN: This elegant little biped has long been valued as a delicacy. . . ." Running away to escape being hunted by the Harfang giants, the children plunge further underground.

With them in Puddleglum is a marsh-wiggle. The marsh he comes from has "something fine and fresh and keen about its loneliness" because "Marsh-wiggles are people who like privacy" (SC, p. 63). The Marsh-wiggle Puddleglum (modelled apparently on an actual gardener) is a manic-depressive, and so is a tower of strength in the schizoid-paranoid predicaments into which the children fall!

> They had thought him a wet blanket while they were still above ground, but down here he seemed the only comforting thing they had. (SC, p. 129)

Like Eustace in *The Dawn Treader*, who feels relief when the worst possible thing happens to him, the Puddleglum is so depressed by ordinary problems that when faced with the ultimate ones he becomes the neurotic hero in a paranoid-schizoid world.

The prince is the black knight, completely bewitched by the white queen. She is the mother who holds her schizoid child in thrall: having failed him as feminine, she holds power over him by impingement. In his bewitchment the Prince experiences as love what normal people would see as hate:

> "I am well content to live by her word, who has already saved me from a thousand dangers. No mother has taken pains more tenderly for her child than the Queen's grace has for me. . . ." (p. 133)
> She is a nosegay of all virtues, as truth, mercy, constancy, gentleness, courage and the rest. . . . (p. 133)

The prince is, in fact, encapsulated in her total moral inversion, proclaiming, "Evil, be Thou my Good!"

In his state of being bewitched, the prince is all pure goodness or, rather, pure inverted good. In his frenzy he resorts to a manic-depressive state—that is, he becomes human, and ambivalent. "He looked a nicer sort of man than he had looked before" (p. 142).

> "There used to be a little pool. When you looked down into it you would see all the trees growing upside down in the water. . . ." (p. 142)

This, as we have seen, is a central image in C. S. Lewis, the pool of birth, or rebirth.

The prince calls on Aslan; and, bound by magic vows, the children release him. He attacks the silver chair. There is a bright flash from it "(for one moment) a loathsome smell" (p. 146).

> "Lie there, vile engine of sorcery," he said, "lest your mistress should ever use you for another victim." (p. 146)

Now comes the conflict with the castrating mother, whose predatory genital has been destroyed.

The Witch tries to lull them all into enchantment, or, as we may say, a sense of schizoid futility: she tries to get them "to give themselves up the joys of hating," to become paralyzed by moral inversion and nihilism. Lewis reveals the seductive joys of giving oneself up to hate and getting what satisfaction one can out of that. Here is the effect of the witch in all her uncreating force:

> "There is no sun" . . . "You are right there is no sun." It was such a relief to give in and say it.

But, as positive meaningful realities are denied by the witch, resistance develops, and the depressive marsh-wiggle eventually protests that human meanings are the only reality:

> "Suppose we have only dreamed, or made up, all those things—trees and grass and sun and moon and Aslan himself. Suppose we have. Then all I can say is that, in that case, the made-up things seem a good deal more important than the real ones. . . . Not that our lives will be very long. . . ." (SC, p. 136*)

We may glimpse behind this Lewis's own struggles to hold

---

*This theme is as some have pointed out, based on Plato's figure of the Cave: see p. 123.

on to a sound sense of reality, after his mother died, in his confusion of fantasy and reality. But the efforts of Puddleglum, the manic-depressive, have their good effect. The spell of nihilism is broken. The witch immediately turns into a serpent—a malignant phallus, that has in its turn to be castrated:

> With repeated blows they hacked off its head. The horrible thing went on coiling and moving like a bit of wire long after it had died: and the floor, as you may imagine, was a nasty mess.* (SC, p. 159)

The prince says that "all these years I have been the slave of my mother's slayer" (SC, p. 158) that is, as we may interpret it, "I have been overwhelmed by Oedipus feeling, about what my father's penis did to my mother, so that she died; and I was left with a revived Castrating Mother who imprisoned me by her male-doing in dreadful obsession with her vagina." This is the unconscious message, and the reason for the long underground exploration of this world peopled with lost penises—the pale, bald, horned little people the children encounter at every turn.

Yet, strangely, and despite the presence of Aslan, at the end comes a banal relapse into spitefulness and sadism endorsed by the author when Aslan is used to frighten the inhabitants of an experimental school, as we have seen.

\* \* \* \*

The Silver Chair is a useful story over which to test the psychoanalytical interpretation. I turned to Lewis's own essay "Psychoanalysis and Literary Criticism" in Selected Literary Essays.

Psychoanalysis, in relation to the arts, has come a long way since Lewis expressed his very intelligent doubts about the reductive effect of Freudian analysis. No one today would suppose that psychoanalysis would say of a work of art that the reason why one was really enjoying it was that the garden in it is an erotic symbol. Literary judgements are by no means in ruins because of the insights of psychoanalysis; nor is the image regarded as merely a "disguise."

I held my breath, however, while reading Lewis's comment

---

*The characteristic lapse into banality here reveals an inability to know what is the right tone: it is hebephrenic like Ransom's, "Here goes—I mean 'Amen,'" in Perelandra. This kind of lapse often accompanies sadistic fantasies in Lewis. See p. 236.

on wish-fulfilment, and his discussion of the universal meanings of symbols. Freud argues that there are objects in the real world whose images, when they appear in dreams or stories, bear a constant meaning.

> These images with constant meanings he calls symbols—the words, so to speak, of a universal image-language. He gives us a few specimens. A House signifies the human body; Kings and Queens, fathers and mothers; Journeys, death; small animals (here come my poor mice, after all, you see) one's brothers and sisters; Fruit, Landscapes, Gardens, Blossoms, the female body or various parts of it. (Selected Literary Essays, p. 291)

Lewis is trying to defend literary values against the reductionism of a form of interpretation which reduces everything to what the symbols "simply mean": "If it is true that all our enjoyment of the images, without remainder, can be explained in terms of infant sexuality, then, I confess, our literary judgements are in ruins" (p. 293).

But Lewis also suggests, in his emendation of Freudian theory, that there are two kinds of activity of the imagination. One is free, the other "enslaved to the wishes of its owner for whom it has to provide imaginary gratifications" (p. 290). This other "servile" kind is not "elaborated" into a work of art. Lewis spends much of his essay resisting the Freudian kind of sexual interpretation, to protect the literary approach. And he finds Jung more sympathetic. The mystery, he declares, of primordial images is deeper, "their origin more remote, their cave more hid, their fountain less accessible than those suspect who have yet dug deepest. . . ." And he ends, "for why should I not be allowed to write in this vein as well as everyone else." But he fails to penetrate to the problem of hate: to those forms of wish-fulfilment in fantasy in which the deepest impulse to live at the expense of others is indulged—the fantasy indulgence in power. He says that there is a peculiar "tang" of the merely personal wish-fulfilment. "Surely this is utterly different from the unpredictable ecstasy, the apparent 'otherness' and externality of disinterested imagination" (pp. 288–89). But in his own work, surely, Lewis himself is a presence, "enjoying his power," and this indulgent presence (which often addresses the reader directly) goes with a literalness, in which, for instance, the leading character Aslan is not simply a character in a fantasy, but a personal deity, the big dog, who guarantees the validity of his world and faith, and links him with a cosmic system in which he as literally believed?

The essay, therefore, although it displays no hostility to psychoanalysis, is something of a defence against its insights, though he confesses to day-dreaming and fantasying in the ways he is discussing. He sees that day-dreaming may "become the source of literature" but assumes too easily that there is a "disappearance of the self who was . . . the raison d'etre of the original dream" (p. 290). A phenomenological study reveals that the self is not so easily jettisoned as that. His own kings and queens, his typography, his journeys and small animals and his houses (and wardrobes) are integral with a psychic tissue which has its own obsessions and urgent needs.

Intensely personal to his own self is Lewis's Christology. The solemn tone around Aslan is not so much a religious awe as a special emotion associated with the meaning of this "lion" to his own mythological world and topography. At one moment we have the gravity of imagery drawn from the most potent Christian symbols, as when Eustace drives a thorn into the lion's pad: "And there came out a great drop of blood, redder than all redness you have ever seen or imagined" (SC, p. 202). But almost at once, after this serious discussion of death, resurrection, redemption and hope for eternal life, the book collapses into the silly and spiteful assault on "Experiment House," led by the same Aslan!

This is more than a failure to find the appropriate emotions: it is a lapse into indulgence. It robs the book of proportion, it represents private values; and it is surely intemperate and banal? All we can do is to try to understand it in phenemonological terms.

Lewis went to a very formal and authoritarian school: he is envious and contemptuous of schools where the teachers try to talk out the reasons for trouble and wickedness. Because of his experiences at "Belsen" Lewis became attached to the patterns of painful chastisement—and so comes implicitly to commend it to his child readers, as an act of which Christ would approve, directed by Aslan against people who are so foolish as to be "progressive" in their approach to schooling.

These people at "Experiment House" did not have much time for the Bible. One may see a parallel with his criticisms of the educationists in The Abolition of Man; but here it is "the abolition of authority" that he is chastising. (Perhaps he would prefer the schools to have their knowledge rationed, like the treatment given to the Lady in Eden in *Perelandra*?) But Christ, it seems, is prepared to thrash teachers and children who do not recognize the authority of those, "close to God," who wrote the Bible.

*   *   *   *

Apart from this, of course, one may read *The Silver Chair* simply as an adventure. As such, much of it is well written and exciting. Many passages are benign, and transcend the unconscious roots of the story into art, such as the description of Cair Paravel:

> On the near side was a quay of white marble, and, moored to this, the ship: a tall ship with a high forecastle and high poop, gilded and crimson, with a great flag at the mast-head, and many banners waving from the decks. (SC, p. 35)

In that vein Lewis creates a dream world which is quite appropriate for children as art as are his dealings with the elder King Caspian, and the Marsh-wiggle—who is a real character, comic, brave, warmly engaging: really very human.

The journey in this book again is about death: it is once more a penetration into the "inner world" where the "bad mother" holds the potentialities of the self in a spell. (The Green Witch is described as being of "the same kind as that White Witch," p. 193.) Prince Rilian's imprisonment in a silver chair may also perhaps be a signal of the mother's inadequate handling, and her whole "grip" on the self; that is, the "genital" symbol is a symbol of Lewis's experience of "impingement." But I refer to the genital symbol because of the intense genital-oral elements clearly there in the story. The Harfang king and queen are parents (giants are surely adults as experienced by small children?); and we have seen Lucy's glimpse of the king's penis-tongue.

There are intense oral dangers in this world of infantile sexuality so the children are to be eaten by the Harfangs. (Then they realize that the Harfangs are eating "talking stag," Puddleglum, who was Narnian born, was sick and faint, and tells them he felt as you would feel—"*if you found you had eaten a baby*," p. 113.)

The book is about the long period during which Lewis felt he had not completed mourning. So Father Time is asleep, while in this underworld the prince is either trapped in the Silver Chair or riding, without speaking, in a suit of armor with the

Green Queen. He is like Hamlet, haunted by the ghost of a dead parent. In this predicament he has suffered deep disturbances of his relationship with reality. He is bewitched into believing all kinds of false things about the Witch herself, and about the world, while later the Witch tries to persuade Lucy, Eustace, and the Prince that Narnia does not exist, and that the creative imagination does not exist.

This is an allegory which, although Lewis takes it as being about belief, also refers to Lewis's difficulties with reality and imagination. The manic-depressive Puddleglum asserts that *play is primary*:

> . . . the made-up things seem a good deal more important than the real ones. . . . We're just babies making up a game if you're right. But four babies playing a game can make a play-world which licks your real world hollow. (SC, p. 156)

The "bad" mother threatens to take out of the world all that primary imagination can put there. Puddleglum asserts the triumph of that *play* by which the infant creates his world.

In a sense the book is the play which is an attempt to break the spell, but Lewis is so desperate he must make two other attempts to find a new reality: Puddleglum puts his foot in the fire, and the prince and other men kill the queen, now turned into a green snake (a predatory penis or anima symbol). Of the former, Lewis comments typically, "There is nothing like a good shock of pain for dissolving certain kinds of magic" (p. 116). Of the latter, Prince Rilian says: ". . . it would not have suited well my heart to have slain a woman" (p. 158). The trouble with the solutions is their "external" quality; that is, everything happens in terms of "split-offs." Of course Lewis does not want to kill a woman. He wants to eliminate the "bad" part of mother, the serpent of false male doing, and hate: he needs to push something of himself "into Mother." But the fantasy (and its recipe) is like some dangerous forms of acting out.

The best part of the book is in the delineation of the loyalty and endurance of the children through the mountains and the snow, and the underground worlds. Here, I believe, there is genuine creative achievement; but there remains a desperation that expresses itself almost in an autistic way, as by Puddleglum putting his foot in the fire, which is a desperate act, like that of an autistic child trying to find reality. Also, in a sense, the (external) chopping off of the Witch's head doesn't solve the problem either, even though the prince cries, "My Royal Mother is avenged!" (SC, p. 158). Again, it is too much enacted, this redemption of the mother, in terms of split-off entities by castration.

The adventure story seemed to me, in this book at least, unobjectionable—the oral content being simply like that of many fairy stories. But the serious weaknesses come, in Lewis's own terms, from areas where the imagination remains "servile": especially where Aslan is demeaned by becoming the agent of hate, directed not against those who have "sinned" even, but merely against those whose life-style is disliked.

# 11

## The Horse and His Boy

The Horse and His Boy is perhaps the most benign of C. S. Lewis's "Narnia" books for the same reason, perhaps, that the passage about the Houhynhymns has more benignity than the rest of Gulliver's Travels ('Hwin' is surely a Houhynhym?). Quite often a writer who fears human emotion is happier with animals than with man, and in this book the horses dominate.*

There is also some very good writing about topography—and, indeed, in all the books the topographical descriptions of imagined territories are much their best features.

This territory in The Horse and His Boy has a symbolism related to the universal symbolism of the "Narnia" books. Such spiritual journeys as Lewis's (like George MacDonald's) represent a quest to seek beyond the deadness (or desert) of "False Male Doing," to find the lost world of the mother where a new birth (of "Female Element Being") can take place. Here the desert is full of phallic tombs, and the quest is made through a dead land seeking the sphere of "Female Element Being." (There is in the map a long valley between hills marked "narrow gorge.") At the end of this journey, they come to a "broad pool":

> Before them a little cataract of water poured into a broad pool: and both the Horses were already in the pool with their heads down, drinking, drinking, drinking.
> "O-o-oh," said Shasta and plunged in—it was about up to his knees—and stooped his head right into the cataract. It was perhaps the loveliest moment in his life. (HB, p. 115; my italics)

This is the fantasied moment of rebirth, of which there are many examples in George MacDonald and C. S. Lewis.

Again, at the explicit level, the book is an odd combination: it has both a sickly Sunday school morality, and an underlying

---

*Henry Williamson is much happier with Tarka in Tarka the Otter than with the human beings in his other books.

brutal primitivism. For instance, after one important episode, Bree, the horse, is deeply ashamed of being cowardly. (This is, of course, the worst of all evils in Lewis's paranoid world.)

> "Yes," said Bree, "Slavery is all I'm fit for. How can I ever show my face among the free Horses of Narnia?—I who left a mare and a girl and a boy to be eaten by lions which I galloped all I could to save my wretched skin!"
>
> "I know." said Aravis. "I felt just the same. Shasta was marvellous. I'm just as bad as you, Bree. . . ."
>
> "It's all very well for you," said Bree, "You haven't disgraced yourself. But I've lost everything. . . ." (HB, p. 128)

The language, and the ethical values, are those of "jolly dee" little boys at a prep school. But can school standards be reconciled with the grave savagery of Aslan's moral intervention on the basis of an "eye for an eye, tooth for a tooth" morality, administering painful punishment?

> Before they reached him the lion rose on its hind legs, larger than you would have believed a lion could be, and jabbed at Aravis with its right paw. Shasta could see all the terrible claws extended. Aravis screamed and reeled in the saddle. The lion was tearing her shoulders. Shasta, half mad with horror, managed to lurch towards the brute . . . her back was covered with blood. (p. 123)

Aslan has a nice, genteel, explanation for this attack. The imagery is a play on the fantasies of primitive sadism, but the cruelty is associated with eating and so with sexual undertones. Hwin turns masochistic:

> Then Hwin, though shaking all over, gave a strange little neigh, and trotted across.
>
> "Please," she said, "You're so beautiful. You may eat me if you like. I'd sooner be eaten by you than fed by anyone else."
>
> "Dearest daughter," said Aslan, planting a lion's kiss on her twitching velvet nose. "I know you would not be long in coming to me. Joy shall be yours." (p. 169)

He tells Aravis he will not be torn this time:

> "It was I who wounded you. . . . Do you know why I tore you?"
>
> "No, sir."
>
> "The scratches on your back, tear for tear, throb for throb, blood for blood, were equal to the stripes laid on the back of your stepmoth-

er's slave because of the drugged sleep you cast upon her. You
needed to know what it felt like."

"Yes, sir. Please——." (p. 169)

Lewis's message seems to be that the important thing is that
one must *accept* the punitive suffering imposed by Aslan without question. It would not do (for instance) for Aravis to *imagine*
the suffering of the slave girl. It must be *acted out on her.*
Again, we encounter Lewis's strange literalness, and his sadomasochistic acceptance of the capronic solution.

We may recognize again the origins of the idolized punitive-
ness of Aslan in "Belsen" school, but what is the effect on
children? Surely Lewis's stories might persuade children with
a penchant for acting out primitive sadistic or masochistic impulses *to feel they were fully justified in doing so?*

At the end Aslan turns Rabadash into a donkey. While such
punishments often happen in fairy stories (as in *A Midsummer
Night's Dream*), there is surely something perplexing about
Aslan doing it? To Lewis, it is an earnest of hope and joy that
one's enemies can be turned into donkeys:

> There was a brightness in the air and on the grass, and a joy in
> their hearts, which assured them that he had been no dream: and
> anyway, there was the donkey in front of them. (p. 184)

Surely, there are, in this recurrent theme of deserved punishment, severe artistic and ethical weaknesses in the "Narnia"
books? Should one really experience joy in the humiliation of
another?

# 12

## The Last Battle

In *The Last Battle*, which is the last of the series, C. S. Lewis turns to that ultimate battle which, in so many mythologies, has to be fought to find one's way through to the final meaning of life. This last battle is, of course, celebrated in many hymns such as *Soldiers of Christ Arise* or *Onward Christian Soldiers*. It belongs to the old human ambition to conquer all our enemies finally—and that even appears in the *Internationale* that summons the Proletariat: "the last fight let us face."

This is the conscious Christian intention, and as we have seen, Lewis offered this story as a testimony to his conviction. There is a concern with the true God and the false God, or, rather, true Alsan and false Aslan. At a deeper level, there is anxiety about the possibility of elements in the world, which should be reliable and protective, suddenly becoming hostile; and creatures which should be trustworthy turning out to be otherwise. I have interpreted the "lamp-post" in the other world as a symbol of male protection. Here something terrible has happened to "Lantern Waste":

> Right through the middle of the ancient forest—that forest where the trees of gold and silver had once grown and where a child from our world had once planted the Tree of Protection—a broad lane had already been opened. It was a hideous lane like a raw gash in the land. . . . (p. 25)

In the first chapter we meet two representatives of the forces of evil that obviously represent human proclivities: Shift the Ape, and his poor dupe, Puzzle the Donkey. The ape is cunning and ugly. He can exploit Puzzle because the donkey is stupid. Between them, they represent two aspects of human nature for which Lewis has much contempt—beastly and cunning barbarity, and good-natured and weak-willed stupidity. It is not difficult, I think, to trace these attributes to Lewis's experience of his appalling preparatory school. I believe we can see the origin of his impulse to feel contempt for such "enemies" in the appalling experience of trying to hold his world together, in an anguish of grief, when it was threatened by the father's deranged instability on the one hand, and the brutality and inhumanity of Capron on the other.

Shift and Puzzle find a lion skin; that is, the mere empty skin of Aslan-ness: the mockery of Christianity. Shift persuades Puzzle to wear it. He protests:

> "I don't think it would be respectful to the Great Lion, to Aslan himself, if an ass like me went about dressed up in a lion skin." (LB, p. 12)

"What does an ass like you know about things of that sort?" retorts Shift. "Why don't you let me do your thinking for you?" (p. 12). When Puzzle tries the skin on, Shift says:

> "You look wonderful, wonderful. . . . If anyone saw you now they'd think you were Aslan, the great Lion, himself."
> "That would be dreadful," said Puzzle.
> "No, it wouldn't. . . . Think of the good we can do. . . . Everyone would do whatever you told them." (p. 15)

The ape is to "set everything right" by such manipulative, duplicitous power not the least by making certain there is an adequate supply of oranges, bananas, and sugar. As Shift speaks of Aslan, there is a thunderclap which he quickly interprets as a sign that Aslan (God) wants them to carry on. The chapter resembles episodes in George Orwell's *Animal Farm*. It is an ironic parody of man's quest to exert his will even by employing false gods and persuading others to revere them.

In the next chapter, King Tirian is discussing with his friend, the unicorn, the possibility of Aslan's coming. "'Yes,' said the King with a great sigh, almost a shiver of delight. 'It is beyond all that I ever hoped for in my life'" (p. 18).

King Tirian, however, is in for a shock. He takes it that there are signs that Aslan has returned to Narnia again, and this will be the fulfilment of his faith. However, creatures from the mythological world appear with grim news. A centaur declares that the rumors that Aslan has come back cannot be true because there have been no indications in the stars. Then the unicorn Jewel argues that Aslan is not the slave of the stars, but their maker, so he might come although the stars tell otherwise. "Is it not said in all the old stories that he is not a Tame Lion" (p. 20).

So, even the acceptance that Christ may be a tiger is seduced into the misrepresentation of religion. A dryad comes in wailing and dying, because the great beech trees in Lantern Waste are being felled—apparently by Aslan's orders. Who dares do this in the name of Aslan? On their way to deal with the problem, they meet a water rat who is steering a raft of timber, cut down and sold to the Calormenes, apparently by the orders of Aslan himself.

Here there is one strangely give-away sentence: could Aslan be felling the holy trees and murdering the Dryads? "'Unless the Dryads have all done something dreadfully wrong—' murmured Jewel" (p. 24). That is, it could be divine punitive retribution, which is, it seems, an acceptable reality in Lewis's devotional system. However, it is not.

Appropriate Christian questions are raised, of course, as in the book of Job: "Even that it would please God to destroy me . . . Then should I yet have comfort . . ." (Job 7:9–10). How do we know when a catastrophe is a mere manifestation of God's wrath—perhaps because His rules have been broken? Or when it is a manifestation of human hubris, as, say, with the devastation of the rain forests, as in this real world of ours?

We may also detect an energy that belongs to the underlying mythology of Lewis's unconscious. In the devastation of Lantern Waste, the felling even threatens the tree which was planted by Digory, the Tree of Protection which grew from the mother's body; that is, the restorative power which the "Narnia" stories themselves represent is now threatened. This means, in my terms, that in this book Lewis confronts the fact that the reality of the human world must be brought up against the imaginary world in order to grapple further with the question he was left with after his mother's death: what is real? Behind Lewis's intense energy of belief lies the dread that is like that of Marie Von Naevestad's patient "Marion," that she might become "unable to discriminate between past and actual, between inner and outer reality." This accounts for the autistic feeling one sometimes has about the story—it is itself an act of shoving one's foot in the fire to see what is real. Of course, also from the beginning, Lewis once more sets up a paranoid-schizoid situation, in which there is a terrible menace which must be counteracted by summoning one's aggression and being prepared to use one's sword—not forgetting to wipe it afterwards, of course.

Yet here the killing does not seem quite so satisfactorily justified as in the earlier stories. Questions of the effects of inflicting pain and killing are raised, as by the recognition that the horses being misused are talking horses—they have a human kind of consciousness. And even in reacting to this outrage, the king and Jewel act swiftly and in heat only to become aware of what they have done in a truly concerned way.

So, the story becomes painful. Here the king finds a talking horse being exploited by Calomenes.

> It was then that the really dreadful thing happened.
>
> Up till now Tirian had taken it for granted that the horses which the Calormenes were driving were their own horses: dumb, witless animals like the horses of our world. And though he hated to see even a dumb horse over-driven, he was of course thinking more about the murder of the Trees. It had never crossed his mind that anyone would dare to harness one of the free Talking Horses of Narnia, much less to use a whip on it. But as that savage blow fell the horse reared up and said, half screaming,
>
> "Fool and tyrant! Do you not see I am doing all I can?" (LB, p. 26)

The king gets into such a rage that he and the unicorn kill the Calormenes:

> Next moment both the Calormenes lay dead, the one beheaded by Tirian's sword and the other gored through the heart by Jewel's horn. (p. 26)

The same compassion is not offered to the Calormenes as it is to the talking horses, because the Calormenes are "not human." But the killing is not quite taken to be as self-righteously justified as elsewhere in the earlier Christian campaigns.

The strange obsession with "drying one's sword" has already been discussed. It emerges again in The Last Battle: "of course he dried his sword very carefully on the shoulder of his cloak, which was the only dry point of him, as soon as they came to shore" (p. 22). That this is related to problems of guilt seems confirmed, for now, after killing, there is much guilt:

> "Jewel," said the King. "We have done a dreadful deed."
> "We were sorely provoked," said Jewel.

> "But to leap on them unawares—without defying them—faugh! we are two murderers, Jewel, I am dishonoured for ever."
> Jewel drooped his head. He too was ashamed. (p. 28)

Now the story takes a strange turn for the king decides to put his fate in the hands of Aslan.

But (of course) we know that the Aslan nearby is false—a donkey in a lion's skin.

True guilt needs the true Aslan to absolve it. The king is prepared to face death as punishment. He says:

> "Do you think I care if Aslan dooms me to death?" said the King. "That would be nothing, nothing at all. Would it not be better dead than to have this horrible fear that Aslan had come and is not like the Aslan we have believed in and longed for? *It is as if the sun rose one day and were a black sun.*" (pp. 28–29, my italics)

The black sun is a symbol found in the symbolism of R. D. Laing's (schizoid) patient Julie in *The Divided Self*. It seems to symbolize the total inversion of all values and qualities, and here perhaps we glimpse C. S. Lewis's fantasy of the worst thing that could be imagined (parallel to the black voids discussed above). Supposing—after all this labour to find renewed life and meaning—the quest proves sterile?

> . . . as if you drank water and it were dry water . . . this is at the end of all things. . . . If you are dead and Aslan is not Aslan what life is left for me? . . . (p. 29)

When Tirian and Jewel give themselves up, they find the ape ruling the world: "There was a great pile of nuts beside him and he kept cracking nuts with his jaws and spitting out the shells. . . ." (p. 30). Here is the complacent hedonism of the petty tyrant, exerting his power by virtue of his subjects' fear of the god whom he hides and will not display to them. This ape claims manhood because of his human attributes. "'I hear some of you saying I'm an Ape. Well, I'm not. I'm a Man'" (p. 32).

He promises the creatures of Narnia *slavery*—and because of their love of Aslan, they accept it, bewildered as they are. The story becomes a parable of all those who have accepted obeisance and drudgery in the name of a super-Saviour, of false religion. The ape promises oranges and bananas, "and roads and big cities and schools and offices and whips and muzzles and saddles and cages and kennels and prisons—oh, everything" (p. 33). The talking animals, indeed, are promised *the human world*: "'but we don't want all those things,' said the old Bear. 'We want to be free. And we want to hear Aslan speak himself'" (p. 33).

This is a parable of the search for freedom, and what is offered by Shift is a travesty of *en la suetade e nostra pace*:

> 'What do you know about freedom? You think freedom means doing what you like. Well, you're wrong. That isn't true freedom. True freedom means doing what I tell you.' (p. 36)

A lamb asks why the animals have anything to do with the Calormenes—for they have a god called Tash, who had the head of a vulture, and to whom they sacrificed men. How could this be reconciled with Aslan, their god? "'They are only different names for you know Who . . . Tash is Aslan: Aslan is Tash. . . .'" (p. 34). That is, hate is love. The animals are more bewildered; the king cries out:

> He meant to go on to ask how the terrible god Tash who fed on the blood of his people could possibly be the same as the Good Lion by whose blood all Narnia was saved. . . . (p. 36)

Before he can say another word, two Calmormenes "struck him in the mouth with all their force."

Some mice and other small animals come to feed the king, but they dare not set him free.

"Do you think it really is Aslan?" he asks. But the animals believe Aslan is punishing them for something. Of course, like Bunyan, Lewis is using a fable mode to make us feel reinforced in our concepts of the "True Faith"; we aren't to be led by such delusions, are we? Yet at the unconscious level, the dread of being deceived by a false follower of the faith (as the child Lewis was by the insane clergyman) is touched on. So, as the king sees the donkey in the lion's skin in the light of a bonfire he reflects:

> How could one be sure? For a moment horrible thoughts went through his mind: then he remembered the nonsense about Tash and Aslan being the same and knew the whole thing must be a cheat. (p. 42)

Rilian thinks of all the Narnian past, and he thinks the present time must be worst of all. The children who used to help in the past—can they help again? Aslan—could he return? "He called out 'Aslan! Aslan! Aslan! Come and help us Now'" (p. 43). Nothing happens. Then he calls the children. He has a vision of them seeing him like a ghost. They experience this as a week ago, before they actually enter Narnia.

Later we discover the children enter Narnia *by dying in a railway accident*. So, to save King Tirian it is necessary for these child protagonists of the "Narnia" books to actually die. Moreover, they die into an "other" world in which Tash exists as a terrible split-off embodiment of hate, and in which the Ape-Aslan deception is possible. Prince Caspian there has "been dead two hundred years"; and it is a terrible blighted world again, much more menacing than earth.

At the end, C. S. Lewis tries to convince us that we shall "be happy dead"; but it is very difficult to reconcile the gravity of this religious parable with the child adventure story mode borrowed from E. Nesbit: "'Oh, hurrah!' said Jill. 'Disguise! I love disguises'" (LB, p. 53). At once (characteristically), the children, as they die into Narnia, enter into a very menacing situation—and have to toughen themselves. They put brown coloring on themselves, Calormene helmets, swords and shields.

> There was no sword light enough for Jill, but he gave her a long, straight hunting knife which might do for a sword at a pinch. (p. 55)

Jill is not bad at archery. She shoots a rabbit (not, of course, a talking rabbit!). It was now already skinned, cleaned and hanging up. "He had found that both the children knew all about this chilly and smelly job. . . ." (p. 56).

So, they are properly "blooded" children. Eustace has to learn how to use a Calormene scimitar: "Both seemed to be already much stronger and bigger and more grown up than they had been when he first met them a few hours ago" (p. 56).

> It is one of the effects which Narnian air often has on visitors from our world. (LB, p. 57)

When we die, the implication is, we shall go to a world in which we shall need to toughen ourselves, and prepare for further painful trials. This makes no kind of sense in Christian terms. It may, however, make sense in terms of the unconscious meaning—even when you reach the land where the dead mother is, the World of Death, the problem has only begun. The struggle for which the child Lewis has prepared himself has engaged him. So, here, the incident in which Jewel is freed is very much like an incident in a James Bond novel. Eustace is told, "If he [the sentry] moves, rive him to the heart" (LB, p. 61). Jill captures Puzzle, the false Aslan, but will not let Tirian kill him. Yet it seems at least that the ape's rule is at an end.

So exciting is the battle drama, however, that we fail to ask what it can possibly mean in the Christian parable, and once more our solution is to ask what it may mean in the fairy story of unconscious legend. The two children and King Tirian meet a party of dwarfs with four Calormene guards. Eustace kills one.

> Eustace, who had drawn his sword when he saw the King draw his, rushed at the other one: his was deadly pale, but *I wouldn't blame him for that*. And he had the luck that beginners sometimes do have. He forgot all that Tirian had tried to teach him that afternoon, slashed wildly (Indeed, I'm not sure his eyes weren't shut) and suddenly found, *to his own great surprise*, that the Calormene lay dead at his feet. And though that was a great relief, it was, at the moment, *rather frightening*. . . . (LB, p. 67; my italics)

Here the rather polite language adapted from E. Nesbit (who has an irony directed at her children's gentility that is very comic at times) is used virtually to *seduce* the child reader into the enjoyment of hate. Violence is only *rather* frightening, and it is only a *Calormene* who is "settled." "Three cheers for Aslan"—and the dwarfs (Jill tells them) can "have fun again." The passage could almost be accused of being a recommendation of "fun killings": "then he too had killed his man" (p. 67). Of course, it is only an adventure story. Yet we may once more recall that Lewis offered seriously the book as evidence of his loyalty to Christ's promises. So the bloodthirsty enthusiasm must be offered as a serious lesson, too. What are our objections? They must be, surely, that if there are so-called bad elements in ourselves and others, it is to evade the problem to set these up as "enemies" with which we should be in deadly contest. The lesson of psychotherapy is that we should exorcise these "bad" elements by understanding them, not by regarding them as *nonhuman* entities, fit only for *destruction*: the problem calls for love not hate—but that, surely, is also the Christian message?*

The dwarfs are a case in point. In the parable, what do they

---

*It wasn't, of course, even at the time of the Crusades, the horror and idealism of which is now coming to light. When a Catholic protested that there were Catholics among the victims in Beziers church a Papal Nuncio replied, "Kill them all. The Lord will know his own."

symbolize? The dwarfs, instead of being grateful, since King Tirian says the real Aslan is "not a tame lion," become ever more suspicious because this is what Shift has always told them. The dwarfs now become (as it were) a kind of disaffected working class in the parable, deprived of their religious belief, impelled solely by self-interest and hedonism, recognizing none of the bourgeois virtues or courtesies, aggressive in their egalitarianism. "We're going to look after ourselves from now on and touch our cap to nobody. See?" They are egoistical nihilists: "The Dwarfs are for the Dwarfs" (LB, p. 112). What Tirian thought was going to be a beautiful moment was turning out "more like a bad dream."

In Lewis's story, being ungrateful for being saved, they deserve only contempt: "'Little beasts!' said Eustace. 'Aren't you ever going to say *thank you* for being saved from the saltmines?'" (p. 70). One renegade Dwarf however, joins the allies: Poggin, who turns out to be a useful kind of batman. At least there is *one* grateful workman! Of course I don't argue that the "Narnia" books will encourage children to despise working men! But, as with so much else in the "Narnia" books, the attitude towards the dwarfs must encourage a contempt for those (split-off) "enemies" whom one has devalued: selfish sinners are treacherous and deserve chastisement.

Such hate must, at the most serious, also be guiltless. Eustace is found to have put back his sword in the sheath "all messy from killing the Calormene":

> He was scolded for that and made to clean and polish it. (p. 73)

As elsewhere, this reveals that under the surface of the killing, there is an obsession with dangerous "inner contents" of one's enemies from which one fears contamination.

That the dangers in this world are real becomes plain in the nightmarish spectacle of Tash:

> At a first glance you might have mistaken it for smoke for it was grey and you could see things through it. But the deathly smell was not the smell of smoke . . . the grass seemed to wither beneath it. . . . It was roughly the shape of a man but it had the head of a bird; some kind of bird of prey with a cruel curved beak. It had four arms which it held high above its head, stretching them at Northwards as if it wanted to snatch all Narnia in its grip. (p. 77)

What does Tash symbolize? Martha Sammons does not have much to say about Tash, though she hints he is anti-Christ.

He seems at times to be a threat of annihilation that gestures towards nihilism: he is the real death that lurks behind the ("good") Christian death of Lewis's faith. What I believe we can say is that Tash represents an ultimate form of "male doing." He is the predatory penis that killed the mother; he has the beak of oral hunger; the grip of voracity. He has many hands, and so symbolizes that intense lure of masturbation which has behind it an intense need to bring back the dead mother, but which is followed by a sense of sin and doom (one could say, in vulgar cant, that Tash is "wanker's doom"). Yet Tash is a *necessary* power in Lewis's cosmology.

It is characteristic of C. S. Lewis that conscience should not be a natural development springing from concern but should depend on individuals being terrified by such external or "objective" threats. Puzzle is as frightened by Tash as a dog is by a thunderstorm:

> "I see now," said Puzzle, "that I really have been a very bad donkey. I ought to have listened to Shift. I never thought things like this would begin to happen." (LB, p. 78)

It is the castigation offered by Tash that makes Puzzle conscientious, it should be noted—and later he becomes an agent of Aslan.

Tash, then, is a split-off, representing the dynamics of the destructive phallus. Another is the unicorn who, as we have seen, is fantasied elsewhere as injecting a dehumanizing poison with his horn. So, as well as the attempt to recognize death in *The Last Battle,* there is also some gesture at encountering the dangers of adult sexuality. By page 81 Jill has "as you might say, fallen in love with the unicorn."

> She thought—and she wasn't far wrong—that he was the shiningest, delicatest, most graceful animal she had ever met: and he was so gentle and soft of speech that, if you hadn't known, you would hardly have believed how fierce and terrible he could be in battle. (LB, p. 8)

This is, actually, a moment when Lewis approaches as closely as he ever does to love: sexual affection. Yet he must emphasize the prowess of the unicorn in the macho world of battle.

It is a high moment, not least in terms of the archetypal woman. Jewel reminisces of the time before the White Witch, when the ideal original mother (as we may say) existed in Narnia with powers of infinite reflection.

He spoke of Swanwhite the Queen who had lived before the days of the White Witch and the Great Winter, who was so beautiful that when she looked into any forest pool *the reflection of her face shone out of the water like a star by night for a year and a day afterwards.* (p. 82; my italics)

. . . "Oh, Jewel, wouldn't it be lovely if Narnia just went on and on. . . ."
"Nay, sister," answered Jewel, "all worlds draw to an end: except Aslan's own country." (p. 82)

Jill is dead when she says this. Lewis has a fervent desire to believe in Christ's promise and the afterworld. He believes the Christian cosmology; yet behind his portrayal of this "other" world there is a deep uncertainty, and we may detect behind it the child's desperate need to invest a fantasy world to live in, "beyond Animaland," which offers an escape from the unbearableness of the world of human mortality in which he felt no existential security, and yet brings him no real security.

At this moment the Eagle Fairsight arrives with news of the end of Narnia—captured by Calormenes, by Shift's treachery.

Narnia is no more (see p. 85). Roonwit the Centaur, in his last hour, sends a message to the king. "To remember that all worlds draw to an end and that noble death is a treasure which no one is too poor to buy."

How can we estimate Lewis's dealings with death from the point of view of existentialism? Existentialism finds mortality as a feature of our lives which, if we can recognize it, urges us to find our authenticity in the limited time alloted to us. As Frankl says: ". . . death as a temporal, outward limitation does not cancel the meaning of life but rather is the very factor that constitutes its meaning" and "The meaning of human existence is based upon its irreversible quality. . . ." (Frankl 1969, p. 65). Man "should be conscious of the full gravity of the responsibility that every man hears throughout every moment of his life: responsibilities for what he will make of the next hour . . ." (*Ibid*, p. 65). This, of course, directs us to find the meaning of life in this life. Lewis, as a Christian, sees death as a gateway to another world.

As we have seen, death is much present throughout the Narnia stories. Indeed, each going through into the "other" world is a kind of death and such deaths are also rebirths. Are Lewis's dealings with death adequate? (We must of course bear in mind the Christian belief that "death is our door.")

Again, we come to the problem of the general fault in Lewis noted by Owen Barfield, W. W. Robson and others: that certain disastrous boyishness or immaturity in this author. Artistically, it seems to me catastrophic, not least in the stories for children. In the end this most serious fable becomes pathetic.

The point may be made by looking at a critical section of this sombre book, *The Last Battle*. In Chapter twelve we have an account of the most tremendous battle; and the protagonists, Jill, Eustace, and King Tirian are overcome and thrust into the dreadful hut where Tash is annihilating creatures by his mere looks. "And then the last battle of the Last King of Narnia began" (LB, p. 118). Aslan dismisses the hideous Tash, with his Calormene prey, to "his own place." Then the seven kings and queens of Narnia appear in their glittering clothes. Jill is restored to life and queenliness. This cannot but be a powerful moment in the whole fantasy—and it is full of sexual feeling, by which I mean (for Lewis) a surprising encounter with female authority, almost erotic:

> He [Tirian] stared hard at her face, and then gasped with amazement, for he knew her. It was Jill: but not Jill as he had last seen her, with her face all dirt and tears and an old drill dress half slipping off one shoulder. Now she looked cool and fresh, as fresh as if she had just come from bathing. And at first he thought she looked older, but then didn't, and he could never make his mind up on that point. (p. 122)

The last hesitation is to be noted.
But then, on the next page:

> . . . They knew how to make things that felt beautiful as well as looking beautiful in Narnia: and there was no such thing as starch or flannel or elastic to be found from one end of the country to the other. . . . (p. 123)

The only word for this kind of (characteristic) lapse is bathos, but it is a perplexing kind of weakness. We have noticed it elsewhere, when Aslan is punishing schoolteachers in the kind of school C. S. Lewis doesn't like, and when he encourages school girls to take off some of their clothes in a Bacchanalian orgy.

The language is at first heightened and even biblical, at a moment of survival "through" death: "for he knew her." But then we descend to starch, flannel, and elastic—in a defiance of nursery wear appropriate to perhaps 1900 or 1910 but certainly not to the prep-school child of 1950, when *The Last Battle* was published.

But this is not all, for on the same page, there is a lapse into yet another kind of bathos. There is a "royal" kind of exchange:

> "Has not your Majesty two sisters? Where is Queen Susan?"
> "My sister Susan," answered Peter shortly and gravely, "is no longer a friend of Narnia." (p. 12)

But there is little gravity in Eustace's outburst:

> "Yes," said Eustace, "and whenever you've tried to get her to come and talk about Narnia, she says, 'What wonderful memories you have. Fancy you still thinking about all those funny games we used to play when we were children.'"
> "Oh, Susan!" said Jill, "she's interested in nothing now-a-days except nylons and lipsticks and invitations. She always was a jolly sight too keen on being grown-up."
> "Grown-up, indeed," said the Lady Polly, "I wish she *would* grow up. She wasted all her school time waiting to be the age she is now, and she'll waste all the rest of her life trying to stay that age. Her whole idea is to race on to the silliest time of one's life as quick as she can and then stop there as long as she can." (p. 124)

This conversation takes place between the tremendous last battle, the resurrection of the children as kings and queens, and their tasting of the fruit of Paradise. ("Well, don't let's talk about that now." said Peter. "Look! Here are lovely fruit trees. Let us taste them."—for this is "the country where everything is allowed" [p. 125]). It is surely a strange moment, for a peevish (and silly) jibe at a girlhood adolescence and early adult sexuality?

The remark put in the mouth of Lady Polly even has misogynist undertones, of the kind a boy of nine or ten might make. It appears ridiculous at a moment when the span and meaning of human life is meant to come into focus, just after the horror of conflict that has gone before. There is even a touch of vinegar in the momentary erotic glimpse, of Jill with her dress slipped off her shoulder, but then transformed to queenly freshly bathed beauty in the eyes of Tirian. What we get is a glimpse of a strange area of the personality of C. S. Lewis—emotionally inept, childish, frightened by female sexuality (and even so jealous of Tirian) so that he can only be spiteful of his own girl character once she becomes a woman. The effect is a sudden lapse into petty mindedness, at a moment of glory and encounter with meaning and death. The tone becomes hopelessly wrong and the creative seriousness must come into doubt, lapsing as he does here into petty hostility to women, as in his letters.

In *The Last Battle*, the strain on Lewis's sensibility is enormous. Narnia is the world of death where the mother is: in a sense the country *is* the mother, too. As King Tirian says at the end of *The Last Battle*, when he sees Narnia wound up: ". . . I have seen my mother's death. What world but Narnia have I ever known. . . ." (LB, p. 199). This is a message from C. S. Lewis's unconscious mind to us. It says, "I have never known a world except that in which the problem of living was not bound up with my mother and my experience of her death. In entering Narnia I was seeking another world where the mother was, to complete the process of mourning. . . . Now I have penetrated its depths, this Mother-world may be wound up."

But what about Tash? Can we recapitulate to say that Tash is the embodiment of the predatory father's penis that threatens annihilation? His bird's beak seems an archetypal image of the "biting" phallus, while the name perhaps refers to the moustache-like male pubic hair. His many hands suggest that masturbation and masturbation fantasies are not far away, so perhaps Tash is the destructive lure, which Lilith brings, of "sin," which may destroy one, too?

Tash, then, being inside the hut at the last, in the last battle, is the predatory penis that killed the mother, confronted at last and sent by Aslan (the parent who cares) to his "own country." To put it in other words, the Oedipus conflict is concluded to the satisfaction of the child. At once the child protagonists seem about to grow to puberty: they are "changed." (But the conscious Lewis cannot bear the growth to maturity and so he plunges back into banality.)

If these strange fantasy elements are doubted, let us see how *The Last Battle* ends with a powerful vision of the Combined Parents: this is the end of Narnia.

Then the Moon came up, quite in her wrong position, very close to the sun, and she also looked red. And at the sight of her the sun began shooting out great flames, like whiskers or snakes of crimson fire, towards her. It was as if he were an octopus trying to draw her to himself in his tentacles. And perhaps he did draw her. At any rate she came to him, slowly at first, but then more and more quickly, till at last his long flames licked round her and the two ran together and became an huge ball like a burning coal. Great lumps of fire came dropping out of it into the sea and clouds of steam rose up.

Then Aslan said, "Now make an end." (LB, p. 143)

A study of the words used here surely suggests that this is a vision of the primal scene—a kind of cosmic intercourse between the father and mother that (as a child fears) may bring the end of the world? The giant—Time—performs a final act of castration:

The giant threw his horn into the sea. Then he stretched out one arm—very black it looked, and thousands of miles long—across the sky till his hand reached the Sun. He took the Sun and squeezed it in his hand as you would squeeze an orange. And instantly there was total darkness. (p. 143)

There is laughter in Aslan's eyes. A stage has been reached, at the end of seven books: Narnia (which is the mother world) has been entered. There have been found the mother and the father, in all their various forms, bad and good. The combined parents have done their worst, and the father has been castrated by Time. Yet Peter, High King of Narnia, can shut the door with a golden key, and has locked it. And the children survive.

Now, perhaps, there can be a return to life and development? Aslan shoots away like a golden arrow and cries: "Come farther in! Come farther up!" (p. 199).

And the cry is taken up by Farsight the Eagle. They are approaching the Great Waterfall.

What we have to speak of here, I believe, is reptation, the word Winnicott uses for the movements of being born:

. . . the Unicorn. . . . You couldn't tell whether he was swimming or climbing, but he moved in, higher and higher. The point of his horn divided the water just above his head, and it cascaded out in two rainbow-coloured streams all round his shoulders. . . . (p. 56)

Jill seems to be "climbing up light itself":

And then at last one came to the lovely, smooth green curve in which the water poured over the top and found that one was out on the level river above the waterfall. . . . (p. 157)

(Interesting, Lewis says "one" as though he had been "with" Jill.) "'Farther up and farther in,' cried Jewel. . . ." We find they are in the country where Digory went in *The Magician's Nephew*, finding at last the "smooth green hill," where, in the Garden of Eden, are found many of the heroic figures of Narnia. As Tumnus (who is there) tells Lucy, it is a Narnia within Narnia, a World within World.

"The farther up and the farther in you go, the bigger everything gets. The inside is larger than the outside—like an onion: except that as you go in and in, each circle is larger than the last." (p. 163)

Let me put this in interpreted terms: up to now the world Lewis has explored on the other side of the mother's body has been blighted by the bad mother and the bad father. Then, these combined, have made an end. The key has been turned on them. But there is another world yet, in a different kind of time and a different kind of space. This is the world into which the good father has penetrated in his creative aspect, and this is indicated by Aslan and other creatures calling "Fa(r)ther up and fa(r)ther in." Now, looking into this world, Lucy finds a "new and beautiful thing had happened to her." She can see everything—including England.

. . . "But you are now looking at the England within England, the real England just as this is the real Narnia. And in that inner England no good thing is destroyed." (p. 163–64)

Peter and Lucy see their father and mother, waving back at them across the great deep valley. We may also say that in this we have a vision of Lewis's mother reconciled with the father and made benign: "It was like when you see people waving at you from the deck of a big ship when you are waiting on the quay to meet them" (p. 169). It was a real railway accident. The father and mother and the children are "—as you used to call it in the Shadowlands"—dead. "The term is over: the holidays have begun. The dream is ended: this is the morning" (p. 165). Significantly, Lewis related life after death to the holiday after boarding school.

And as He spoke He no longer looked at them like a lion; but the things that began to happen after that were so great and beautiful that I cannot write them . . . now at last they were beginning chapter one of the Great Story which no one on earth has read: which goes on for ever: in which every chapter is better than the one before. (p. 165)

My Christian reader will tell me: there you are—that ending

is a loyal expression of belief in Christ's promises. It is true that the end of *The Last Battle* has a kind of elated excitement.

But there is a sense in which it was also obviously *too easy to write*. There has been no real reconciliation of ambivalence. My own doubt concerns those very last words. Would Lewis, who needs so constantly a "battle situation" to carry his parable on, ever be happy in a heaven without conflict? What kind of things could "begin to happen" in Aslan's heaven which were not glorious engagement with evil? Throughout the "Narnia" books, what engagements with dynamics of the spirit have brought us to this peace? (Compare, say, *Four Quartets*, or Hopkins' poems, or Herbert?*)

The truth is that conflict in Lewis's books is a way to escape real inner conflict. So the phrase we have to use for Lewis's stories, I believe, is *manic defence*. Manic defence is a phrase from psychoanalysis; and it is used to describe the way in which the patient seeks to avoid the pain of reality, his own and the world's, and especially the pain of depression arising from the recognition of the problem of love and hate, of the impulses to preserve and destroy, in their ambivalence, that are exacerbated in mourning. If the problems of love and hate, of destructiveness and concern, are not realistically confronted, grief cannot be "worked through."

As Winnicott says, "In manic defence mourning cannot be experienced."

> Its characteristics are omnipotent manipulation and control and contemptuous devaluation. (Winnicott 1958, p. 132)

These are exactly the characteristics of the "Narnia" fantasies: everything is controlled by magic while the "bad" forces are split-offs subjected to exactly that kind of control.

Let us look back over *The Last Battle*. It is an attempt, through fantasy, to encounter the realities of pain and death, and to complete the process of mourning, towards ultimate meaning. At the moment we have reached in the tale, even Narnia, the country of the mother, seems menaced. Characteristically, we have yet again a paranoid situation, in which a good place has been overwhelmed by evil agencies. The ape, Shift, having duped all the Narnian talking animals by dressing up the donkey

---

*In *That Hideous Strength* the characters feel in harmony most with the Universe when preparing for battle. Lewis's heaven would be intolerable, one supposes, if it didn't provide for such paranoid ecstasy.

Puzzle in an old lion's skin, has turned the Aslan myth to his own selfish ends of obtaining more bananas. So, there must be military action:

> The Unicorn stamped the ground with his hoof. . . .
> "We see that the Ape's plans were laid deeper than we dreamed of. Doubtless he has been long in secret traffic with the Tisroc. . . . Nothing now remains for us seven but to go back to Stable Hill, proclaim the truth, and take the adventure that Aslan sends us. And if, by a great marvel, we defeat those thirty Calormenes who are with the Ape, then to turn again and die in battle with the far greater host of them that will soon march from Cair Paravel." (LB, p. 35)

King Tirian suggests that it is time for the children to go hence into their own world. "'B—but we've done nothing,' said Jill who was shivering, not with fear exactly but because everything was so horrible. . . ." (p. 86). Yet the children came into Narnia to help, in answer to his appeals to Aslan. There is a strange ambivalence about the situation. If Jill is dead, then she cannot get back to her own world. Yet now she is dead, she is faced with catastrophe in the Narnian world. I am not at all clear about what it is that Lewis is trying to say here. Perhaps he was somewhat ambivalent himself about exposing his child protagonists to so much bloodshed and death—obviously needing to do this, but at the same time somewhat doubtful about his own motives. Tirian protests that they have done much to help:

> ". . . You loosed me from the tree: glided before me like a snake last night in the wood and took Puzzle; and you, Eustace, killed your man. But you are too young to share in such a bloody end as we others must meet tonight or, it may be, three days hence I entreat you—nay, I command you—to return to your own place, should be put to shame if I let such young warriors fall in battle on my side."
> "No, no, no," said Jill (very white when she began speaking and then suddenly very red and then white again). "We won't. I don't care what you say. . . ." (p. 86)

Eustace is more pragmatic "we haven't any choice. What's the good of talking about our going back . . . we've got no magic for doing it" [p. 86]), and Jill hates him for being so matter-of-fact. This kind of debate is of great importance to C. S. Lewis. What matters in children (and if you accept the Christian interpretation, what matters to God in children) is that they should be brave enough to fight even the last battle. The ensuing dialogue is "childish" in the E. Nesbit mode, but it is painfully inept—and callow:

"Pole," said Eustace in a whisper, "I may as well tell you I've got the wind up."

"Oh, you're all right, Scrubb," said Jill.

"You can fight. But I—I'm just shaking, if you want to know the truth."

"Oh, shaking's nothing," said Eustace. "I'm feeling I'm going to be sick."

"Don't talk about *that*, for goodness sake," said Jill.

They went on in silence for a minute or two.

"Pole," said Eustace presently.

"What?" said she.

"What'll happen if we get killed here?"

"Well we'll be dead, I suppose."

"But I mean, what will happen in our world? Shall we wake up and find ourselves back in that train? Or shall we just vanish and never be heard of any more? Or shall we be dead in England?"

"Gosh. I never thought of that."

"It'll be fun for Peter and the others if they saw me waving out of the window and then when the train comes in we're nowhere to be found! Or if they found two—I mean, if we're dead over there in England."

"Ugh!" said Jill. "What a horrible idea."

"It wouldn't be horrid for *us*, Eustace. We shouldn't be there."

"I almost wish—no I don't, though," said Jill.

"What were you going to say?"

"I *was* going to say I wished we'd never come. But I don't, I don't, I don't. Even if we are killed. I'd rather be killed fighting for Narnia than grow old and stupid at home and perhaps go about in a bathchair and then die in the end just the same."

"Or be smashed up by British Railways."

"Why d'you say that?"

"Well when that awful jerk came—the one that seemed to throw us into Narnia—I thought it *was* the beginning of a railway accident. So I was jolly glad to find ourselves here instead." (LB, pp. 88–89)

The "Narnia" stories were written to explore the problem of death; but here the subject is really only toyed with, and dealt with in terms which derive from an archaic jingoism. The effect is unsatisfactory, because the tone and manner (belonging to manic defence) implicitly deny death. The children are dead: now they have to face a death in battle. But what they reach is a dangerously false-solution position, in which it seems actually better to die in war than live one's old age in a bathchair. We have thought a great deal about war, since Lewis's time; and we have advanced in our recognition of its deadly fascination. We are surely now very doubtful of the argument which prefers a glorious death in combat to becoming old *"and stupid"* in Civvy Street, to die in the end, just the same? The danger is that of attaching the sense of being meaningfully alive to aggression. The effect could be to persuade children that violence is a satisfactory way of establishing meaning in life, when a sense of significance is lacking, and when normal existence and mortality seem threatening.

The others are discussing how to deal with the formidable enemy against whom they are pitting themselves (without, it seems, the support of Aslan):

> Why not hide in the wood, or even up in the Western waste beyond the great waterfall and lurk like outlaws? And then they might gradually get stronger and stronger. . . . (p. 83)

But such a solution seems impossible. Tash seems like an evil force which no one could imagine likely to be defeated by waiting, or by anything but suffering and attrition. King Tirian kisses the unicorn. It is a romantic parting between two warrior lovers:

> "Kiss me, Jewel," he said. "For certainly this is our last night on earth. And if ever I offended against you in any matter great or small, forgive me now."
> ". . . Farewell. We have known great joys together. If Aslan gave me my choice I would choose no other life than the life I have had and no other death than the one we go to." (p. 91)

They arrive as more deceptions are to be put over the "people" by yet another ritual bonfire.

What follows is a horror sequence conveyed with all the solemn gravity Lewis can commend. As we have already seen, Narnia is haunted not only by a false Aslan and all the evil consequences of Shift's exploitation of this false god, but by an actual demon.

The effect of encountering Tash turns Ginger the cat from a sleek, sophisticated, talking cat into a dumb and horror-stricken wild animal. It is the destruction of human attributes that is feared terribly:

... everyone of them had been taught ... how Aslan at the beginning
of the world had turned the beasts of Narnia into Talking Beasts
and warned them that if they weren't good they might one day
be turned back again and be like the poor witless animals one
meets in other countries. . . . (p. 101)

The punishment for being wicked is to be dehumanized like
those injected by the unicorn in Lewis's other story—and this
means annihilation: "Ginger disappeared further up into the
tree. No one ever saw him again" (p. 101). A young Calormene
goes in—and falls dead. To look on the face of Tash means
death. Tash is, as it were, the utter other extreme from reflection
by the mother—he is the possibility of total *unreflection* or
*dereflection*.

Lewis knows of no way of dealing with Tash than *fighting*.
Some animals now come to the king's side; but there must be
a battle, and the children are put to the final test of blood.
"Eustace stood with his heart beating terribly hoping and hoping
that he would be brave. . . ." (p. 109).

Jill is hard at work killing:

> She heard twang-and-zipp on his left and one Calormene fell: the
> twang-and-zipp again and the Satyr was down. "Oh well done
> daughter!" came Tirian's voice. . . .
>
> Eustace could never remember what happens in the next two
> minutes. It was all like a dream (the sort you have when your
> temperature is over 100°. . . . (p. 109)

The Calormenes retire: the scene is satisfyingly bloodthirsty:

> Two lay dead, one pierced by Jewel's horn, one by Tirian's sword.
> The Fox lay dead at his own feet, and he wondered if it was he
> who had killed it. The Bull was also down, shot through the eye
> by an arrow from Jill and gashed in his side by the Boar's tusk.
> But our side had its losses too. Three dogs were killed and a fourth
> was hobbling behind the lines on three legs and whimpering. The
> bear lay on the ground, moving feebly. Then it mumbled in its
> throaty voices, bewildered to the last, "I don't—understand," laid
> its big head down on the grass as quietly as a child going to sleep,
> and never moved again. . . . (p. 109)

The illustration shows dogs tearing at a fallen satyr, sword
play, and a fallen Calormene with an arrow in his back. Now
the Talking Horses come rushing up—only to be shot by the

Dwarfs. "'Little swine,' shrieked Eustace, dancing in his rage. 'Dirty, filthy treacherous little brutes'" (p. 112).

We may notice certain aspects of Lewis's language. He talks to us directly (about a temperature of 100°). He is deliberately childish (and the effect is rather silly: "Oh well done . . ."). And he talks of "our side." The child reader is *seduced* into identifying with anger and hate: he is taught here that to be godly and good is to be righteously hostile to creatures who are subjected to that "contemptuous devaluation," and to attack them.

What we must never be (according to this instruction) is *tender.* Tirian says to Jill: "If you must weep, sweetheart [this was to Jill], turn your face aside and see you wet not your bowstring" (p. 112).

Such a lapse would be like failing to dry your sword. Like the Nazi Rauschning, Lewis declares, "we will have no weakness or tenderness in our youth."

> Feeling terribly alone, Jill ran out about twenty feet, put her right leg back and her left leg forward, and set an arrow to her string. She wished her hands were not shaking so.
>
> "That's a rotten shot!" she said as her first arrow sped towards the enemy. . . . Then one of her own arrows hit a man, and another hit a Narnian wolf. . . .
>
> The Unicorn was tossing men as you'd toss hay on a fork . . . Eustace seemed to Jill . . . to be fighting brilliantly. The Dogs were at the Calormenes' throats. It was going to work! It was victory at last. . . . (p. 114)

At this point the Calormenes are reinforced. One grabs Eustace and hurls him into the hut containing Tash:

> Even then Jill remembered to keep her face turned aside, well away from her bow. "Even if I can't stop blubbing, I won't get my string wet," she said. (p. 115)

The battle is long and drawn out. Now the Calormenes attack the Dwarfs—and they, too, are flung into the hut.

> "I feel in my bones," said Poggin, "that we shall all, one by one, pass through that dark door before morning. I can think of a hundred deaths I would rather have died." (p. 117)

The primitive fantasy is terrifying because, with Tash inside it, the hut now becomes a parallel to the wardrobe. That is, it is the mother's body, or womb, through which (again) we pass to the other world of death. Yet now we face "the dreadful dreads" of utter incorporation into nothingness, in that very womb where the malignant father (the internalized penis) now threatens annihilation. In another sense, we could say that that womb now incorporates all the ferocity by the combined parents threatening to eat the child, and all the *oral* dread associated with this.

> "It is, indeed, a grim door," said Tirian. *"It is more like a mouth."*
> "Oh, can't we do anything to stop it?" said Jill in a shaken voice.
> "Nay, fair friend," said Jewel, nosing her gently. "It may be for us the door to Aslan's country and we shall sup at his table tonight."
> (LB, p. 119; my italics)

Again we have a nod to Christian myth. But what is this battle the wretched children have to fight *after their death?* In our terms, of the unconscious mythology, I think we must say that the redemption of the "bad mother" could only have come by love, compassion, and acceptance. All Lewis can offer is *mental rage*, which only seems to hold self and world together. Like the schizoid, besides his high drama of paranoid distortion, ordinary life and love seem "pallid and artificial."*

Now the children are fighting against the spears of the Calormenes. The author tells us, cheerfully, in his most pimpish tone (as an advocate of perversion):

> In a way it wasn't quite as bad as you might think. When you are using every muscle to the full—ducking under a spear-point here, leaping over it there, . . . you haven't much time to feel frightened or sad . . . out of the corner of one eye he saw, but only just, a big Calormene pulling Jill away somewhere by her hair. . . .
> (p. 119)

The sadism is at its most intense. All seems lost, and a strange, excited recklessness overtakes the reader. The writing enacts the false solution of "giving oneself up to the joys of hating."

Tirian lures the Calormene leader into the hut; and Tash confronts them.

> A terrible figure was coming towards them. . . . It had a vulture's head and four arms. Its beak was open and its eyes blazed. (p. 120)

---

*See the essay on the "Schizophrenic and the Mad Psychiatrist" in Farber 1966.

This vulture carries out the vengeance "our side" wish on Rishda Tarkaan.

> He was shaking like a man with a bad hiccup. He was brave enough in battle: but half his courage had left him earlier that night when he first began to suspect that there might be a real Tash. The rest of it had left him now. . . . (p. 120–21)

We are invited to enjoy his ignominious end:

> With a sudden jerk—like a hen stooping to pick up a worm—Tash pounced on the miserable Rishda and tucked him under the upper of his two right arms. (p. 122)

But a voice orders the hideous bird away with its prey. Or, to put it in my terms, magic is employed once more, to dispel threats by enchantment.

And now seven kings and queens stand before the astonished Tirian. As we have seen, one queen is Jill, erotically presented. This girl, striving to keep her bow-string dry, has been virtually raped by a Calormene; and we glimpse her being dragged off by her hair, her dress slipping off her shoulder, but then revived like a girl fresh from the bath.

I have already pointed to the strange banality by which Lewis retreats from this movement forward to developing sexuality. Has there been any real development? Or is the advance merely manic? Now, after the last battle, the protagonists eat the golden fruit from grove of trees. They are momentarily touched by guilt:

> Everyone raised his hand to pick the fruit he best liked the look of, and then everyone paused for a second. This fruit was so beautiful that each felt, "It can't be meant for me. . . . Surely we're not allowed to pluck it."
> "It's all right," said Peter. "I know what we're all thinking. But I'm sure, quite sure, we needn't. I've a feeling we've got to the country where everything is allowed." (p. 125)

Now that the children have fought the last Christian good fight, they are to have their rewards. But these rewards, too, are characerically manic. For a moment it seems they are transformed into adult human beings; but there is no growth towards maturity of character or benignity of satisfaction: no access to grace. Lewis's goals are conceived in characteristically small boy terms: treats! Also, in another sense, good breast (while the White Witch's treats were bad breast):

What was the fruit like? Unfortunately no one can describe a taste. All I can say is that, compared with those fruits, the freshest grapefruit you've ever eaten was dull, and the juiciest orange was dry and the most melting pear was hard and woody, and the sweetest wild strawberry was sour. And there were no needs or stones, and no wasps. If you had once eaten that fruit, all the nicest things in the world would taste like medicines after it. But I can't describe it. You can't find out what it is like unless you can get to that country and taste it yourself.

When they had eaten enough. . . . (p. 125)

What makes the difference? With the Witch's Turkish Delight, to be greedy was to lay oneself open to sin—and to forfeit one's autonomy. What is the difference between Edmund's greed and the appetite of these kings and queens? Of course, we can see that they are in heaven and may indulge without guilt: it is the place where "everything is allowed." The point surely was that one should not be self-interested, but think of others (like Digory). Is heaven, then, simply a place for *guiltless* self-indulgence? The fruit brings no deeper knowledge, or self-knowledge, or *concern*, or compassion, or love. This is simply, to take a phrase from Winnicott, the "use of opposites in reassurance." (See "The Manic Defence," Winnicott 1958, p. 134).

Death meanwhile is nothing. It is no longer merely having the pain of a sore knee.

". . . There was a frightful roar and something hit me with a bang, but it didn't hurt. And I felt not so much scared as—well, excited. Oh—and this is one queer thing. I'd had a rather sore knee, from a hack at rugger. I noticed it had suddenly gone. And I felt very light. And then—here we were." (LB, p. 126)

Digory says he and Polly "felt that we'd been *unstiffened*" (a strange word for becoming "a stiff"). The language is inappropriately childish. Such trivial language about human mortality reveals the extent to which Lewis has failed to solve his problem, failed to complete mourning, by really encountering the real problems of death and the pain and depression associated with it: the real dread, and the existential questions of meaning, such as he does confront in *Till We Have Faces*.

There is a more serious theme: nothingness from time to time really threatens in this last battle.

This seems to be a door leading from nowhere to nowhere. . . .

Tirian put his eye to the hole. At first he could see nothing but blackness . . . he knew he was looking out through the Stable door into the darkness of the Lantern Waste where he had fought his last battle. . . . (p. 128)

It seems, then," said Tirian, smiling himself, "that the Stable seen from within and the Stable seen from without are two different places."

"Yes," said the Lord Digory. "Its inside is bigger than its outside."

"Yes," said Queen Lucy. "In our world, too, a Stable once had something inside it that was bigger than our whole world." (p. 128)

The Stable, when we first encountered it, contained Tash, and was a place into which men and creatures were thrown to die of fright or annihilation by a terrible vulture-like creature. How is this dreadfulness overcome? Surely now we must face the problem of death? Again, the solution is manic defence—again by contemptuous devaluation of one's "enemies." In the course of explaining the elaborate comings and goings in the stable, Edmund says:

". . . Someone flung a monkey through the door. And Tash was there again. My Sister is so tender-hearted she doesn't like to tell you that Tash made one peck and the monkey was gone!"

"Serve him right!" said Eustace. "All the same, I hope he'll disagree with Tash, too." (p. 130)

Even in the thick of this last engagement with his faith, Lewis lapses, in his emotional ineptitude, into childish hostility: "good job!" The danger is clearly that, from this, child readers will learn contempt for anyone whom, they decide, is fit only for aggression? "'I hope Tash ate the dwarfs too,' said Eustace. 'Little swine. . . .'" (p. 130). The dwarfs, however, do reach the new world. Everyone tries to forgive them, but they can only see the inside of the stable at dark. Aslan appears and sets a feast before them—but they see it as rubbish—because "The Dwarfs are for the Dwarfs." Presumably this was meant to be a homily about egoism and the way it cuts you off from grace. Aslan says: "The prison is only in their own minds, yet they are in that prison and so afraid of being taken in that they cannot be taken out . . ." (p. 135).

What are the ethical or religious implications of these episodes? By contrast with the dwarfs, what are the motives of the protagonists? They are perhaps for Narnia and Aslan rather than for themselves, as are the dwarfs? This is again simply a matter of "believe and have faith," and of loyalty. The good protagonists do little by way of serving causes beyond themselves, in any creative way, of devoting themselves to the good of others, or indeed, to any acts of true reparation. They don't come to understand themselves or others any better. The externalized conflict and the inhuman nature of their enemies forestall any attempts to win over antagonists or to offer them redemption. They suffer no dark night of the soul, for battle is so glorious and exciting. In the end their rewards are a good feast rather than a bad one. There is certainly no sense that the children are any more free in their minds than the dwarfs. The latter, it seems, are "bad" because they cannot imagine Lewis's magical world. (They are, perhaps, humanists?)

There follows the vision of the end of Narnia as we have seen. A massive contemptuous devaluation of the talking animals is even undertaken by Aslan, while the author himself carelessly reports that he doesn't know what happened to them:

> The expression of their faces changed terribly—it was fear and hatred: except, that, on the faces of the Talking Beasts, the fear and hatred lasted only for a fraction of a second. You could see that they suddenly ceased to be Talking Beasts. They were just ordinary animals. (p. 140)

They merged with Aslan's shadow "and I don't know what became of them." But the others looked in the face of Aslan and loved him, "though some of these were very frightened at the same time" (p. 140). Narnia is left to the dragons and lizards; but these die, and then everything is swamped by the sea. The sun turns dark red and dies.

> As its rays fell upon the Great Time-giant, he turned red too and in the reflection of that sun the whole waste of shoreless waters looked like blood. (pp. 142–43)

In this vision of universal catastrophe, we have something akin to the myth of entropy in positivist scientific theory. This vision of the ultimate sterility and death of the world (Narnia though it may be called) surely calls into question all the validity of the choices and acts of the protagonists in all those long stretches of Narnian time covered by the "Narnia" books? Of course, the presence of Aslan in heaven suggests an ultimate transcendental source by which the acts are judged. The vision of the end of all things (like the catastrophe at the end of George MacDonald's *The Princess and Curdie*) has a deeply undermining effect on the reader's existentialist need, to find his own

authenticity in the face of nothingness and death. The effect
is as though, failing to solve his problem, Lewis destroys the
world, and tears everything down on himself and us, like Sam-
son.

This vision expressed even a strange "longing for non-being."
It conveys a sense of the futility of ever establishing an inten-
tional perception of a real and meaningful world. This sense
of futility is surely the consequence of the manic defence nature
of Lewis's fantasy of finding the mother?

> The children weep: Lucy says,
> "I am sure it is not wrong to mourn for Narnia. Think of all
> that lies dead and frozen behind that door."
> "Yes and I *did* hope," said Jill, "that it might go on for ever.
> I knew *our* world wouldn't. I did think Narnia might." (p. 144)

There follows more accounts of recent events and more topography. Then it turns out that they are in Narnia still after all
because what they have seen destroyed is not the real Narnia,
and they are now in a new Narnia.

> That has a beginning and an end. It was only a shadow or copy
> of the real Narnia which has always been here and always will
> be here: just as our own world, England and all, is only a shadow
> or copy of something in Aslan's real world. (p. 153)

Here is the end of the quest which began when the child
Lewis found his world of reality blighted by his mother's death,
and then found himself in a cruel world which he could not
report to his father in his (wrecked) world of home. Where,
in heaven's name, is "reality"? The best answer, in manic defence, is to have a number of realities so one can slide from
one into the other. Lewis is here trying to get us to believe
that his imagined other world (Heaven?) is "as different as a
real thing is from a shadow or as working life is from a dream"
(p. 154). ("It's all in Plato, all in Plato; bless me, what *do* they
teach them at these schools": his theme comes from the parable
of the shadows and the cave again.) Here he is still compromis-
ing over the problem of feeling real in a real world, left him
by his mother's death.

Significantly, the real heaven is a looking-glass world:

> Perhaps you will get some idea of it if you think like this. You
> may have been in a room in which there was a window that looked
> out on a lovely bay or the sea or a green valley that wound away

among mountains. And in the wall of that room opposite to the
window there may have been a looking glass. As you turned away
from the window you suddenly caught sight of that sea or that
valley, all over again, in the looking glass. And the sea in the mirror,
or the valley in the mirror, were in one sense just the same as
the real one: yet at the same time they were somehow different—
deeper, more wonderful, more like places in a story: in a story
you have never heard but very much want to know. (p. 154)

To Lewis the reflection in the mirror seems *more real* than
the real world. So, too, to him, the transcending Christian cosmos is more real than this world. The Christian Cosmos is *literally* true. But the problem of finding the mother and finding
a creative (reflective) relationship with this world, to give it
meaning, remains unsolved. It is evaded, and dissolved into
mere promises of good opposites to depression: alive, colored,
light, luminous, rather than dead, grey, dark, and heavy.

Discussing this, the children are solemn: "There is a kind
of happiness and wonder that makes you serious. It is too good
to waste on jokes" (p. 154). And in the next chapter they are
all reborn, as we have seen, by walking up a waterfall. "It was
the sort of thing that would have been impossible in our world"
(p. 157). We have seen many attempts to reenact rebirth in the
"Narnia" books. Here is the last effort: "It seemed as if you
were climbing up light itself . . . in that world you could do
it" (p. 157).

The end is not a real creative achievement. It remain manic:
a dream world, a religious promise, vague gestures towards spiritual triumphs. The book concludes in a profusion of archaic
words, in which many of the old characters appear, in the New
Narnian Garden of Eden, in which "'The farther up and the
farther you go in, the bigger everything gets. The inside is larger
than the outside'" (p. 162).

The children are not yet happy dead. Aslan says:

"You do not look as happy as I mean you to be."
Lucy says, "We're so afraid of being sent away, Aslan. You have
sent me back into our own world so often." (p. 165)

There follows the passages quoted above. But what kinds of
things could the new joys be? It would have been interesting
to have C. S. Lewis's account of them.

If "Heaven" is to offer anything, it must surely be in terms
of the satisfaction of existential problems, and to find the chal-

lenges of life met? The messages of the "Narnia" book does not really touch on the real problems of meaning to be served, in terms of mysteries of this world, the potentialities of oneself or men in general, the satisfactions of interpersonal encounter between human beings or of meaningful living such as are found, say, in the philosophical religious writers of Gabriel Marcel, Martin Buber, or Karl Jaspers. There is only plotting, marching, moving about the terrain, and killing—in opposition (mostly) to nonhuman creatures, helped by magic, in world after world in which events are already determined by the "deeper magic." The children never escape from magical control and a kind of determination (of the Emperor's Magic): they seldom question what they do, or their motives for killing and they seldom make existential choices (apart from Digory). Even Tash is made an instrument of execution, while the world, the universe, and even transcendental realms beyond are governed and manipulated between the White Witch, Tash, Aslan and the unseen Emperor.

Aslan's power seems often to be exercised by whim, and by menace. Nowhere does he operate *within the heart* as a prompting to choice. He has a smell and a sound; but insofar as he essentially manipulates people, his magic essentially robs human beings of their autonomy—and so of their freedom, and their quest for authenticity. It seems at times as if thoughts of Aslan remind people of their "duty" and of "right": but he seldom allows them to be out of control—he is more like a pantomime fairy than Christ.* He controls rather than redeems, or draws out good in others. The more seriously we take him, the more he represents Lewis's own urge to control us; and to will us into his interpretation of existence, and his morality, based on the strange logic and ethics of his unconscious mythology, with its perverted and sadistic undercurrents, taken in from Capron.

---

*Compare the gnomic statement attributed to Christ in the Gnostic Gospels, so easily reconciled with psychotherapy: "When you make the two one, and when you make the inside like the outside and the outside like the inside, and the above like the below, and when you make the male and the female one and the same . . . then will you enter the Kingdom. . . ." *The Gospel of Thomas, The Nag Hammadi Library*, p. 121.

# Part 3
## The Adult Fantasies

# 13

## That Hideous Strength

Here I shall concern myself with the adult fantasies of C. S. Lewis only insofar as they seem to confirm my phenomenological interpretation. As I have suggested earlier, I was perplexed by some of my own conclusions as to the meanings of certain symbols in his work, only to find them confirmed by other evidence, such as the Greeves letters. When I turned from the "Narnia" stories to the adult fantasies, I was equally startled by the confirmation they seemed to offer of the themes and proclivities that I had discovered in those fables.

I shall look at two of the "space fiction" stories, *That Hideous Strength* and *Perelandra*, and then *Till We Have Faces*, which is the retelling of a classical myth. In each of these, a predominant feature is a tendency for the action to be extremely violent. In *That Hideous Strength* the wicked scientists are trampled to death; in *Perelandra* the hero kills an "Un-Man" in a particularly violent way; and in *Till We Have Faces*, there are killings and a castration with much pain and blood. The problem, however, is not the violence itself, but its place in the tales. As in the "Narnia" tales, not only is there an intense satisfaction to be found in violent acts; but as we shall see, in *That Hideous Strength*, the militant action, the preparation for battle, and the assault on the enemy mark the highest point of spiritual experience. In *Till We Have Faces*, however, we experience something somewhat different: the violent acts bring real pain, there is concern for the results of militant acts, and a sense that this kind of solution no longer works.

*That Hideous Strength* is the third book of a trilogy—the first two books are *Out of the Silent Planet* and *Perelandra*. *That Hideous Strength* is called "a modern fairy tale for grown-ups"; (sub-title) and it has a preface in which Lewis declares that he is following traditional fairy tales by using "humdrum" scenes and persons, his magician, "pantomime animals" and planetary angels being analagous to "wood cutters, and petty kings." The fairy tales he is following were realistic and commonplace he says, "for many German peasants had actually met cruel stepmothers, whereas I have never, in my university, come across a college like Bracton" (*That Hideous Strength*, p. 7). What, then, exactly, is the relationship between this fairy story and the "truth"?

This is, says Lewis, a "tall story" about devilry, though he claims it has behind it the kind of serious point he makes in *The Abolition of Man*. In the latter Lewis castigates some educational writers for not upholding absolute values. The point of *The Abolition of Man* and of *That Hideous Strength* is that the modern impulse to make "man immortal and man ubiquitous" is wrong: diabolical. There are dangers in man's use of science to manipulate, exploit and control nature: these are not only environmental, but moral and spiritual.

Lewis was an intelligent and intellectual man, and so one takes from his preface that he is offering in this fairy tale a serious point, a responsible criticism of the kind of tendency to be found in man in modern times. The title refers to Sir David Lindsay's *Ane Dialog*:

> The Shadow of that hyddeous strength
> Sax myle and more it is of length.

(p. 6)

—a reference to the Tower of Babel.

So we expect a parable about the dangers of man overreaching himself and becoming proud and arrogant in his relationship with the universe, while denying absolute values: being hubristic, like Faust. In the story, a scientific organization, the National Institute of Controlled Experiments (NICE) persuades a college to sell its woodlands, to build a vast new center for its work. This is not only an environmental threat to the college and an offense to its humane, urban setting; it is a breakthrough (like the perversion of science under the Nazis) into a nationalization of scientism, into a fanatical program, to which everything must be subjugated. A new kind of pragmatic utilitarianism, in which scientific scepticism becomes combined with fanatical idealism, such as Michael Polanyi discusses in *Knowing and Being* ("Beyond Nihilism"), is coming to pass in Bragdon Wood. The account of how the dons of Bracton College are seduced into selling their land for this treachery to human values is wholly convincing, and there is a sense in which the fairy story is gripping and "relevant" to modern times, in its first chapters.

So far, so good. When my Christian friends urge me not to write this book, they tell me that I would find myself very close to Lewis's position, because I too am trying to resist "scientism" and the menace to values coming from the objective, empirical, scientific tradition that has itself failed to find man, and even points to the "abolition of man," in some of its activities.

*That Hideous Strength* is the nearest Lewis got to an adult novel, and it is in some ways a gripping and engaging book. It even contains a measure of self-analysis and "moral teething" on the part of two of the characters, Mark and Jane Studdock. They, especially the woman, undergo some degree of existential torment. As we go on, this becomes less a development of the capacity to choose, than an inclination of the character towards giving himself or herself into submission, to one "side" in an existing structure of conflicting entities. That is, the problem is approached in terms of "split-off" entities in conflict, "out there," and of putting oneself under an absolute authority.

Given that this is a fairy story, does it portray a Christian, or indeed any kind of intelligent way of dealing with hubristic scientists? The theme is struck in a discussion between Jane and one of the "bad" scientists, Filostrato, of the time of the Babel movement. "It is the beginning of all power. He live forever. The giant time is conquered" (p. 217). The concept of the horrid invention is itself schizoid—a human head kept alive forever, and developed so that it grows a superbrain, to issue master orders. The schizoid tendency to live in an intellectual structure turned into a mechanical superbrain:

> "It is the beginning of Man Immortal and Man Ubiquitous," said Straik. "Man on the throne of the universe." (*That Hideous Strength*, p. 213)

Filostrato is contemptuous of the "canaglia": what he seeks is the power of *some* men over Nature, an elite. Mark Studdock is exposed to the "exciting horror of the man God." The good forces, by contrast, discuss the "cerebral hypertrophy artifically induced to support a superhuman power of ideation" (p. 240).

Dismally, we can today believe in such a horrific possibility. We can recognize the wrongness of Filostrato—a new version of the sin of pride. Outraged humanity, we feel is urgently obliged to find a new source of ethical living in relation to science, technology, and life.

This is not Lewis's direction. The god-head as detached intellect is only one facet of his nightmare. For him the problem is not an existential one for each human being to face up to, and to find responsibility for. For him the question is externalized and a matter again of objective conflict, split-off, "out there." The problem with the scientists is not their responsibility. They are *possessed*. The scientists are being manipulated by Dark-Eldils so there is need for recourse, in resisting them, to "atlantean magic": Logres is involved, and there is Merlin's body buried under Bragdon Wood.

Ransom is the hero of the trilogy, God's "Director" on earth; and his is the kind of intelligence which (Lewis is telling us) will save us from the wicked scientists—the worst threats in the modern world. Yet his reflections manifest a strange occultism. Are we to believe that our salvation lies in alchemy?

> Ransom agreed. He thought that Merlin's art was the last survival of something older and different—something brought to Western Europe after the fall of Numinor and going back to an era in which the general relations of mind and matter on this planet had been other than those we know. It had probably differed from Renaissance Magic profoundly. It had probably (though this was doubtful?) been more effective. For Paraclesus and Agrippa and the rest had achieved little or nothing: Bacon himself—no enemy to magic except on this account—reported that the magicians "attained not to greatness and certainty of works." The whole Renaissance outburst of forbidden arts had, it seemed, beed a method of losing one's soul on singularly unfavourable terms. But the older Art had been a different proposition. (p. 246)

It is worth pausing on that paragraph, and examining it for its tone and intention. It sounds well-written, scholarly, and elegant; it impresses us with the learnedness of a don who can throw out his reference to Paraclesus and Agrippa, and place Bacon with a *bon mot*. But what about "Numinor"? In the preface we read, "Those who would like to learn further about Numinor and the True West must (alas!) await the publication of much that still exists only in the MSS. of my friend, Professor J. R. R. Tolkein" (p. 8). We thought the book was a serious engagement with the "abolition of man" theme; but then after all it turns out to be a mere donnish fantasy game.

Cultural activity can be a dissociated joke; yet one may use it to frighten people into joining one's religious position—and so gloat on one's power over them. Significantly, Lewis quotes

Pope's couplet in one essay, calling it a "sublime poetical image": "Yes, I am proud; I must be proud to see / Men not afraid of God, afraid of me" (*Selected Literary Essays*, p. 155). There is a sense in which Lewis makes his Christianity a cloak and justification for his need to coerce people by threatening them. But if he is not serious, why should we accept his minatory homilectics?

In *That Hideous Strength* we abandon the conflict we thought we were going to see between values and intelligence—between *Christian faith*—and the misuse of human powers. We enter instead into a fantasy of the occult:

> If the only possible attraction of Bragdon lay in its association with the last vestiges of Atlantean magic, this told the company something else. It told them that the N.I.C.E. at its core, was not concerned solely with modern or materialistic forms of power . . . there was Eldilic energy and Eldilic knowledge behind it. It was, of course, another question whether its human members knew of the dark powers who were the real organisers. (*That Hideous Strength*, p. 246)

The "theory of sails, or air, or etheric tensions" which scientists produce may therefore, Lewis suggests, really be meant to cover up acts which are really organized by demonic powers of which the scientists are ignorant. If this is part of the point of this fable, in relation to *The Abolition of Man*, how are we to take it?

And what of the black magic of the Christians? Under Bragdon Wood is Merlin's body. We might accept this in a fable, but what can it possibly symbolize to any intelligent reader? The long-preserved existence of this body is now offered to us as an act of God:

> To those high creatures whose activity builds what we call nature, nothing is "natural" . . . or then there are no basic assumptions . . . all springs with the wilful beauty of a jest of a tune from that miraculous moment of self-limitation wherein the Infinite rejecting a myriad possibilities, throws out of Himself the positive and elected invention. That a body should lie uncorrupted for fifteen hundred years, did not seem strange to them: they knew worlds where there was no corruption at all. (*That Hideous Strength*, p. 247)

The words here are dense and the language elevated: "incarnation," "elected invention," etc. But it is all false, and essentially a misuse of language. It is really occultism. It is the language usually employed for theological and philosophical argument; but it is prostituted for a yarn—a yarn which is offered as having a point, but one that is undermined by that "voulu" element. One might call it a "pastoral" if it were not so full of hate, and the usual obsessions with war:

> It was not as a marvel in natural philosophy, but as an information *in time of war* that they brought the Director their tidings. (p. 247; my italics)

To put it another way, the composition of paranoid-schizoid fables permits the author to fudge natural philosophy, science, history, belief, cultural history, in any way he pleases.

The liberties he takes relieve us of any necessity to examine Lewis's arguments about scientific scepticism or whatever. On the "good" side, there are no arguments: there is only a deepening magic and mumbo-jumbo about "Viritrilbia in Deep Heaven" and so forth. "The detachment of the spirit not only from the senses but even from the reason . . . was now his. . . ." (p. 307) With Merlin and his magic, elves, ogres, and wood-wooses, we sink deeper and deeper into abracadabra. There is a great deal in the book whereby Lewis is trying to purge Merlin and make him suitable as an instrument of the goodies, as if he is uncertain of the relevance of this goblin to his fable.

The reaction of Lewis's protagonists is, in any case, a child's reaction, and studied in the light of his "internal" myth, the book becomes yet another child fantasy over the problem of grief. There is talk of "the Great Atlantean" and of "Long before the great Disaster." The reference to Atlantis makes it clear that this "Disaster" is the mother's death. So Merlin is the *mother's* body, and is "Something that people had been trying to find since the beginning of the world" (p. 33); that is, as in Narnia, there is a quest for a parental, omnipotent figure to set the world to rights. "The universe should have backed him up" (as when Lewis the boy prayed for the mother), but it did not (p. 237). What is needed is the exercise of an occult strength in the paranoid-schizoid situation. ("Good is always getting better and bad is always getting worse," p. 350. "The whole thing is sorting itself out all the time, and the conflict is getting sharper and sharper.") The fact that the scientists are possessed by demons gives one a justification for resorting to demonic weapons, not least because "No power that is merely earthly will serve against the hideous strength" (p. 357). They have pulled down deep heaven on their heads, and deserve all they get: "The Director'll bring it all right in the end. You see if he don't" (p. 374). Everything points to an excitement of fully vindicated revenge—almost a kind of justified terrorism, because the enemy have been deprived of their human value.

Lewis plunges back into his private unconscious mythology of his quest for his dead mother, and magic modes of dealing with it. The Atlantean magic is the magic of the "sunk continent"; Merlin asleep is the dead mother; Logres is the country of the dead in the light of day.

So we descend, even in the language of debate in the area of the philosophy of science, into sheer voodoo and mumbo-jumbo (pp. 246–48), all the worse for being offered in "scientific" and intellectual disguise, and being all served up in a pseudo-scientific sauce, with references to the "heat death of the universe" and so forth. In the end, in the crisis, it all culminates in bloodthirsty violence as primitive as anything in the pulp thriller or sadistic film. The delight we experience with fairy stories is in *meeting* what we recognize to be human problems in fantasy, albeit unconscious ones. With Lewis we do not often feel this meeting. *Where we do meet is at the bone and blood:* that is where Lewis can, at last, find "reality," and our response will be some satisfaction for him. We will be shocked, at least, and so some sense of "real" will be experienced. This resembles the sense of being real that the soldier feels:

> I'd like to be able to say as an old sergeant said to me in the first war, about a bit of a raid we did near Monchy. Our fellows did it all with the butt end you know. "Sir," says he, "did ever you hear anything like the way their heads cracked?" (*That Hideous Strength*, p. 401)

We often get a sense that only when fantasying wounding or death does Lewis feel secure; the threat of such conflict brings excitement and even *love:*

> ". . . But I was just thinking as you awoke that I don't feel afraid of being killed and hurt as I used to do. Not tonight."
> "We may be, I suppose," said Jane.
> "As long as we're all together," said Mother Dimble. "It might be . . . me, I don't mean anything heroic . . . it might be a *nice* way to die." And suddenly all their faces and voices were changed. *They were laughing again, but it was a different kind of laughter. Their love for one another became intense.* . . . (p. 401; my italics)

At such high points, we have a kind of biblical tone, and read of:

> The long banner of the Virgin fluttering above the heavy British-Roman cataphracts, the yellow-haired barbarians. . . . There was no fear anywhere: the blood inside them flowed as to a marching song. *They felt themselves taking their place in the ordered rhythm of the universe, side by side with punctual seasons and patterned atoms and the obeying Seraphim.* (p. 402; my italics)

His enraptured excitement here goes with an argument that such aggressiveness is at one with the order of the universe.

> They had outlived all anxieties; care was a wind without meaning. . . . Ransom knew, as a man knows when he touches iron, the clear, taut, splendor of that celestial spirit who now flashed between them vigilant Malacandra, captain of a cold orb, whom men called Mars and Mavors, and Tyr who put his hand in the wolf-mouth . . . &c. (p. 402)

In the description of the massacre the prose gloats on the desperate penetration of bodies. Of course, Lewis avoids responsibility by making out it is not he, or men, who are committing the violation, but *agents of a righteous God* (the animals are agents of Merlin's dark forces):

> . . . kicking, struggling, leaping on tables and under tables, pressing on and pulling back, screams, breaking of glass. . . . It was the smell more than anything else which recalled the scene to mark in later life: the smell of the shooting mixed with the sticky compound smell of blood and port and Madeira. (p. 431)

The pleasure offered the reader is the pleasure of terrifying people—terrifying and destroying them, because they are "enemies":

> Suddenly the confusion of cries ran all together into one thin long-drawn noise of terror. Everyone had darted very quickly across the floor between the two long tables and disappeared under one of them . . . a glimpse of black and tawny . . . it was a tiger. (p. 431)

The scene is not, actually, very disturbing, because the idea is so ridiculous: besides the tiger, a dog or wolf, then a snake—and finally an elephant trumpeting and trampling—continually trampling like a girl treading grapes, heavily and soon wetly trampling in a pash of blood and bones, of flesh, wine, fruit and sodden table-cloth. Something more than danger darted from the sight into Mark's brain. The pride and insolent glory of the beast, the carelessness of its killings, seemed to crush his spirit even as its flat feet were crushing women and men. Here, surely, came the king of the world. . . . (p. 434)

On the next page Merlin is chanting *Qui Verbum Dei contempserunt, eis auferetur etiam Verbum hominis.* It all seems very "educated," cultured, and full of scholarship; but these postures disguise a strange tendency to lure the reader, once more, into an indulgence in mental rage into the joys of sadism.

The militant cruelty seems "justified"; but even in our imperfect exaction of justice, we do not subject the monsters of crime to cruel torments, but modify our sense of horror by recognizing the ways in which the human mind can be twisted by false solutions. Our justice is tempered by pity and understanding: "judge not that ye be not judged."

Lewis, clearly, believes in punishment, and at this point can lecture us on the problems of penal reform. Compassion, charity, apparently, could deprive the convict of his *right to punishment.*

An educated man in his circumstances would have found misery streaked with reflection; could have been thinking how this new idea of cure instead of punishment, so humane seeming, had in fact deprived the criminal of all rights, and by taking away the *name* punishment made the thing infinite. (p. 435)

So, with the destruction of the scientists, despite what might seem to be an attempt to experience guilt in fantasy, no guilt is felt, no anguished development of the sense of being human.

Love seems to mean control and submission: love is actually the impulse to frighten others into submission, by authoritarianism and the threat of punishment. Throughout the story there are subtle vindications of the authoritarian and cruel attitude to "enemies":

"The Pedragon tells me," he said in his unmoved voice, "that you accuse me for a fierce and cruel man. It is a charge I have heard before. A third part of my substance I gave to widows and poor men, I never sought the death of any but felons and heathen Saxons. As for the woman, she may live for me. I am not master in this house. But would it be such a great matter if her head were struck off? Do not queens and ladies who would disdain her as their tire-woman go to the fire for less? Even that gallows bird (cunciarius) beside you . . . even that cutpurse (sector zonarius) . . . yet the rope should be used on his back not his throat. . . ." (That Hideous Strength, p. 346)

This speech, one could say, might have been made by Capron. It is a bit of special pleading for the convinced sadist. Despite all the bits of history and Latin, there is the subtle implication that it is acceptable to give a dog a bad name and hang him: "felons" and "heathen Saxons" do not count. Merlin, like Lewis, has a primitive impulse to deal ruthlessly with anyone who can be shown to be an enemy. This may be taken "Pickwickianly" for the purposes of a child's fairy story or a space fiction fantasy; but Lewis's very religious fervour, by which he offers his stories, makes it extremely dangerous, in the way in which it might possibly influence habits of mind.

These habits could be dangerous because they are inimical to openness, such as science, at best, cultivates. Lewis's scientists are not wicked because of pride, greed, or vanity. They are wicked because they are *possessed*, servants of the "Bent Ones." In dealing with them there has to be an invocation of the Emperor's Magic, as in the "Narnia" books, of Merlin, and "What the Renaissance called magic" (p. 245). "No power that is merely earthly will serve against the hideous strength" (p. 357). The "good" side takes to the "older art" of necromancy. With the conflict thus externalized, it is removed from the individual conscience, the personal human breast however much Lewis may talk of the fact that "souls and personal responsibility exist" (p. 357) for the only responsibility is to be on one side or the other.

The objection to Lewis's bloodthirsty scenes, then, is not that they are bloodthirsty (there are bloodthirsty scenes in *Huckleberry Finn*, *Live and Kicking Ned*, but these prompt one into a *dismay* about human cruelty, not into an excitement about it), but that they subtly involve one in delighting in violence, and its vindication, supposing that one's cause is just.

The invitation appears from time to time in phrases that almost taint one, without one's becoming aware of it, as here: ". . . his present instinctive desire to batter the professor's face into a jelly would take a great deal of destroying. . . ." (That Hideous Strength, p. 366).

What is worse, the joys of hate are linked by Lewis with

the modulation of one's soul on to a higher plane with his Christian warriors. As the followers of Ransom contemplate battle, "they felt themselves taking their place in the ordered rhythm of the universe" as "the blood in them flowed to a marching song" (p. 402). And when the crunch comes, in this "spiritual" battle, it is described in revealing oral terms. There is a "pash of blood and bones"—as with the bear (a "pantomime" bear) which seeks the "warm salt tastes, of the pleasant resistance of bone, of things to crunch and lick and worry" (p. 402). These "things" are the "bad" scientists, who have been depersonalized—as depersonalized, one might say, as the "enemies" that all human beings are ready to torture and kill once they have been given that label.

At the beginning of *That Hideous Strength*, the "I" of the book reflects, "But when alone—really alone—everyone is a child: or no one? Youth and age touch only the surface of our lives" (p. 19). *That Hideous Strength* is yet another attempt to solve the timeless existential problems of the tormented child, who cannot find his world. Lewis is also haunted by that dread that "the real universe might be simply silly" (p. 376). As for oneself, there is often the dread that, "suppose one were a thing, a thing designed and invented by someone else and valued for qualities quite different from what one had decided to regard as one's true self" (p. 393). However deeply hidden, Lewis seems to have had fundamentally schizoid insecurity about what was his true self, and a deep uncertainty about what was real.

So again, examined phenomenologically, everything happens in terms of externalized "split-offs." In *That Hideous Strength* the hideous strength itself, the tower, is such a split-off subject, a huge penis with a shadow six miles long. Against it have to be sent split-off aggressive entities. The climax of the story is the moment when these frightening entities meet. When (one might say) all the oral-aggressive dynamics of the dissatisfied infant engage with the salty taste, pash, crunch, and blood of the combined parents, who are (in any case) engaged in a dangerous (if not fatal) mutual eating. The great bad-male-doing penis is destroyed; but there is no gain in understanding.

So, the victory at the end of *That Hideous Strength* is not a victory of human conscience, or courage, or devotion, against hubristic arrogance. It is a victory of irrational wish-fulfillment—of magic—against "science" (but a science that is heavily caricatured and misrepresented as being possessed by the devil).

What is endorsed here is mumbo-jumbo—the deliberate cultivation of irrationality and superstition. Even if we take them as symbols, what do Merlin's dogs, elephants, and snakes in *That Hideous Strength* represent? In what sense, against hubristic "science," does one seek to invoke beasts that will mutilate and kill "bad" scientists who are badly wrong in their philosophies and cause social havoc? These might be brought under examination by reasonable discourse (as over genetic engineering, or germ warfare, or experiments on mental patients, animals, or human embryos). It does no good to any cause to convey to readers that it could somehow be in God's purpose or human interests for them to be eaten by ghostly wild animals, in an orgiastic act of revenge, justified by the allegation that they are serving "bent angels."

In the face of the mechanism and materialism of our age and its blindness, Lewis invokes an entity parallel to the "Big Dog," Aslan, in Narnia—omnipotent phantoms which can solve human problems by magic manipulation. This childish solution is no answer to the spiritual problems of our time, or those posed by the moral failures of the scientific era.

# 14

## Perelandra

Lewis was correct to declare that his "lust" to write space fiction invited a psychoanalytical interpretation. *Perelandra*, for example, displays a passionate yearning, and an intensity of vision and color, which suggest a profound and energetic unconscious impulse behind this cultivated dream. Lewis himself tells us that "all my Narnia books and my three science fiction books began with seeing pictures in my head" (Green and Hooper 1974, p. 246). In *Perelandra*, as we shall see, these *pictures* arise, or so I argue, from a devoted desire to find the lost mother, to reexperience birth, and to complete those processes by which one finds the reality of the world and its meaning.

*Perelandra*, at the level at which the Christian reader takes it, is a story told to an "I" by one Ransom, who has been to the planet Mars (or Malecandra, as its inhabitants call it, Lewis tells us) in a previous space fiction novel, *Out of the Silent Planet*. Earth is the "silent planet" because one does not hear from it the direct expression of the "good" powers in the universe. The universe, in Lewis's cosmology, is poised between the "eldils" who belong to "Deep Heaven," and who are presumably angels (they do not eat, breathe, breed, or die) and the "bent" or fallen angels, demons, who embody hate and destructiveness. In this earth, which in the Lewis cosmos is called Thulcandra, in the "Arbol" region (or Solar system), we have our own especial "Bent One," called Oyarsa. Maleldil, who is Christ, is seeking to overcome the bent ones, and this requires the sacrifice of the crucifixion—Ransom, that is, has been ransomed. "When Maleldil was born a man at Bethlehem this altered the universe for ever" (*Perelandra*, p. 164). A voice says to Ransom, "It is not for nothing that you are named Ransom," and "My name is also ransom" (p. 164). Ransom is "Fallen Man," for whom Christ died. Everything belongs to the pattern, in which this sacrifice was made for man, and Ransom realizes that "It lay with him to save or to spill" (p. 164). But in what way does he display this choice?

Ransom becomes aware that the world, indeed, the cosmos, is threatened by one Weston. Weston is scientific man, in a state of hubris. He is devoted to the conquest of space, and seeks to bring about the domination of the universe by our species:

> He was a man obsessed with the idea that is at this moment circulating all over our planet in obscure works of "scientification" in little Interplanetary Societies and Rocketry Clubs, and between the covers of monstrous magazines . . . ready, if ever the power is put into its hands, to open a new chapter of misery for the universe. It is the idea that humanity, having now sufficiently corrupted the planet where it arose, must at all costs contrive to seed itself over a larger area: that the vast astronomical distances which are God's quarantine regulations, must somehow be overcome. . . . (Perelandra, p. 91–92)

Beyond this lies the hope of "destruction or enslavement of other species in the universe" (p. 92). Over this question there are revealing exchanges between Ransom and Professor Weston, who is an (H. G.) Wellsian figure. He believes in "emergent evolution," and justifies his ambitions in the name of the "Life Force," whose blind impulses must be followed, even though they might be thought to come into conflict with God's law and the limits He has set on human ambition. Pressed to the extremes, Weston is prepared to defy all values, and displays contempt for "our petty ethical pigeon holes" (p. 108). He is a nihilistic fanatic:

> "In so far as I am the conductor of the central forward pressure of the universe, I am it. Do you see, you timid, scruple-mongering fool? I am the Universe. I, Weston, am your God and your Devil. I call that force into me completely. . . ." (p. 109)

At this point, however, something disturbing happens. Ransom has noticed that Weston's face looks different from how it seemed to him in Malecandra. Here, Ransom has a glimpse of the "old" Weston, and the professor cries, "Ransom, Ransom! For Christ's sake don't let them . . ." (p. 109)—but he is at once struck as if by a bullet, and falls down in convulsions. Weston has been *taken over*, by demons, more or less at this moment.

Ransom has a great deal of respect for Professor Weston, and in the end he sets up a tomb for him with an inscription: "He was a great physicist after all." But in the inscription he also says "he gave up his will and reason to the bent Eldil" (p. 109).

Weston, then, is Faust; or we might say he is like Macbeth. At that moment when he cries out "Don't let them . . .", he is like Macbeth at the moment he feels he and his wife should go no further with their dreadful enterprise. If we compare Weston with Macbeth, in terms of our response, we will find ourselves in difficulties. *Macbeth* may be a poetic study in demonology, but we are always aware that Macbeth himself is not a witch, nor is his wife. He is a *man*. By degrees, Weston becomes not only damned (as Faustus is): "it is and it is not Weston talking"—there is a devil inside him, who acts and speaks with only the mechanistic semblance of Weston's body as his exterior. It is like a terrible dream, in which a familiar figure is actually possessed: Weston becomes the "Un-man."

In long and subtle conversations with the "Green Lady," of whom more anon, the Un-man is trying to possess her, too:

> If the remains of Weston were, at such moments, speaking through the lips of the Un-man, then Weston was not now a man at all. The forces which had begun, perhaps years ago, to eat away his humanity had now completed their work. The intoxicated will which had been slowly poisoning the intelligence and the affections had now at last poisoned itself and the whole psychic organism had fallen to pieces. (*Perelandra*, p. 148)

From inside the body of Weston, the Tempter is trying to poison the consciousness of the Lady—to persuade her, as Eve, to take "the great Risk." The Devil seems to be persuading her towards those "progressive" ideas about fulfilment which Lewis so detested.

The strange thing about the whole episode, however, is that Ransom is so persistently silent, and unable to make any headway in his arguments to counter the subtle propaganda of the Tempter. He is supposed to be Maleldil's representative, but he becomes exasperated with mere argument: "Anyway, what can I do?" babbled the voluble self. "I've done all I can, I've talked till I'm sick of it. It's no good, I tell you'" (p. 148).

He gradually comes to the conclusion that it is part of Maleldil's plan that he should come to Venus to oppose this Tempter. But the opposition, it seems, is not going to succeed by argument, persuasion, or prayer. Instead, by degrees, after a contemplation of Christ's ransom, he reaches the conclusion that *he must kill this demon* and cheerfully: "No sooner had he discovered that he would certainly try to kill the Un-man to-morrow than the doing of it appeared to him a smaller matter than he had supposed!" (p. 170). The thing was "going to be done": "predestination and freedom were apparently identical" (p. 170). So, the fulfilment of Ransom's duty to Christ is to kill the Un-man who has taken over Weston's body. He has been chosen for this destiny, and the carrying out of this attack was simply a question of obeying Christ's plan for the cosmos. In our terms, we may see the theme as dealing with spiritual or moral problem in terms of externalized split-offs, projection, and paranoia.

The story develops with such subtle power that the reader goes with it, and enters into the excitement. There are bone-crunching fights, blood flows, and the Un-man tears strips off Ransom. There is a long sadistic fantasy, developing over pages. The horror of the conflict fills Ransom with joy: "*The joy came from finding at last what hate was made for.* . . . He felt that he could fight, so hate with a perfect hatred, for a whole year" (p. 178; my italics). In the end the final annihilation of the Un-man is achieved with almost blasphemous satisfaction:

> "In the name of the Father and of the Son and of the Holy Ghost, here goes—I mean Amen," said Ransom, and hurled the stone as hard as he could into the Un-man's face. The Un-man falls as a pencil falls, the face smashed out of all recognition. (p. 209)

The playful quip, "here goes—I mean Amen" seems to me the most disastrous lapse in Lewis's fiction. And yet the sadistic fantasy is given an endorsement, in a subtle way by references to the crucifixion:

> "And you think, little one," it answered, "that you can fight with me? You think He will help you, perhaps? Many thought that. I've known Him longer than you, little one. They all think He's going to help them—till they come to their senses screaming recantations too late in the middle of the fire, mouldering in concentration camps, writing under saws, jibbering in mad-houses, or nailed on to crosses. Could He help himself?"—and the creature suddenly threw back its head and cried in a voice so loud that it seemed the golden sky-roof must break, "*Eloi, Eloi, lama sabachthani.*" (*Perelandra*, p. 174)

For the Devil to jeer thus is surely intended to infuriate the Christian reader, and so he may be supposed to feel even greater satisfaction when the Un-man is smashed. The failures of tone here seem to me to reveal that Lewis is cloaking an indulgence in sadistic fantasy in the coarsest way as a Christian fable. Yet by my perspectives the basis of the need to indulge the fantasy is the (schizoid) dread of being taken over or "imploded" by evil forces.

Ransom is trying to kill this creature. At one point the broken body seems to become Weston again, and Ransom has a conversation with him. But now the Un-man appears. This is a nightmare we have all had: fighting with a creature who does not die, whatever we do to it.

> Slowly, shakily, with unnatural and inhuman movements a human form in the firelight, crawled out on to the floor of the cave. It was the Un-man, of course; dragging its broken leg and with its lower jaw sagging open like that of a corpse, it raised itself to a standing position. . . . (pp. 207–08)

Joining it come hideous insects: "a huge, many legged, quivering deformity, standing just behind the Un-man so that the horrible shadows of both danced in enormous and united menace on the wall of rock behind them" (p. 208).

When Ransom kills him:

> . . . The Un-man fell as a pencil falls, the face smashed out of all recognition. . . . All that he had felt from childhood about insects and reptiles died at that moment died utterly, as hideous music dies when you switch off the wireless. Apparently it had all, even from the beginning been a dark, enchantment of the enemy's. . . . (p. 209)

Lewis's fantasies had their origins in their nightmares; and as we know, he was afraid of insects. In *Perelandra*, at this moment, Ransom resists these apparitions as if they were invasions of his brain. Again, we have the theme of implosion:

> "They want to frighten me," said something in Ransom's brain, and at the same moment he became convinced both that the Un-man had summoned this great earth-crawler and also that the evil thoughts which had preceded the appearance of the enemy had been poured into his own mind by the enemy's will. The knowledge that his thoughts could be thus managed from without did not awake terror but rage.

He yells at the Un-man: "Do you think I'm going to stand this," he yelled. "Get out of my brain. It isn't yours I tell you! Get out of it" (p. 209).

After the killing, there is a passage that is revealingly "academic" and detached. It is offered like something in an autobiography; but we may learn more from the schizoid dissociation by which it appears at this moment:

> Once, as he had sat writing near an open window in Cambridge, he had looked up and shuddered to see, as he supposed, a many-coloured beetle of unusually hideous shape crawling across his paper. A second glance showed him that it was a dead leaf, moved by the breeze; and instantly the very curves and re-entrants which had made its ugliness turned into its beauties. (*Perelandra*, p. 209)

The passage is strangely cool and detached, at such a tense moment. And by this we get a clue to why Lewis needs to indulge in murderous fantasies.

There does seem to be, at the moment of the smashing of the Un-man in *Perelandra*, an admission that Lewis is almost fantasying the destruction of his own paranoid nightmares. After the Un-man's death, Ransom thinks (in a passage that comes immediately above that just quoted):

> But where had the horror gone? The creature was there, a curiously shaped creature no doubt, but all the loathing had vanished clean out of his mind, so that neither then nor at any other time could he remember it, nor ever understand again why one should quarrel with an animal for having more legs or eyes than oneself. All that he had felt from childhood about insects and reptiles died that moment: died utterly, as hideous music dies when you switch off the wireless. Apparently it had all, even from the beginning, been a dark enchantment of the enemy's. (p. 209)

This insight should surely indicate a warning against projection, throwing out horrors from one's inner world and attacking them in others out there in the world? And if this kind of phenomenon is a trick of the "enemy," perhaps all that Ransom has done is to be caught by a prompting to commit an evil act in the name of good? Is Ransom's horrible act of hate to be so delighted in? Or could it not be the psychopathological response of a man to a misled projection, like the reported response to a leaf in Cambridge?

Ransom reflects that the giant beetle "intended him no harm—

has indeed no intentions at all" (p. 209). Ransom almost laughs when he sees it disappear "like an animated corridor train" (p. 209). But the absence of emotional substance in the passage is chilling. Just as Ransom kills the Un-man, he turns to make an aside to a giant insect, then to an academic reminiscence, and then despatches the body with cold detachment

> He turned to the Un-man. It had hardly anything left that you could call a head, but he thought it better to take no risks. He took it by its ankles and lugged it up to the edge of the cliff: then, after resting a few seconds, he shoved it over. He saw its shape black, for a second, against the sea of fire: and then that was the end of it. (p. 210)

What is frightening about Lewis's bloody murders, battles, and ordeals is that *he displays no awareness of the agony people (or Un-people) suffer from bodily injury.* Nor does he have any idea of the misery a person may experience when he hurts another, until we come to *Till We Have Faces.* Ransom, like Lewis, has to resort to compulsive intellectual rituals in order to defend himself against intolerable dread:

> He recited all that he could remember of the *Iliad,* the *Odyssey,* the *Aeneid,* the *Chanson de Roland, Paradise Lost,* the *Kelevala,* the *Hunting of the Snark.* . . . He tried to rough out a chapter for a book he was writing. But it was all rather a failure. . . . (p. 199)

This seems to give us a clue to Lewis's own tremendously energetic intellectual activity, and his need for it to stave off anxiety.

In *Perelandra* another perplexity is over the Green Woman. *Who is she in Christian cosmology?* And why does the Un-man have to be destroyed especially to save her? Christian interpretations here provide no answers. Oh, yes, she is Lilith in a sense. But we may find more profitable insights if we begin with the conversations between Weston and the Green Woman. Reading them, as they progress for long hours, as Ransom overhears them enviously and impotently, we may develop a sense of sharing the experience of a small boy listening to the parents talking in bed. From time to time, I return to the theme in Lewis's work, of the "Combined Parents"—that image that Melanie Klein discovered as a factor in infant fantasy. The infant fears that the parents, in the oral intensity of their sexual hunger, may turn on him, and destroy him. I need to bring in here, too, the recurrent image in Lewis of the unicorn-like creature impregnating others with poison from its horn; and the secret unconscious fear that the father killed the mother by sexual intercourse. The tension behind the end of the story here has to do with intense and vengeful hate aroused in a child by the incomprehensible progress of sexual congress between mother and father. The destruction of the Un-man is thus an intense vision of an Oedipal act, by a child enraged by intense feelings around the mother, and the way in which the father is taking her over in a way the child cannot understand, but which seems very menacing.

This interpretation, of course, directs us into quite another myth; and *Perelandra* can be interpreted in a very different way from the "Christian" gloss. Every now and then there is a clue to this other myth. For instance, in a last exchange between Ransom and Professor Weston about whether or not the universe is *bearable:*

> "I'll tell you what's truer," said Weston presently.
> "What?"
> "A little child that creeps upstairs when nobody's looking and very slowly turns the handle to take one peep into the room where its grandmother's body is laid out—and then runs away and has bad dreams. . . ." (*Perelandra*, p. 191)

That child knows something about the universe, says Weston, that all science and religion is trying to hide. This is that a whole continent can sink, and all your sense of living in a real and meaningful world can sink with it. We have seen above how Lewis felt himself to be so traumatized by seeing his mother's dead body, she having become an "it"; and we may assume this conditioned his feelings about all matter and reality.

The floating islands, which are the land for the most part in Venus in *Perelandra*, are Atlantises; that is, they are the mother-world before it sank. Venus is the planet of love and of woman, and so it is the "other" world where the mother is to be found and reexperienced. Again, as in Macdonald, the trouble is that once the lost mother is found, the bliss that was expected is clouded by the fact that all the old troubles of being human are forthwith reexperienced—not least the problem of the father, who inevitably breaks in upon the visionary innocence that the infant tries to preserve. The oral intensity that prompts the very quest is so strong it is feared it may prove too destructive. In *Perelandra*, Lewis yearns for a "trans-sensuous life and a non-sensuous life," but this cannot be sustained.

In the end, Ransom at first does find a new birth, and he is fed again at the breast:

> Indeed, it was a second infancy, in which he was breast-fed by the planet Venus herself: unweaned till he moved from that place . . . the delicious life that he sucked from the clusters which almost seemed to bow themselves into his upstretched hands. . . . (*Perelandra*, p. 213)

*Perelandra*, then, may be read as a vision in which Lewis hopes to make his world benign, by finding rebirth—but then finding that the wounds of the psyche cannot be so easily healed. The symbolism of rebirth is so clear in the story that one feels that Lewis must himself have been aware of it. The "celestial coffin" in which Ransom is enclosed for his journey to Venus has all the symbolism of schizoid rebirth, that ultimate regression which is to lead to a new parturition. Note at the end of his journey:

> . . . as he spoke the figure in the coffin began to stir and then sat up, shaking off as it did so a mass of red things which had covered its head and shoulders and which I had momentarily mistaken for ruin and blood. (p. 32)

The intense feelings of color, of falling and of movement, and of being "turned out" seem clearly to be imaginings of being reborn:

> He was moving his limbs, encumbered with some viscous substance . . . there was a delicious coolness over every part of him . . . he had for some time been performing unconsciously the actions of a swimmer. . . . (p. 32)

Lucy feels coolness as she goes through the wardrobe in the first "Narnia" book—the coolness is that of being born into the air from the womb.

The physical feeling is of what Winnicott calls "reptation," the physical movements of being born, like swimming, as often recalled by patients. The passages in *Perelandra* are striking, as Lewis fantasies the experience of birth as he so profoundly desires it.

For page after page, Lewis expresses the sense of this quest

for the world where the lost mother is, from the original statement by Ransom:

> "It's on hot summer days—looking up at the deep blue and that
> thinking that in there, millions of miles where I can never, never
> get back to it, there's a place I know. . . ." (p. 23)

That "place" is the womb, and later the mother's breast. The
fantasied rebirth brings intense feelings of delight:

> . . . the coolness of the water and the freedom of his limbs were
> still a novelty and a delight; but more than all these was something
> else at which I have already hinted and which can hardly be put
> into words—the strange sense of excessive pleasure which seemed
> to him to be communicated to him through all his senses at once. . . .
> There was an exuberance or prodigality of sweetness about the mere
> act of living which our race finds it difficult not to associate with
> forbidden and extravagant actions.* (p. 40)

He even feels that "his reason might be in danger" because
of the "unearthly pleasure" that he experiences in Venus, not
least when he begins to find the delights of the breast:

> Now he had come to a part of the wood where great globes of
> yellow fruit hung from the trees—clustered as toy-balloons are clus-
> tered on the back of the balloon-man and about the same size.
> He picked one of them and turned it over and over. The rind was
> smooth and firm and seemed impossible to tear open. Then by
> accident one of his fingers punctured it and went through into
> the coldness. After a moment's hesitation he put the little aperture
> to his lips. He had meant to extract the smallest, experimental sip,
> but the first taste put his caution all to flight . . . it was so different
> from every other taste. . . . It was like the discovery of a new genus
> of pleasure, something unheard of among men, out of all reckoning,
> beyond all covenant. For one draught of this on earth wars would
> be fought and nations betrayed. (p. 47)

The oral hunger is intense behind these rhapsodic passages on
being breast-fed by Venus.

Not only do the breast objects in Venus give this profound
delight, there is a new discovery of a transcended reality: "he
saw reality and thought it was a dream" (p. 49). I have said
that Lewis's problem in part was that he had had an unsatisfac-

---

*The latter is surely a reference to masturbation as a way to bring the mother
back?

tory experience of the mother, and of play, by which to discover reality. The imaginative dynamics between mother and child have not completed themselves: the fantasies are an attempt to complete the process. The reality of Venus is to Ransom "the most vivid dream I have ever had" (p. 49).

In George Macdonald's fantasies, there appear often translucent shining objects which are clearly breasts, as they might be supposed to be imagined by a hungry infant. They are the focus of a yearning to find something, some illumination about the world, some ecstasy of meaning which the spirit seeks. In *Perelandra* we find similar objects, which are described with a kind of ecstasy:

> Suddenly his whole attention was attracted by something else. Over his head there hung from a hairy tube-like branch a great spherical object, almost transparent, and shining. It held an area of reflected light in it and at one place a suggestion of rainbow colouring. So this was the explanation of the grass-like appearance in the wood. And looking round he perceived innumerable shimmering globes of the same kind in every direction. He began to examine the nearest one attentively. At first he thought it was moving, then he thought it was not. Moved by a natural impulse he put out his hand to touch it. Immediately his head, face, and shoulders were drenched with what seemed (in that warm world) an ice-cold shower bath, and his head, face, and shoulders were drenched with a sharp, shrill, exquisite scent that somehow brought to his mind the verse in Pope, "die of a rose in aromatic pain." . . . When he opened his eyes . . . all the colours about him seemed richer and the dimmest of that world seemed clarified. A re-enchantment fell upon him. (*Perelandra*, p. 52)

The intense oral needs of Lewis are clear as we follow Ransom in this ecstasy:

> The things were not fruit at all but bubbles. The trees (he christened them at that moment) were bubble-trees. Their life, apparently, consisted of drawing up water from the ocean and then expelling it in this form, but enriched by its short sojourn in their sappy inwards. . . . Looking at a fine cluster of the bubble which hung above his head he thought how easy it would be to get up and plunge oneself through the whole lot of them and to feel, all at once, that magical refreshment multiplied tenfold. (p. 53)

In this world, the Green Woman is encountered. She is later described as a madonna. At first she is Mother Nature who "stood up amidst a throng of beasts and birds as a tall sapling stands among bushes." "Was this the beginning of the hallucinations he had feared?" (p. 72). He is puzzled by the expression on her face. She points to him and laughs because, while she is green, he is piebald. As the longed-for process of reflection begins, he is made aware by her response of his own strange mixture of aspects; but the Green Woman is nonhuman. She is a goddess, beautiful, shameless, and young. She is the mother idealized:

> The alert, inner silence which looked out from her eyes overawed him; yet at any minute she might laugh like a child, or run like Artemis or dance like a Maenad. . . . It was not really like a woman making much of a horse, nor yet a child playing with a puppy. There was in her face an authority, in her caresses a condescension, which by taking seriously the inferiority of her adorers made them somehow less inferior—raised them from the status of pets to that of slaves. (p. 72)

She belongs to the king. Who is this king? asks Ransom. "He is himself" she replies. Ransom asks her if she had a mother: "I am the Mother" is the answer. Ransom says that "Our Mother and Lady is dead," and this is meant to mean in the Christian sense—but we may take this to be from Lewis's unconscious, and believe that Ransom is talking not of the Virgin Mary but of his own mother. If find it hard to make sense of the mother and king in Christian terms; but there is no doubt what they mean in terms of Lewis's private mythology.

In the fantasy he has found the creative reflection of the mother's face. By degrees, Ransom is redeemed by Venus (Perelandra):

> Looking down at his own body he noticed how greatly the sunburn on one side and the pallor on the other had decreased. He would hardly be christened piebald if the Lady were now to meet him for the first time. . . . He felt pretty certain that he would never again wield an un-maimed body until a greater morning came for the whole universe, and he was glad that the instrument had been thus tuned up to concert pitch before he had to surrender it. "When I wake up after Thy image, I shall be satisfied," he said to himself. (Perelandra, p. 172)

The need to experience Venus, thus, in Christian terms, means preparing oneself for heaven. In my terms, it means finding out a sense of a meaningful existence by being reflected in the mother's face.

At this moment, Ransom nearly trips over the sleeping form of the Lady, who is seen now for the last time.

> "I shall never see her again," he thought; and then, "I shall never again look on a female body in quite the same way as I look on this." As he stood looking down on her, what was most with him was an intense and *orphaned* longing that he might, if only for once, have seen the great Mother of his own race thus, in her innocence and splendour. . . . (p. 172; my italics)

This is just before the beginning of the ferocious sadistic fantasies of Ransom's fight with the Un-man.

As I have suggested, another problem arises when the mother is found because the problem of the father arises again. It is also true to say that a great deal of Ransom's energy has to be given to what must be called a reexperiencing of a small boy's ghastly responses to being brutally attacked by a man who was in the place of his father, who seemed to wear the uniform of a good man, a clergyman, but who was insane, and so possessed by a devil. Who can read the dreadful episodes of the conflict with the Un-man without finding in them revengeful fantasies directed by such a child's soul, against inhuman (or Un-man) treatment, at his most unhappy period of grief? Weston "possessed" is Capron mad and mad most because of the loss of his wife.

There are from time to time indications that in Lewis's consciousness much remained of the small traumatized child, to whose state of consciousness he now and then returns. On page 147, for example, when the Un-man is exerting his destructiveness on the planet, there is a quite odd return to the time and language of his school: "The more childlike terror of living with a ghost or a mechanised corpse never left him for many minutes together. The fact of being *alone* with it sometimes rush upon his mind with such dismay. . . ." Combined here seem to be reminiscences of Capron with those of public school perversions:

> With Ransom himself it had innumerable games to play. It had a whole repertory of obscenities to perform with its own—or rather with Weston's—body: and the mere silliness of them was almost worse than the dirtiness. (p. 147)

One wonders what this could mean? It must surely refer to the perversions of Wyvern? When Weston surfaces in this body, he speaks not like a scientist as much as a schoolmaster or a pupil: "That boy keeps shutting the windows . . . so when they didn't want me in the first Fifteen they could jolly well do without me, see. We'll tell that young whelp it's an insult to the examiners to show up this kind of work. . . . It's not fair. Not fair. I never meant any harm. . . ." Lewis speaks of "the frightful abyss which parts ghosthood from manhood" (p. 147) and here follows the passage quoted above about the poisoning of intelligence. Who can doubt that here Lewis has released from suppressed memory hideous memories of his endurance at school, and the sense that even within his own sensibility are suppressed horrors from that time, which deeply threaten his equanimity? We may even hear Capron's voice, in these utterances from the hated Weston. I have suggested that the intense oral need indicates a need to reexperience the discovery of reality through the mother's creative reflection. Lewis also expresses through his character a fear that too much may harm:

> But he was restrained by the same sort of feeling that restrained him overnight by from tasting another gourd. He had always disliked the people who encored a favourite air in an opera—"That spoils it" had been his comment. But his now appeared to him as a principle of far wider application and deeper moment. The itch to have things over again, as if life were a film to be unrolled twice or even made to work backwards . . . was it possibly the root of all evil? (Perelandra, p. 53)

This seems to reveal a fear that, in some way, the release of the intense oral impulse will somehow damage the hard-sought relationship between himself and reality. If one sought to intensify satisfaction too much, it would be as if one were rolling back life like a film: the true progress of intentionality might be damaged.

We may associate this doubtfulness with the obvious links in his symbolism between the oral hunger and masturbation. It often seems clear from episodes in Perelandra that the breast hunger in Lewis was the impulse behind his masturbation fantasies. "The tube or branch, deprived of its pendent globe, now ended in a little quivering orifice from which there hung a bead of crystal moisture. . . ." (p. 53). The little globes burst and swell, and we can see that the orgasmic episode I have quoted above is a kind of masturbatory crisis. We may note that throughout Perelandra the relationship between Ransom and the Green Woman is totally sexless, and here the only relationship he has is with a dragon:

> If a naked man and a wise dragon were indeed the sole inhabitants of this floating paradise, then this also was fitting, for at that moment he had a sensation not of following an adventure but enacting a myth. (p. 52)

The dragon is thus as significant in Lewis's myth (and nothing to do with Christianity) as the dragon is in the "Narnia" books.

The dragon in the "Narnia" books seems to be associated with the rejection of the flesh. Eustace is peeled because his flesh is sinful, and working this out from Lewis's poems, we can surely see that behind this lies guilt about masturbating. This guilt is a very deep one which has to do with being human at all so that Lewis can only conceive of Christ becoming a man in terms of being like "a slug." He is, however, also fascinated by rending, peeling, and tearing the flesh; and much of the symbolism here has to do with inner contents.

This symbolism has to do with *penetrating the interior of the other*, and this we may relate to the oral impulses, and the fascination with the breast objects. Lewis's fear is that the delight he experiences in taking the breast, albeit in fantasy, may get out of hand and become destructive: hence the guilt. The guilt at masturbation follows the same path. Oddly enough, here the problem is, as it were, displaced on to the dragon, with which Ransom has a kind of man-and-dog relationship of a mildly physical kind:

> He decided that he had better make friends with it. He stroked the hard dry head, and the creature took no notice. Then his hand passed lower down and found softer surface, or even a chink in the mail. Ah . . . that was where it liked being tickled. It grunted and shot out a long cylindrical slate-coloured tongue to lick him. It rolled round on its back revealing an almost white belly, which Ransom kneaded with his toes. His acquaintance with the dragon prospered exceedingly. (p. 54)

In this the sexual impulses and the dread (as of the unknown dynamics in the animal kingdom) are reconciled by domesticity, and by the comedy of the life of pets. But to Lewis it is one of the worst manifestations of evil when curiosity about the insides of living creatures becomes the focus of sadistic deeds.

In Chapter Nine there is an appalling description of the trail of damaged frogs, which Weston has left behind him in his grisly progress:

> The whole back had been ripped open in a sort of V-shaped gash, the point of the V being a little behind the head. Something had torn a widening wound backward—as we do in opening an envelope—along the trunk and pulled it out so far behind the animal that the hoppers or hind legs had been almost torn off with it. (p. 122)

There has been so far nothing spoiled or dead in *Perelandra*—the "Fall," we might say, had not yet arrived there. The destruction of the frog, to Ransom, was "an intolerable obscenity which afflicted him with shame" (p. 122). Ransom tries to kill the wounded frog, but this makes the creature's suffering worse. Lewis's reflections at this moment are like those one endures, as a sensitive child, when one first discovers the realities of pain and death. This has to do with the first discoveries of reality: "The milk-warm wind blowing over the golden sea . . . all these had become . . . the illuminated margin of a book whose text was the struggling little horror at his feet"—that is, we are back at the problem of the dead mother, and the light this cast, in the child's mind, on the reality of the world, to whose reality she had not completely managed to bring him. Ransom finds Weston "tearing a frog—quietly and almost surgically inserting his forefinger, with its long sharp nail, under the skin behind the creature's head and ripping it open" (p. 124). The face of the body of Weston with the demon inside it does not have human compassion or concern:

> The face which he raised from torturing the frog had that terrible power which the face of a corpse sometimes has of simply rebuffing every conceivable human attitude one can adopt towards it. The expressionless mouth, the unwinking stare of the eyes, something heavy and inorganic in the very folds of the cheek said clearly, "I have features as you have, but there is nothing in common between you and me." (p. 124)

That face, surely, is the face of Capron? And the face of Capron, moreover, as it may have seemed to the boy, after his world had been shattered by witnessing his mother's dead unresponsive face? It is also the face of one who seeks, by his vicious acts, to find concern; and what Weston is doing, in his "pleasures beyond vice" is, surely, also a form of masturbation? Behind this deeply disturbing scene, we may find many clues to the intensity of Lewis's fantasy—and clues, too, to how, in the end, despite his positive impulses to find his humanness, he turns to the indulgence in the satisfactions of hate because he can only *feel real through hate*. It was Capron who taught him that kind of false solution. This hate belongs to false solution, and to manic defence.

Because of this, Lewis's attitudes towards death and mortality seem puerile, and lacking seriousness. Towards the beginning, speaking of his coming ordeal, Ransom says: "I think I feel as a man who believes in the future life feels when he is taken out to face a firing party. *Perhaps it's good practice. . . .*" (p. 28; my italics). It is this note that I mean (whatever Owen Barfield meant) by the word *voulu*: to me it is on a par with that embarrassing comment of Peter Pan, about dying being an awfully great adventure. From this I go on to find the same radical insincerity in the comment, "The joy came from finding at last what hatred was made for" (p. 28). Lewis doesn't mean it: not as we would mean it. The failure to mean it means that he has not found the reality of existence, and the painful consequences of one's actions, the sense which must come with *concern*. Yet it is very quality, of a disastrous failure to find the moral sense while substituting for it delight, fulfilment, and harmony in hallucinations of righteous hostility, that is what people take to be a sound expression of Christianity in Lewis.

Christian commentators fail to see the dangers of Lewis's attempt to persuade us of the truth of his paranoid picture of the cosmos. Yet Lewis moves from fantasies of this kind to homiletics about the world based on his paranoia. Hooper says:

> The end of *Out of the Silent Planet* hints at the "force or forces" behind Weston which "will play a very important part in the events of the next few centuries, and, unless we can prevent them, a very disastrous one": and "the dangers to be feared are not planetary but cosmic, or at least solar, and they are not temporal but eternal." (Green and Hooper 1974, p. 166)

From the above quotations, it is clear that his fantasies are erected in this way into a general philosophy of existence; and Lewis insists that we accept this view of existence as true—otherwise we may suffer some cosmic disaster.

At the same time, Lewis reveals a strange dissociation, whereby the writing is also a game, meant but not meant:

If you are writing a book about pain and then get some actual pain
. . . it does not either, as the cynic would expect, blow the doctrine
to bits, or, as the Christian would hope, turn it into practice, but
remains quite *unconnected* and irrelevant, just as any other bit of
actual life does when you are reading or writing. (Green and Hooper
1974, p. 186)

Really to engage with the problem of death and meaning,
which are the central problems in Lewis's quest, one must face
one's mortal predicament without prevarication. Lewis does pre-
varicate, I believe. Instead of attending to his existential problem
he believes in smuggling "theology" into other people's minds
by his fantasies. He adheres to the attitude expressed above
the reading and writing about "Numinor" can intrude into what
seems, at first, a genuinely honest confrontation with scientific
endeavour and hubris. One may alter myths to suit one's own
psychic needs, perverse as these may be, and invert values,
even while declaring that the Christian myth one is using is
simply "true," and that values are absolute and must be deferred
to as the "Tao." In these duplicities, I believe, we find an essential artistic and ethical insincerity in Lewis.

# 15

## Till We Have Faces

Lewis wrote *Till We Have Faces* after his marriage. It is a retelling of the Psyche myth, which is about jealousy and envy among other things. This story was told by Apuleius (b. 124 A.D.). Psyche is a princess so beautiful that Aphrodite is jealous of her and orders her son Cupid to punish her. Her father is commanded by an uncle to sacrifice his daughter to a monster. When she is abandoned on the mountain, the west wind, Cupid, rescues her and carries her to a palace, making her his bride. But they only meet in the darkness, and she must not look in his face. Psyche takes a lamp and looks at her sleeping husband's face: he awakens, reproaches her for her lack of faith, and vanishes; the palace vanishes, too, and she finds herself alone on the mountain.

She attempts suicide, but the river bears her gently to the opposite bank. From there she is pursued by Aphrodite's anger, but she survives and completes all the impossible tasks set her even to descend to the underworld. Finally, Cupid pleads with Zeus for his unfaithful wife, asking that she be permitted to join him. Zeus makes her immortal; Aphrodite forgives her; the wedding is celebrated on Olympus.

C. S. Lewis, Margaret Patterson Hannay (1981) tells us, was fascinated by this story; and it is not difficult, in my perspective, to see why.* It is about a beautiful object of the yearning of love, who is also the subject of envy, who is subjected to various forms of sacrifice, and who goes down eventually to the underworld. Psyche is thus here very much like the figure of the lost mother (while the story resembles the fantasies of George MacDonald that are also about such a pursuit). Here I shall only deal with those aspects of this complex story that seem to confirm my interpretation.

Phenomenologically speaking, the most significant element

---

*Margaret P. Hannay, *C. S. Lewis*, New York: Ungar, 1981.

in the story is the moment at which Psyche looks at Cupid's face. In many of MacDonald's stories we have a moment of ecstasy in which it seems the mother's face (or *breast*—meaning the whole experience of creative reflection) is about to be found. In this case, it is Psyche looking at Cupid. It is this kind of moment that excites the bereaved mind seeking the still-needed lost object: somehow the veil which separates the living and the dead is to be lifted (in the story, between the mortal and the immortal). But when this veil is lifted, it could be that bad things will follow, as they did from the original encounter (in MacDonald's fantasies this happens continually). So, there must be a long and painful progress to the ultimate goal of reunion and renewal. This seems to be an unconscious recognition of the truth, that the ecstatic immediate rediscovery of the longed-for face will not at once solve the problem of being. What is needed is a long redemptive experience in which the soul can be recreated.

Here, too, we come to the underlying significance of the Cupid and Psyche myth. Psyche represents the human, explicit mode of knowing: love belongs to the higher realm of *sub specie aeternitatis*. Expose love to explicit analysis, and it vanishes: the need is always to trust and be faithful to the loved one. But, of course, as with MacDonald and Lewis, once the love object has, despite all your trust, offered the final rejection by dying and has destroyed your world, that trust and faith seem impossible.

In light of these interpretations, it is not difficult to see how C. S. Lewis was fascinated by the Cupid and Psyche myth, or why he wrote out of it this new version. In this, as we might expect, there is much about modes of identity, trials, faces, and veils. But Lewis introduces a new feature: Orual, an ugly sister to Psyche. As Hannay says:

Her [Orual's] veil is her major identification with the faceless goddess, an ugly image. Her father first made her wear a veil to hide her ugliness; in her vision, it is her father who rips off the veil. She is stripped of both veil and clothing when she is judged, symbolising the baring of her soul before the gods. The veil is also important in the story of Istra, as told by the priest. The goddess's face is covered: "the thing that marred it was a band or scarf of some black stuff tied round the head of the image so as to hide its face—much like my own veil, but that mine was white." (Hannay 1981, p. 126)

Orual's story is of self-recognition, repentance, and redemption. But Christianity, as Hannay points out, is never mentioned—it is a pre-Christian story. Hannay calls it a "profound psychological story" and a "significant myth."

So it is the myth of Lewis's own psychic topography, and the psychological story of his own dealings with male and female within him. The story is dedicated to Joy Davidman, whom he married, and in it, as Hannay declares, "the misogyny of Lewis's earlier works is reversed" (Hannay 1981, p. 126). The story marks the discovery of love by Lewis.

Under his hearty exterior, says Hannay, Lewis was a sensitive and gentle person, one who believed he had an ugly soul (and this ugly soul, as we have seen, had sadistic fantasies and was guilty about masturbation). He loathed himself. Like Mark in *That Hideous Strength*, he was aware of "the lout and clown and clodhopper . . . the coarse male boor with horny hands . . ." (Hannay 1981, p. 125)—in himself. Orual then is the female element in Lewis himself, only a female element that is not right, not benign. She is too mannish; she is conscious of her mannish features, her unfeminine appearance, and she has a consequent shame. Her mother died when she was young and her father scorned and beat her. She is in this exactly parallel to Lewis, with Capron as the father-substitute, at the moment of his grief.

Psyche is the figure for whom he longs—the object of his *sehnsucht*, joy: "the sweetest thing in my life has been the longing, to reach the mountain, to find the place where beauty came from" (*Till We Have Faces*, p. 83). This is Orual, but it could be Lewis speaking of himself. Somewhere (as Howard puts it in *The Achievement of C. S. Lewis*, as with Lewis, "Somehow (where did the case go wrong? where?) . . . there is the frightening spectacle of love turning into tyranny and thence to hate. . . ." (Howard 1980, p. 164). The whole story is of hate, as is clear from the publisher's blurb:

> This re-interpretation of an old story has lived in the author's mind, thickening and hardening with the years. . . . That way, he could be said to have worked at it most of his life . . . the straight tale of barbarism, the mind of an ugly woman, dark idolatry and pale enlightenment at war with each other and vision, and the havoc which a vocation . . . works on human life. (*Till We Have Faces*, prelims, p. 1)

This introductory note makes great deal of sense, according to my interpretation.

As a footnote to the quest and the *sehnsucht,* we may add
Lewis's remark made in July 1963, "I had forgiven the cruel
schoolmaster who so darkened my childhood. I'd been trying
to do it for years" (quoted by Hannay 1981, p. 6). *Till We Have
Faces* was part of this process, too; and I believe its very painfulness is an indication of the way in which, in this story, Lewis
genuinely confronted his inner problems without falsity.

I believe that this story indirectly tells the "inner" story of
Lewis's psychic life when his mother died. Orual writes: "I
will begin my writing with the day my mother died, and they
cut off my hair" (*Till We Have Faces,* p. 12). We may recall
the cutting of Aslan's mane, and the castration theme that under-
lies the story: the loss of the mother drives the meaning out
of reality ("Oh, what a pity! All the gold gone!").

Throughout there are images of faces and veils, doubts about
one's appearance, and of inner fears. In one scene the children
are veiled because the king says "Do you think I want my queen
frightened out of her senses. Veils of course. And good thick
veils, too" (*Till We Have Faces,* p. 19). This brings Orual to
realize she is ugly. Somehow, the yearning to do with face-to-face
encounter is thought to be menacing in its intensity. A character
called the Fox, who has capronic qualities, urges the girls to
sing: ". . . and he kept on frowning and smiling and nodding
at us while we sang, and once he held up his hands in horror—
*pictures of things that had been done to girls in the stories
were dancing in my mind. . . .*" (*Till We Have Faces,* p. 20,
my italics). When the king's new bride, her stepmother, is carried
in "it was as if they were lifting a child." She is veiled. When
they take her veil off she is beautiful and frightened: "indeed
terrified." She has had her first view of the king:

> His was not a brow, a mouth, a girth, a stance or a voice to quiet
> a girl's fear . . . we . . . left the shivering, white body with its staring
> eyes in the king's bed. (p. 20)

Sexual intercourse has killed the first mother. Here is a revived
female from whom a new female element in the self is to be
born, but it is frightening, because of the intense need.

A later chapter is about the birth of Istra, who is Psyche,
from this wretched second wife. The king was hoping for a
prince. When he finds the baby is another girl he goes berserk,
killing a slave boy, who slips in a pool of sacrificial blood
with his wine cup. I believe this terrible scene reenacts the

monstrous Capron brutally attacking, in the little boys, the weakness he feared in himself.

Again, the atmosphere is full of images of the dying mother and Capron's violence, distributed among the female and male figures. At the heart of it is the problem of male and female—and, as Hannay sees, the problem of the female element in Lewis the child himself. Hannay is very insightful on this issue: "Again and again in the novel people say that it is a pity she is not a man; Orual herself says, 'The one sin the gods never forgive is that of being born women'" (quoted in Hannay 1981, p. 226).

I think we have to interpret this in the light of Lewis's insistence in Narnia that the girls should never become vulnerable by wetting their bowstrings. The sensitive female element in Lewis himself was brutally hurt by his experiences after his mother died, and he had to steel himself—it was as if he were being taught that this sensitive female self was ugly and bad. It is this aspect of the self that is embodied in Orual. As Hannay says. "There is more of Lewis than of Joy (Mrs. Lewis) in Orual," and declares that the three sisters Redival, Orual and Psyche may represent body, mind, and soul.

> The real struggle is between the rational mind, symbolised by Orual and her teacher the Fox, and the Soul, symbolised by Psyche in her *sehnsucht*, her longing for the god. (Hannay 1981, p. 126)

It is this kind of interpretation, of the inner dynamics of the self, that I have been trying to apply to *all* Lewis's fantasies. But I would suggest that while Orual may have represented in Lewis's explicit intentions a Platonic, rational mind, she rather represents that need and impulse which, taken as love, is, rather, *hate*.

In early chapters the analogies between birth and death are emphasized. The doors in the palace are kept open "the shutting of a door might shut up the mother's womb" (p. 22); "the sound of women wailing and beating the breast as I had heard them do it the day my mother died" (p. 22). Lewis has returned to the atmosphere of his mother's death chamber, with its blood and knives; and to Capron's school, with its boy victims and the king acting like an automaton. ("My father stared for a moment at his own dagger; stupidly, it seemed") (p. 23). He goes back to the time when the Psyche—his *sehnsucht*, his intellectual effort to hold his world together—was born.

The father, too, is clearly like the insane Capron: "the voice came roaring out of his chest loud enough to raise the roof."

. . . "He caught me by the hair, shook me to and fro . . ." (p. 24); "he was shaking the Fox by the throat." Then the king cries: "Faces, faces, faces! What are you all gaping it? It's made a man mad" (*Till We Have Faces*, p. 24). Whether or not Capron ever cried out so, it seems clear that the reference is to the bereaved child, cut off from his mother's face forever, who gazes at the father-figure who is in her place, and the hungry eyes provoke an insane response. (By contrast, Aslan offers a gaze that confirms the soul.) The Fox, by the way, seems to be the wise advisory aspect of the teacher, whether Capron or Kirke, Lewis's more benign tutor.

The topography here is like that of MacDonald. The escape from Glome ( = depression) is over the ridge of the Grey Mountains: the Fox must fly, and needs a poison as a possible means of escape (though Orual warns that those who go that way lie wallowing in filth in the land of the dead). They are all in terror of the king's murderous jokes. In this book, Lewis seems to be placing his own sadism as well as rejecting Capron's.

At one significant moment the king says "It's I who am asked to give up part of myself." Lewis's whole problem, which he addressed in this myth, is his loathing of part of himself. He is investigating why he wants to eliminate the more beautiful aspect of his female element being, while embracing his uglier aspect in this mode. The ugliness is emphasized by the king taking Orual into his chamber where he has a big mirror: since Ungit has asked for the best he can't "Give her that."

One can say that Lewis exploring the nature of woman, and thus his misogyny, in complex with the female element in himself. There is the primary phantom woman, Ungit, envious and full of oral hate. There is Psyche, love and beauty of being. There is Orual, deformed and ugly, yet full of concern and potential love but driven by a ruthless egoism; and there is the *femme moyen sensuelle* Redival. In the face of the imagined crises, the value of woman is rising. When the king declares "It's not in nature" for one sister to care for another, we are not on his side; in this story Lewis is genuinely groping towards love and to understand ambivalence.

At one point, Lewis suggests that only by becoming like a man can Orual get in touch with Psyche. From now on the story pursues the self's search for fulfilment by the *male* modes. In the end, as we shall see, the desire is to embrace the female element in oneself: but Orual's whole impulse (as was the child Lewis's) is to act by male doing modes. Orual seeks to see Psyche before she is sacrificed; so, she takes a sword and attacks

Bardia, who is the sympathetic guard. He wards off her blows, but wishes she were man, so he could train her. He is so impressed with her desperation and courage that he lets her in to Psyche, on condition she comes out when he knocks.

Lewis, as we have seen, has a penchant always to see his solutions in terms of assertive courage and the wielding of swords. The answer to his problems, even in fantasy, do not lie that way; and by degrees here, I feel, he comes to place these as *false* solutions. It is characteristic of his "false solution" assertiveness that there is as much beating, stabbing, sword-fighting, threats, physical assaults, and such violence throughout this story as in the others—only here the painful *consequences* are more real. "Sister, what have they done to you" (p. 74); "you'd be dying. . . . It's only in tales that a man dies the moment the steel's gone in and come out" (p. 73). The imagination begins to penetrate to the reality of bodily harm beyond the Cimmerian imaginings of infantile sadistic fantasy.

In the face of her impending doom, Psyche is resolute. I sense that Lewis felt that, under the duress of his misery as a child, he had to steel himself: "You must hold together and fight the closer . . . like soldiers in a hard battle. . . . Oh, your heart is of iron, I said" (p. 77). The only thing Psyche is afraid of is a world without gods. We glimpse Lewis's horror of a world that is only matter and has no point: the world of the "It" to which his dead mother was reduced.

> . . . Supposing—how if there were no God of the Mountain and even no holy shadow brute, and those who we tied to the tree, only die, day by day, from thirst and hunger . . . or are eaten piece-meal by the crows. . . . (p. 78)

Here there is an analogy with Christ: "How can I be the ransom for all Glome unless I die?" declares Psyche. "And if I am to go to the god, of course it must be through death. . . ." (p. 80). The Christian will try by this to pin the tale down to his mythology. I read it as expressing the need for ultimate regression: unless the individual who feels he has never been born experiences real ultimate regression, he can never begin to be.

> ". . . death opens a door out of a little, dark room (that's all the life we have known before it) into a great, real place where the true sun shines and we shall meet—." (p. 81)

Here, the language and thought are very close to those of George MacDonald.

As I hope I have shown, it is in feelings about the mother and death that we find the origins of Lewis's misogyny, for a bereaved child inevitably hates the mother who has died and rejected him, and wishes to be revenged on her. In one sense his restoration to full being *does* demand the death of the mother: it is necessary to let her go into the world of death, and this parallels the preoccupation with death as rebirth.

The story is too complex to examine in more detail. But one can say of it, I believe, that in every episode Lewis engages, in a "felt life" way with the inner needs that impel his fantasies. Each character seems to symbolize a dynamic in the unconscious. For example, Bardia relieves Orual's apathy at one point by giving her lessons in sword-fighting: we may, I think, conjecture that Lewis is telling us that when he was sunk in a deeply depressed state after the loss of his mother what relieved him was false-male-doing: "Sweat is the kindest creature . . . far better than philosophy as a cure for ill thoughts. . . ." (p. 99). Her frock gets in the way of her sword-fighting; but even though she is a girl, her ugliness makes her ineligible as a potential bride. Bardia declares, "if a man was blind . . . she'd make him a good wife" (p. 100).

Orual has moments of delight when she sees how beautiful the world is, and moments of despair under the frightful cliffs (the literary analogy of this journey is that of Sir Gawaine in *Sir Gawaine and the Grene Knight*). As with so many perilous journeys, it seems in the end as if it were futile: "I had not thought of our journeys being so vain: nothing to do, nothing to gather. The emptiness of my life was to begin at once" (p. 107).

They find only a ruby (a relic of the mother's eyes?). But, beyond the mountain, they find the fertile secret valley of the god. Suddenly, on the far side of a river, stands Psyche. She seems perhaps a goddess, she is so "brightface." It is like one of those moments in MacDonald when (at last) the dead mother is found:

> She was tanned by sun and wind, and clothed in rags; but laughing, her eyes like two stars, her limbs smooth and rounded, and (but for the rags) no sign of beggary or hardship about her. (p. 111)

Only those with god's blood in their veins can cross into that other country. The way Psyche feeds Orual reminds her of childhood: "It brought back so many of her plays in childhood"

(p. 113). Here we have, as so often in MacDonald, memories of the mother's care and play. There follow characteristic passages in which one individual disbelieves another, when the other has found a new reality, for Orual's nonbelieving response is very threatening to Psyche. The episode recaptures Lewis's problems as a child as what was "real"—the bleak dull reality of reality, the literal pretend-worlds of Animal Land, the imaginary fantasies. Winnicott (above) discusses the case of the boy who was ordered about by a "wizard" who ran to his (lost) mother only to find traumatically it was not her. Here, where Orual has "really" found Psyche (but she is in the mysterious world of the god), we have a parallel moment (very similar also to some moments in MacDonald's fantasies):

> You have seen a lost child in a crowd run up to a woman whom it takes for its mother and how the woman turns round and shows the face of a stranger, and then the look in the child's eyes, silent a moment before it begins to cry. Psyche's face was like that; checked, blank; happiest assurance suddenly dashed all to pieces. (*Till We Have Faces*, p. 125)

Where is the god's palace? You are in it, declares Psyche: ". . . with white face, staring hard into my eyes, she said, 'But *this* is it, Orual! It is here! You are standing on the stairs of the great gate'" (p. 125).

In the scene that follows, Lewis is, I am sure, exploring his own strange ambivalence about what is real. The disturbing problem is a deep distrust of reality, a fear that (as she experiences later in life) things may change unexpectedly:

> Everything I saw was different from what I touched. I would lay my hand on the table and feel warm hair instead of smooth wood, and the corner of the table would shoot out a hot, wet tongue and lick me. (p. 129)

When she believed she was looking at Psyche's palace and did not see it: ". . . the horror was the same; a sickening discord, *a rasping together of two worlds, like the two bits of a broken bone*" (p. 129; my italics). The confusion of reality is near-autistic. It also records a failure of the process of "disillusionment" (as Winnicott calls it) between mother and infant; that positive process by which we find ourselves relating to a real world. This arises after the mother's death, when the yearning for her is so strong that it seems as if her vision (which is Psyche) is more real than the real world.*

This problem has its origins in some failure of the processes by which the mother presents the world to us, and is bound up with the processes of seeing and being seen.

The anguish of Orual is spun from Lewis's problems over the reality sense, his strong fantasy life, his literalness (as about demons), and his terror that the one world (the fantasy world where the dead, idolized mother was) might flow into the other as well as his deep distrust of the nature of reality itself—a legacy of the time when Atlantis, the "Mother Continent," sunk away beneath his feet.

In the very painfulness of some of the episodes, we experience feelings that are not those of enjoying the humiliation and punishment of others, but something like the discovery of *concern*, the reality of the effect of our actions on others: the root of all "ethical living" as psychoanalysis sees it.

At another significant moment, although Orual supposes she is acting for love, Psyche sees that what she has to deal with is hate:

> You are indeed teaching me about kinds of love which you did not know. It is like looking into a deep pit. I am not sure whether I like your kind better than hatred. Oh, Orual—to take my love for you, because you know it goes down to my very roots and cannot be diminished by any other, newer love, and then to make of it a tool, a weapon, a think of policy and mastery, an instrument of torture. . . . I begin to think I never knew you. . . . (*Till We Have Faces*, p. 174)

Psyche declares she will trust her husband to understand her compliance with Orual's blackmail. In this she shows her capacity for a kind of love, involving trust, that contrasts powerfully with Orual's mode, which Lewis is coming to see as *hate*: hate being the impulse to force the other to obey one's will.

This is, I believe, an important moment in Lewis, when he realized that the demand made upon a love object can be hate, and that the blackmailing will is hate, for this is what he calls love elsewhere: the submission to an authoritarian insistence.

---

*On the philosophical issues involved here, from a very different point of view, see "Seeing and Knowing: the Epistemology of C. S. Lewis's *Till We Have Faces*," Peter J. Schakel, VII, vol. 4, p. 84.

But what is it that Orual is seeking, in terms of Lewis's inner mythology? If Psyche is his sensitive female self, what is it that his ugly self is seeking to do to her? Presumably, the problem is to become reconciled to the nature of her sensual life—the face of female sexuality and to make that which is dark and filthy clearly visible as divine? In all this, we have the discovery of ambivalence, of pity, and concern, as

> I never heard weeping like that before or after; not from a child, nor a man wounded in the palm, nor a tortured man, nor a girl dragged off to slavery from a taken city. If you heard the woman you most hate in the world weep so, you would go to comfort her. You would fight your way through fire and spears to reach her. And I knew who wept, and what had been done to her, and who had done it. (p. 183)

Again and again in this story Lewis explores the ways in which one may develop solutions to one's vulnerability. Orual builds up her (male-like) prowess by sword lessons:

> My aim was to build up more and more that strength, hard and joyless . . . by learning, fighting, and labouring *to drive all the woman out of me.* (p. 193)

—as Lewis as a boy did when his mother died. In this story, we encounter again the question as to whether women should fight. Orual proposes a challenge to Trunia's enemy brother Argon, and offers to fight him herself. Bardia, who has taught her swordsmanship, declares: "Oh lady, lady, it's a thousand pities they didn't make you a man" (*Till We Have Faces*, p. 206). Lewis is at his happiest, bracing for a battle; but the context reveals that this enthusiasm springs out of the need to steel oneself after the loss of the mother, and the need to deny one's femininity. Orual declares: "Nature's hand slipped when she made me anyway. . . . If I'm to be hard-featured as a man, why shouldn't I fight like a man, too?" (p. 207).

Orual is determined to fight Argon; but as she contemplates it, she thinks of Psyche, and comes to feel that *Psyche is her enemy*—that is, her female element may, in these aggressive circumstances, be inimical to her. But then she thinks that if Argon does kill her, it would be the best thing in the world. She was losing herself in queenliness: "If Orual could vanish altogether into the Queen, the gods would almost be cheated" (p. 210). As they prepare for the fight, Bardia warns Orual that the actual killing, plunging a sword into flesh, is the greatest difficulty. She practices on a pig; but at least here, we have a contemplation of the real effects of violence. The Fox is thinking of leaving her. If she lives after the fight, she may have to live without the Fox: "He had been the central pillar of my whole life" (p. 218). This is all characteristic Lewis territory: preparation for a fight, and especially a *woman* preparing for a fight, while there is an associated fear of relinquishing the male stance.

Orual is prepared for the fight in a hood or mask of fine stuff. The female must be given a strong exterior. When she goes out, she feels like Psyche going out to heal. Is this what the god meant when he said "You also shall be Psyche"? Is it that she, too, shall take on the reparative mode?

When she sees Argon, she thinks of the word *kill*; and Lewis here again reveals his own sadistic excitement about this. Here we are surely involved in his profoundest misconception that the exercise of ultimate hate is the way to solve his problems? Lewis is fascinated by the details:

> I gave the straight thrust and then, all in one motion, wheeled my sword round and cut him deeply in the inner leg where no surgery will stop the bleeding. . . . (*Till We Have Faces*, p. 228)

She jumps back: "so my first man-killing bespattered me less than my first pig-killing." And Lewis is fascinated also by the look of a man dying (like "Rudolph," whose fantasies this much resembles):

> [T]he change that presently came over his face. . . . I have since seen the faces of other men as they began to believe, 'This is death'. You will know it if you have seen it; life more alive than ever, a raging, tortured intensity of life. . . . (p. 228)

There is a hint that this killing is a sexual act and so perhaps this represents that sexual act that is to restore the world, as the original parental act has blighted it?

> I felt myself changed, too, as if something had been taken away from me. I have often wondered if women feel like that when they lose their virginity. (p. 229)

Such a hint reveals that Lewis's fantasied sword-fights (and all the preoccupation with weapons) have a deeply sexual connotation, to do with the link between life and death (again, like "Rudolph's"): no doubt to be traced to his sexual excitement when being beaten by Capron, when he was in a state of grief while dreading that his mother died from sexual acts performed by the father. Somehow, there is a strange satisfaction in these fantasies, to do with a rediscovery of the mother: "a little sweet-sharp prickle of pride thrust up inside me" (p. 229). She becomes ultimately male, and yearns for the breast: "Oh, for that bowl of milk, drunk alone in the cool dairy, the first day I ever used a sword" (p. 229). A feast is prepared, even with, as Orual says, "my sword not yet wiped from the blood of my first battle."

> Now for the first time in all my life (and the last), I was gay. A new world, very bright, seemed to be opening all round me.
> It was of course the gods' old trick; blow the bubble up big before you prick it. (p. 231)

Behind such feelings about women lurk, surely, the most complex fears to do with the breast and the sadistic fantasies of the infant that focus on it?

We can read *Till We Have Faces* as a dramatization of various psychic entities or dynamics in the inner life of Lewis himself. We can read it as an attempt to seek what the Jungians call 'individuation', by discovering and embracing components of the self. Bardia has gone to his wife who is in labor. Orual feels a double loneliness:

> . . . for Bardia, for Psyche. Not separable. The picture, the impossible fool's dream, was that all should have been different from the very beginning and he would have been my husband and Psyche our daughter. Then I would have been in labour . . . with Psyche . . . and to me he would have been coming home. (p. 233)

Orual takes to drink; she is not the "girl crying in the garden."

> No one, cold, hungry, and banished, was shivering there, longing and not daring to come in. It was the chains swinging at the well. It would be folly to get up and go out and call again; Psyche, Psyche, my only love . . . I am the Queen; I'll kill Orual too. (pp. 233–34)

It is as if she denies dependence and her need to embrace her true female element being: that element (like the ghost of Cathy in *Wuthering Heights*) can go on crying in the darkness. She is strong since she has killed a man; taken upon herself the ultimate (false) male doing, and in doing so, denied her true self. It is as if Orual, as the (false) female self, has gone as far as she could along the path of false solutions. Here, nothing is solved by the process of learning "not to wet your bowstring."

Throughout her reign, the queen rules, but the true Orual is denied:

> I locked her up or laid her asleep as best I could somewhere deep down inside me; she lay curled there. It was like being with child, but reversed; the thing I carried in me grew slowly smaller and less alive. (p. 235)

This image of an unborn self recurs in the fantasies of schizoid individuals, as Guntrip shows. The essential rebirth has not happened.

During her reign, becoming more male, she kills other men. She remains veiled, but people say she has a beautiful (mannish) face. Her real strength lay in two things: having two good counsellors, the Fox and Bardia ("I learned from them a thousand things about men" [p. 237]; and her second strength was in her veil.

The myth is virtually the story of Lewis's psychic life: he lost the source of knowledge of femininity when his mother (Psyche) died; he learned to steel himself by learning manhood (from the Fox—from Kirke and the benign side of Capron). He, like Orual, had to veil himself because he had not yet found his identity (as we have seen he often, in adult life, postured before mirrors). Some said the face behind the veil was "frightful beyond endurance—a pig's, bear's, cat's, or elephant's face."

> The best story was that I had no face at all; if you stripped off my veil you'd find emptiness. (*Till We Have Faces*, p. 237)

These (schizoid) problems of being nothing, or only repulsive, remain unsolved.

The myth is clearly not a Christian myth about purity of soul; it may derive from Socratic ideas of the good and the beautiful. But, rather, in terms of Lewis's myth of the unconscious, it is about love. Orual's love has been all hate—all incorporative hunger—except her love for Psyche. To Psyche love and its richness are natural, to be simply gathered.

Can the story be read at all as a Christian story? It ends as other Lewis stories end, with a complete rejection or loss of the old ugly self, in a merging with another: but is the last "you" in any sense the Christian God? Or can it be understood in terms of Platonic ideas?

It seems to me only to make sense as a story belonging to Lewis's mythology of the unconscious of the search for the dead mother, and her capacity to "Be For," which is also the search to find one's own female element being, its power and beauty and the search for love—the capacity to love, which is not an envious or rapacious, or a jealous hunger, but a love of the other for the other's sake, in which sense of unique meeting of being to be being lies the sense of meaning in existence.

In this we eventually find our true capacity to be, "when we have faces." The significant thing about this book is that the male-doing "solutions" such as those to which Orual is given are rejected as unsatisfactory: as hate. In the end, by the pictures shown by the Fox, they are even seen to be based in their voracious destructiveness on jealousy, on envy. The impulse to "battle" is even seen as empty by comparison with the quest for inner transformation. But in the other fantasies, whether in Narnia or Perelandra or the world of NICE, the male, "doing", aggressive solutions are not only celebrated, they are portrayed as the essence of Christianity. And yet here they belong to the ugly errors of Orual. *Till We Have Faces* marks a significant departure, and shows the kingdom of God to be an inward condition; the discovery of feminine element being a different kind of quest—of coming to love oneself and "life" rather than hating it and seeking to have it torn away. The redemption of Orual, in her becoming Psyche, is an embracing of the self, in all its ambivalence. It is, one might say, at the opposite pole from the story of the sinful Eustace whose foul (human) flesh is stripped away by an authoritarian Aslan.

Though *Till We Have Faces* is not at all a didactic Christian myth among Lewis's fantasies, it seems to me the most Christian in that it pursues a genuine engagement with ambivalence, with our admixture of love and hate, and a true search for being. I have paid it the devotion of close attention to its detail because I believe it confirms, even in an uncanny way, that my kind of phenomenological interpretation of Lewis's fantasies, in terms of his agony of soul at the unconscious level, is the correct approach to his meanings.

\* \* \* \*

I belong, of course, to a critical school that believes creative writing to be a form of thinking about experience; and Lewis offers his fiction in that spirit, too, though he sees his work as bearing a Christian message. Oddly enough, I suggest, *Till We Have Faces,* although the most pagan in spirit, seems to me the most Christian of his writings. But in the other two stories examined, he offers to write a fable that conveys his kind of mess age. In *That Hideous Strength,* he offered to uphold the Christian faith against the *hubris* of science; in *Perelandra* he offered to uphold this faith against instruments of the powers of evil, including a representative of humanism, Weston, who is "possessed" by the devil, in a world in which the Green Woman is a malevolent influence.

However, as around the latter figure, who seems to have affinities with the White Witch in Narnia, we find the "other" private mythology of Lewis's fantasy intruding. Looked at in my phenomenological terms, these stories become further explorations of the possibility of finding the dead mother and removing from the world the threats which her loss was brought. In *Perelandra,* too, there are intense images, as we have seen, of the longed-for rebirth and the breast, from which primal reexperience a new life is to begin. In *Till We Have Faces,* however, what we have is less a fantasy of refinding the lost mother than a perplexed engagement with the dynamics of male and female element, and an exploration of the ambivalence of the dynamics of the psyche towards the discovery of the possibilities of love rather than hate. Other critics have noted that in this work Lewis becomes less misogynist, and moves closer to the realities of human make-up.

In the two space fiction stories, however, the underlying mythology of Lewis's unconscious mars the creative thinking. I was most interested in Lewis's attempt to deal with the arrogance of science, in *That Hideous Strength,* but sadly disappointed in the event. For instead of exerting against scientific hubris the religious sense that (in Leavis's words) "man does not belong to himself," to emphasize the claims of the "Ahnung," or the obligations imposed upon us by the recognition of the mysteries of the universe that we do not understand, and cannot aspire to control and exploit, Lewis reverts to irrationalism, magic, and "mental rage." Instead of urging us to exert awe and intelligence in the face of the mysteries of life, he plunges into mumbo-jumbo—revives Merlin and black magic in the name of Christianity, and then displays, in an aside, a deeply erosive failure of seriousness anyway, as if engagement with the menace of scientific hubris was only a donnish game. The same effect follows, in *Perelandra*, from a disastrous moment when the hero falls into a playful blasphemy at the very instant he attacks the Un-Man, thereby turning the moment of supreme conflict into one of playful sadistic perversion.

Despite the assumed gravity of tone, and the allegorical assumptions, these fantasies seem to fail seriously as creative art. One does not quite know how to take them, and if one does take them, the upshot is wrong. But here I have been concerned predominantly to convey how they confirm my analysis of the "Narnia" stories.

# Conclusions

# Conclusions: On the "Upshot" of Fantasies

While there can be no simple connection between the morality of fiction and life, it seems clear that some meanings in literature can belong to true solutions to the problem of identity and meaning, while others can be false. But here again we must be careful, as I have already implied, because we would find ourselves in serious difficulties if we began to transfer to life the solutions endorsed in many fairy tales. There are other considerations to be invoked here—the way in which fairy stories bring out into the open subjective dynamics of which both child and parent may be afraid, for instance—so the story generates a relief that (at least) we know life contains these terrors. This is also one of the effects of tragedy: we now have seen the worst that faces us, since we have been thrown into this existence, with all its mutability and mortality. And then there is the element by which deeply troubling elements in our subjective life, like hate and sexual fears, are explored allegorically, as when the princess kisses the toad: in such a form, a child can bear to look at these disturbing realities, just as, in dreams, the child may explore the problem of his or her relationships with adults, in terms of animals that talk, because he or she is not yet ready to explore them in terms of human beings. This is one advantage of the "as if" mode of all fiction and poetry.

With Lewis's "Narnia" books, however, there are a number of points that must be raised in trying to estimate their value as art and especially as art for the child. They and the adult fantasies have an "upshot."*

Probably most children simply enjoy the "Narnia" stories as good yarns of a fairy-tale kind. But there is the question, as we have seen, that for many they are offered didactically as Christian stories—and so analogies about Christ and the spiritual values He offers. There is quite a strong pressure of endorsement

---

*This useful word comes from F. R. Leavis's classic debate with George Santayana about Shakespeare's *Macbeth*. See *Scrutiny* IV, p. 365 and XII, p. 249.

271

here, at large, and this must be taken into account, for the stories seem quite objectionable if they are taken as Christian parables. And this is not either, as I have shown, a question of the enthusiasm of the parish magazine. It is clear from many internal passages that Lewis is offering these tales in that spirit, and he wanted to *teach children* by them.

Moreover, as I hope I have also shown, he does this in a certain way. Behind his tone there is a certain kind of authoritarian insistence, for often in his work he implies that if you do not accept his kind of religion something terrible will happen to you—and, indeed, to the whole world. This, of course, has been the emphasis throughout the ages in a great deal of Christian culture. But Lewis often puts behind his attitude some disturbing persuasive energies—as we manifest in Aslan's growl, his claws, and the more solemn moments of Lewis's fictions, in which he creates a certain kind of ominous dread. There is also in this a certain kind of paranoia—those who are not with us must be against us.

Then, it is clear from other sources as well as from the tales that Lewis himself actually believes in the worlds he creates, despite the "voulu" element that some have detected. He actually believed that the world was threatened by real demons, which were hanging about in the universe trying to conquer man and the world. His belief in Christianity was a *literal* belief, and he believed that the Christian myth was the one myth that was real. So, while he writes what seem to be fairy stories, he really meant them, and wrote them with the deliberate intention to work upon children and to convert them to his faith, to "save" them.

But, if we call the bluff of his grave admonitory tone, what is "wrong" in Lewis's moral scheme? If everything will be "right" when Aslan comes in sight anyway, how are we guided in our exploration of right and wrong, true and false? Certain very petty matters of childish behavior are dwelt on: it is important not to lie, sulk, or tease. It is sinful to be greedy, deceitful, or selfish. Of course, when it comes to treachery, like Edmund's original betrayal, we may fall in with Lewis's sense of the gravity of the offence. There is often a seriousness of discrimination in Lewis, against "sins" which are no more than trivial manifestations of bad manners, and so out of all proportion—except, of course, when one takes into account the *unconscious* meaning.

So, when Aslan is crucified, to save Edmund, we cannot help

feeling this is a disproportionate sacrifice for a grumpy little
boy who has, in any case, been bewitched by a very cunning
wicked queen, and poisoned by her magic Turkish Delight. What
is it that Aslan does for the children? What does it mean when
he commends their taking off their "elastic"? When he urges
them to wipe their swords? When he leads them to fight?

Any fable which symbolizes spiritual struggles must surely
be judged, whether by Christians or by nonbelievers, in terms
of what its implications are for our ethical living here and now,
by its "upshot" which reveals its morality. What must surely
make us doubtful is the tone in these children's fantasies that
encourages such excitement about justified killing. I have discussed this problem at the beginning. Let me once more remind
the reader of this particular tone.

> Eustace stood with his heart beating: terribly, hoping and hoping
> that he would be brave. He had never seen anything . . . that made
> his blood run so cold as that line of dark-faced bright-eyed man. . . .
> Then he heard a twang-and-zipp on his left and one Calormene
> fell: then twang-and-zipp again and the Satyr was down. "Oh, well
> done, daughter!" came Tirian's voice; and then the enemy were
> upon them. . . . The Bull was down, shot through the eye by an
> arrow from Jill. . . . "Little *swine*," shrieked Eustace, dancing in
> his rage. "Dirty, filthy, treacherous little brutes. . . ." "That's a rotten
> shot!" she said as her first arrow sped towards the enemy and flew
> over their heads. But she had another on the string next moment:
> she knew that speed was what mattered . . . one of her own arrows
> hit a man, and another a Narnia wolf. . . .
>     "Oh well done. *Well* done!" shouted Jill. . . .
>     . . . The Unicorn was tossing men as you'd toss hay on a fork. . . .
> Tash made one peck and the monkey was gone. . . .
>     "Serve him right," said Eustace. . . . (LB, passim)

The "enemies" are simply "given" as such: they offer, because
they are enemies, a menace which must be responded to. There
is little or no identifying with their "sins." There is little sense
of "there but for the Grace of God, go I"—indeed, any such
response is inhibited by the way in which those who are depicted as "enemies" are deprived of human qualities, and are
dwarfs, evil spirits, witches, Calormenes, or whatever. They are
"vermin."

As we have seen, this is true in an even more extreme form
in the adult fantasies. Not only is the world caught between
angels, "bent" angels or fallen spirits or demons. Human beings

who become inimical, like the scientists or Weston, are actually taken over so that their bodily shell is inhabited by a possessive spirit that does not deserve human pity, only exorcism or destruction. The problem of good and evil is therefore dealt with exclusively in terms of projection and splitting. I have tried to show how Lewis takes his inner fears of the threatening "baby" inside him, his phantom woman who haunts him, and his sense of threatening vulnerability, and projects these outward over others, and attacks them in them. "Battle" thus becomes a mode of feeling strong, when the real problems are fear of emptiness, weakness, loss of meaning, and the problem of ambivalence, of how to reconcile the admixture in oneself of love and hate. The significant exceptions to this pattern of splitting and projection are the moments with Digory, in his anguish about his mother's decline, and the story *Till We Have Faces* in which the pain of mortality, ambivalence, identity, and gender and meaning are allowed to be encountered, in the creative drama, with pain and grave distress.

For the most part, the spiritual conflict is all externalized; and the individual can only struggle to choose to belong to the "right" party. Here I believe the retreat into primitive modes, of black and white externalization of the moral conflict, may be linked to the powerfully authoritarian position into which Lewis was moulded in his prep school, by the brutal Capron. For what one finds in Lewis's didactic stories is a sense that the moral problem is externalized into an already existing pattern, "out there." One only has to decide whether or not to "fit in" to it. So *there is no real existential freedom of choice in his spiritual scheme.* But then having become one of the "right" party, one can be completely *self-righteous.* Those who have given in to the demons and devils and eldils or whatever have forfeited their right to be given any kind of quarter or compassion—and in the fantasies, of course, they are often, or more often than not, made into nonhuman entities: the opposition is dehumanized into Calormenes or Monopods or dwarfs, or whatever and so, the protagonists can be totally ruthless in dealing with them. Moreover, there is a strong sense in this, that because they have given themselves over to wickedness, they only deserve what they get; and so are actually *better* sent to the "other world" of death or hell.

Such simple morality is often a feature of fairy stories, but in Lewis it is endorsed with a special kind of fervor and is combined, of course, with the Christian message. But even if one examines them apart from that homiletic impulse, to consider the artistic quality of his fantasies, I believe it mars them. Lewis himself actually made a pertinent analysis of this kind of weakness in discussing George MacDonald. He is writing about *What's Mine's Mine:*

> I wonder did he indulge, (day dreamily) an otherwise repressed fund of indignation by putting up in his novels bogeys to whom his heroes could make the stunning retorts and deliver in real life. I am certain that this is morally as well as artistically dangerous and I'll tell you why the *pleasure* of anger—the gnawing attraction which makes one return again and again to its theme—lies, I believe, in the fact that one feels entirely righteous oneself only when one is angry. Then the other person is pure black, and you are pure white. But in real life society always returns to break the dream. In fiction you can put absolutely *all* the right with no snags or reservations, on the side of the hero (with whom you identify yourself) and all the wrong on the side of the villain. You thus revel in unearned self-righteousness which would be vicious even if it were earned. Haven't you noticed how people with a fixed hatred, say, of Germans or Bolshevists, *resent* anything which is pleaded in extenuation, however small, of their suppressed crimes. The enemy must be unredeemed black. While all the time one *does* nothing and enjoys the feeling of perfect superiority over the faults one is never tempted to commit. (Quoted in Green and Hooper 1974, p. 114)

This is very insightful, but it also describes exactly what Lewis himself does in the "Narnia" books and his adult fantasies. Moreover, underlying the dynamics is his own unconscious deep fear and hatred of woman, as we have seen, and his impulse to put under control forces that threaten him.

I must leave an analysis of the unconscious meaning of the fantasies of George MacDonald for another place; but it is highly significant that Lewis owes so much to MacDonald, whose own problems arose, as I believe, from the loss of his mother and his traumatic weaning. As we have seen, Lewis spoke of MacDonald's work "baptizing" his imagination, and he links the influence with death. Of *Phantastes* he says: ". . . if this was a dream, it was a dream in which one at least felt *strangely* vigilant" (Green and Hooper 1974, p. 45; my italics). I would suggest that this means Lewis recognized it as a kind of paranoid-schizoid fantasy that he could make use of.

The whole book had about it a sort of cool, mourning innocence, and also, quite unmistakeably, a certain quality of Death, *good* Death. . . . What it actually did to me was to convert, even to baptize (that was where the Death came in) my imagination. . . . (quoted in Green and Hooper 1974, p. 45)

What Lewis found in MacDonald was a mythology of the sudden weaning and loss of the mother and of the urgent search for a redemption in her eyes, towards an adequate relationship with reality: the need for a quest in the "other world" to find new birth. It is interesting to note Lewis's remarks about "baptism" and death, "good Death." One infant belief that MacDonald could not escape from was the fear that since the lost mother is in the "World of Death," she may threaten death when found; adored and revived, she may become malignant. Another related fear is that it is sexual intercourse that has killed her so, there is a dread in dehumanized fantasy, that love is deadly. So, MacDonald's woman, in the end, is Lilith. It is clear, surely, that it is this same malignant woman who had blighted the world of Narnia; that Jadis is Lilith, and in Lewis's letters we find that "Lilith" tempts him to masturbate and sin.

What MacDonald's work offered Lewis was a kind of mythology at the unconscious level about woman and death. But from MacDonald, too, he took elements which belong to MacDonald's failure to solve the problems of the "Quest for the Lost Mother." Towards the end of his life MacDonald fell into a deep depression, which meant he spoke to no one for the last years of his life; and this suggests that his problems had to do with "finding reality" and the question of concern and its related issue of gratitude. There are times in MacDonald, as at the end of *The Princess and Curdie*, where he seems to lose all hope for the future. As I have suggested, *The Last Battle* has some elements of this.

C. S. Lewis obviously took much else from MacDonald. The problem for Curdie of whether he believes in the old great-great-grandmother was translated into the problem of whether or not the Pevensie children believe in Narnia and Aslan. The old lady of "Terrible power and authority" (as Naomi Lewis puts it in her introduction to *The Princess and the Goblins*) becomes Aslan. The brutality inflicted on the bad characters becomes the aggressiveness in the "Narnia" books. The end of Narnia is the end of Gwyntystorm.

Lewis also took over the body analogy of quest (see the first pages of *The Princes and Curdie*), the topology of the inside of the mother's body, and the "underground" world where she is. But he also took over something of MacDonald's paranoia: the black and white morality of necessary aggression ("there are plenty of bad things that need killing" p. 32). He took the implication that children have an imaginative power that they later lose ("he was quickly turning into a commonplace man . . ." p. 17). He took the timelessness (the lady says some of Curdie's questions would take "a few thousand years" to answer). He took from MacDonald the concept of flocks of ugly nonhuman creatures opposing one, and the fantasies of vengeance.

But there are more human elements in MacDonald, like Curdie's discovery of concern, and his urge towards reparation over the death of the dove. In *The Princess and the Goblin* and in the first half of the second book, there is a great deal about the "change in a child's heart," and the power of love. MacDonald's fantasy becomes more like Lewis's, towards the end of that second book, when the author seems to lose direction and hope, and to despair, and at certain desperate moments in *Lilith*.

When it comes to the fantasy mother, however, at least in the Curdie books, MacDonald's use of the great-great-grandmother is, I think, very different from Lewis's use of Aslan. She is omniscient, but she isn't omnipotent. She represents the internalization of the good mother, who operates to encourage the child to have faith in love. Her thread which guides is, as it were, the capacity for ethical living by which one guides oneself, by which one finds right action, and judges whether others are genuine (as by touching their hands). The strings which Aslan provides are puppet strings or bowstrings. The old lady's thread is spun from her loving devotion as she works away for her children. She seems a more adequate and benign internalization of the mother. So MacDonald's stories offer more love and hope—more *humanness*—than Lewis's.

A comparison of these writers, however, certainly reveals the urgency of their quest. Writing fantasies was a life-or-death matter for both. Lewis admitted his "lust," for his fantasies, at floating islands, of golden skies, and other realms. ("'Perelandra!' said Lewis with such a passionate longing in his voice.")

But one significant aspect of fantasy that Lewis may have picked up from MacDonald is the inclination to fantasize *justified cruelty* and murder vindicated by that self-righteousness which is convinced that destruction of those who belong to the world or to the devil is entirely acceptable. MacDonald may have picked up this aspect from Calvinism.

The lesson of the "Narnia books" is that true followers of Aslan *must learn to kill,* and must learn to have contempt for the creatures they kill ("All that foul brood . . .") It is Aslan who issues the instruction: "Whatever happens never forget to wipe your sword" (LWW, p. 121); and it is in his name that the "vermin" are flung in the pit.* It is difficult to know how much of MacDonald's work Lewis read, but in his adult novels MacDonald writes a great deal of physical violence. In *Alec Forbes,* for instance, there is gloating on the details of a whipping:

> A swollen cincture, like a red snake, has risen around his waist, and from one spot in it the blood was oozing. It looked as if the lash had cut him in two. . . . (See *The Golden Key* [Wolff 1961, p. 306] and passim on sadism in MacDonald)

In *Paul Faber: Surgeon* Juliet Faber confesses a premarital love affair to her husband, pulls her nightgown over her head, and hands him a whip, kneeling naked before him: "Do, Paul, take the whip and strike me. I long for my deserts at your hand. . . . Will you not be my saviour and forgive my sin?" Her husband, however, throws the whip out of the window. MacDonald, as Robert Lee Wolff points out, condemns Faber for not beating her!

> Had he struck once, had he seen the purple streak rise in the snow, that instant in his pride-frozen heart would have melted into a torrent of grief; he would have flung himself on the floor beside her, and in an agony of pity over her and horror at his own sacrilege, would have clasped her to his bosom and baptized her in the tears of remorse and repentance; and from that moment they would have been married indeed. . . . (Wolff 1961, p. 308)

In the background of this, I believe, we may detect the punitive conscience of Calvinistic tradition. There is a great deal in MacDonald where the infliction of pain is done in full righteousness, and for the purpose of bringing about a good end: "Whip me, and that will make me good" (Wolff 1961, p. 308). In at least

---

*"'Quick!' . . . shouted the voice of Aslan, '. . . I see another wolf in the thickets . . . After him, all of you!'" (LWW, p. 121). Aslan is very much a militant sergeant-major.

one work by MacDonald, murder itself is done in full self-righteousness, and without any kind of remorse or guilt. This is in his first verse play, *Within and Without*, in which the hero Julian stabs a wicked noble who has exerted his power over a woman, Julia, whom he loves. She has not committed any act of unfaithfulness, but that she has been tempted is enough! For a moment she has listened to the voice of an adulterer when her future husband is preoccupied with the voice of God. Wolff points out that "he stabs the villain and *briskly wipes his dagger on the dead man's coat*: and never, throughout the whole play, does he express a word of regret for his action. . . ." (p. 25, my italics). This, says Wolff, is a little hard to reconcile with his "absorbing hunger for individual communication with the source of life."

> But MacDonald puts the explanation into Julian's mouth at the very moment of the stabbings: *"If man will be devils,"* he says, *"They are better in hell than here."* (p. 29; my italics)

MacDonald, says Wolff, "never doubted the righteousness of a righteous blow."

There is behind this pattern of self-righteous violence and murder an element of the belief that this world does not matter; any trial we go through in it is preparation for "the life to come." In the light of this belief, it could be an act of charity, or at least devotional appropriateness, to send a villain to hell. It belongs to a kind of vestige of Calvinistic determinism, and certainly to a kind of thinking in which members of the faith have a clear route mapped out for them towards fulfilment in a future state. From this point of view righteous killing can be "pure," and absolutely proper; it is, virtually "called for," as are the crimes committed by some individuals who are impelled to murder women and prostitutes because they have a "call" from God to do this. (Again, the story of the boy and his "wizard" who commanded him to steal seems relevant.)

Whatever the theology of such beliefs, it seems obvious that they could be combined with a very dangerous kind of solution to the problems of identity and relationship with the world.

As we have seen, C. S. Lewis obviously hated certain infant-like weaknesses of his own and offered the advice to "knock the little bastards' brains out" (*Reflections on the Psalms*, see above p. 77). The belief that righteous acts of violence are justified against sinners could very well take the form of these threats from weakness being projected over others, and attacked in them. This is what I suspect the Reverend Capron did when he went for certain children whose social status he despised; and this, I believe, taught Lewis the pattern of projecting his own weaknesses over those who seemed to embody them and attacking these in them. Moreover, in the "Narnia" books, he makes this a powerful message: to behave like this is only to show one's "loyalty to Christ." Yet they tend to endorse a pattern or structure in dealing with the world that is based on hate.

We tell children fairy stories, even when these seem to endorse aggression, because they are a form of "working out" fears of the conflicting dynamics within the self. As Derek Brewer and others have pointed out, they enact dynamics in the inner world to do with Oedipal rivalry, hungry feelings, and death. On the whole, however, despite their moments when the child is encouraged to feel "good job!" as when the Big Dog throws the wicked people in the air, they do not, on the whole, endorse one particular kind of solution, though they do often display the power of love. On the whole, one might say, they tend not to endorse the power of hate. But Lewis's fantasies do, undoubtedly, endorse the power of hate, not least by making it seem right and exciting.

This tendency in Lewis was not confined to his fantasies. In a broadcast during the War he said:

> What I cannot understand is this sort of half-pacifism you get nowadays which gives people the idea that though you have got to fight, you ought to do it with a long face as if you were ashamed of it. It is that feeling which robs lots of magnificent young Christians in the Services of something they have a right to, something which is the natural accompaniment of war—a kind of gaiety and whole-heartedness. (Broadcast Talks)

It is hardly possible to endorse this, unless one has subjected the "enemy" to "contemptuous devaluation." His morality is very much one of giving a dog a bad name and then hanging him:

> "She's no Daughter of Eve. She comes of your father Adam's first wife, her they called Lilith. And she was one of the Jinn. That's what she comes from on one side. And on the other she comes of the giants. No, no, there isn't a drop of real human blood in the Witch."
> "That's why she's bad all through, Mr Beaver," said Mrs Beaver.

"True enough, Mrs Beaver," replied he, "there may be two views about humans (meaning no offence to the present company). But there's no two views about things that look like humans but aren't."

". . . in general take my advice, when you meet anything that's going to be human and isn't yet, or used to be human once, and isn't now, or ought to be human and isn't, you keep your eyes out and feel for your hatchet. . . ." (LWW, pp. 76–77)

By the most subtle blandishments, Lewis puts this doubtful message into the mouths of those who represent love—the Beavers, Aslan—the "good" characters in his adult fiction. So, the embodiments of a respected faith seem to be urging others, and the reader, to hate.

Morover, as we have seen in the adult fantasies, this giving way to hate seems to Lewis's Christian protagonists as the highest form of spiritual experience. It is in preparing for this kind "battle," or the destruction of one's enemies, that one finds the "harmony of the universe." This, again, seems a seriously harmful "upshot" in Lewis's fictions. At the time of writing, many thousands of wretched men and children were dying in the Iran-Iraq wars in the joyful expectation of being rewarded in heaven for carrying the injunctions of their authoritarian leaders into a futile battle over religious truth. Lewis's message has the same fundamentalist character.

The underlying dynamics developed from the anguish Lewis suffered by his mother's death, and the psychic hunger which her disappearance left with him, compounded by the presence within of an internalized "bad" mother. We may follow parallel dynamics in such case histories as that of "Marion" in Marie Naevestad's (1979) marvellous study, The Colours of Rage and Love. Marion's life was being destroyed by the presence within her psyche of the "bad" mother. Her drawings display the way in which the fear, rage, and suffering she associated with her mother were dominating and destroying her life. But while these seem to be the mother, they are really aspects of her own make-up, and by degrees she has to learn to embrace the "all-bad" mother imago within herself. She has to learn to love herself. Marion's great discovery was, "All the bad colours belong to myself" (Naevestad 1979, p. 196). The appeal of this remarkable case history is in its archetypal quality: it is a universal problem.

Marion's progress under therapy, however, is very different from the path chosen by Lewis in his fiction. Through creative effort in her therapy, Marion integrates the good and bad mother both within herself and "out there"; that is, she learns to see the tragedy of her mother's inadequacy and death as a historical fact in the outer world, while embracing her own hate as part of herself. This means she achieves a full awareness of the ambivalent reality of herself and the world. She now feels "she seems to have slept all her life till now" (p. 190), and can *begin to live*. I believe it is this desire to *begin* that drives many artists—as it certainly drove George MacDonald, and, I believe, C. S. Lewis.

Throughout his work, it is this kind of new beginning that C. S. Lewis sought. There are many places where he yearns for such a beginning, often conceived expectantly in intense color visions. The detailed delineation by Dr. Marie von Naevestad of Marion's quest reveals what is involved—her patient's creativity could not have been achieved without a long and patient relationship with a therapist of profound insight. The study reveals how complex a process is involved to find a true solution to the dreadful inheritance of a psychic ghost. By contrast, we must surely see Lewis's solutions as false— exporting the problems, rather than engaging with them, in such a way as to modify them. The trouble with exports of this kind is that they may tend to encourage others to forfeit their own humanness and their own hope rather than engage creatively with the problem.

Perhaps the most significant issue over which the lessons from psychotherapy might be brought up against Lewis's kind of Christianity is that of whether we can accept our mixed, ambivalent, body-and-psyche human existence at all. One cannot avoid the conclusion that Lewis felt that to be human was a poor thing. I was surprised to hear the Right Reverend Richard Harries, Bishop of Oxford, say on BBC Radio recently that Lewis's was a form of "central Christianity." He followed this remark with an extract from a broadcast by Lewis in which he urged his listeners to give up the self, in favor of a Christ-self. If one looked only for oneself, one would only find "hate, despair, ruin, and death." What came into my mind was that image of Eustace having his flesh peeled away, as if by Christ. And then I remembered a passage in *Beyond Personality* in which Lewis wrote:

> The Eternal Being, who knows everything and created the whole universe became not only a man but (before that) a baby, and before that a *foetus* inside a woman's body. If you want to get the hang

of it, think *how you'd like to become a slug or a crab.* (*Mere Christianity,* p. 142; my italics)

There is a certain vibration behind that last sentence that reveals an impulse in Lewis to reject being human: a certain disgust at being-in-the-body, which I find it difficult to reconcile with what I know of the best in Christianity, and certainly with what (say) that existentialist psychotherapist would believe.

Lewis seemed to want to replace all that was him, both flesh and spirit, with God or Christ, and to seek that the Holy Spirit should replace totally the revolting human thing that he was. Whether or not this is a Christian message must be left to the church. From the point of view of those insights which come to us from psychotherapy, nothing could be more harmful or false, since our salvation lies in becoming able to embrace and love ourselves, not in egoism, but in full acceptance of our ambivalence, and as the product of "life," whatever that may mean. "For everything that lives is holy," Blake said (*The Marriage of Heaven and Hell,* last line). It is no solution to reject ourselves.

It is by no means reductive to see the *sehnsucht* of a man like Lewis as a quest impelled by mourning for a lost mother, since this raises the tragic question of the meaning of life. It is natural and human for man to yearn for meaning, order, and beauty; and the impulse can be understood in many ways. A priest would discuss a man's longing in relation to God; a psychotherapist would seek to find the origins of the impulse in his earliest formative experiences—and his purpose would be to distinguish between true and false experience, in relation to true and false yearning, in his adult life.

I have suggested that the reason why Lewis' world seemed meaningless is because he has lost the mother, and the processes of finding a real and benign world were not completed by her. He wants to complete *play,* and the reality sense. The experience of her death, his father's pessimistic persuasiveness, and the misery of his early school life, left him with a bleak sense of the nature of reality, a tendency to live in fantasy worlds, and a confusion about gender. The White Witch who blights the "other" world is the inner image of the bad mother who wrecks the inner world, while (as in the fantasies) the male figures are often problematic (and the best creature seems in any case an animal).

In this plight there seems at times only certain radical solutions: to dissolve the self altogether; to seek ultimate regression and begin again (as by going through into another world); or to find utter and absolute obedience. When he is lured by the internalized mother into masturbation, at first it seems the vision will return; but afterwards the world seems bleaker. In both his sexuality and his imaginative play, he seems to make no progress.

So, man has been cut off from the truth by sin. Thus, the problem and its solution are not really to do with the heritage of the scientific revolution and the consequent dissociation of sensibility. They belong to Lewis's psychopathology, engrained in his psychic tissue as it was from traumatic experiences in infancy and childhood. His solutions are false solutions to these problems. His world is blighted by destructive fantasies associated with masturbation and directed at the Lilith mother-imago. To counter this impulse he resorts to even more aggressive paranoid fantasies, in which splitting and projection play a large part. The effect is to deepen the division within himself, and instead of seeking to embrace his own ambivalence and that of others, coming closer to the mixed nature of humanness, he tends to develop a world picture in terms of a faith in which gleams of celestial strength and beauty can fall "on a jungle of filth and imbecility," as he puts it characteristically somewhere in his devotional writing. Beneath his homiletic sermons one may detect this persistent sense of the feeling that to be human is loathsome:

He will make the feeblest and filthiest of us into a god or goddess . . . (Mere Christianity, p. 162)

Dozens of people go to Him to be cured of some one particular sin which they are ashamed of (like masturbation or physical cowardice) or which is obviously spoiling daily life (like bad temper or drunkenness) . . . (p. 159)

The solution to our spiritual problem is to give up the present human self, to be reborn by being entirely taken over by God:

Until you have given yourself up to Him you will not have a real self. (p. 177)

There are places where Lewis shows himself aware of the way in which creative art, as myth, can bring about fundamental changes in us. Discussing myth in *An Experiment in Criticism*, he says:

> The nearest I have yet got to an answer is that we seek an enlargement of our being. We want to be more than ourselves. . . . In love we escape from our self into one other . . . to go out of the self, to correct its provincialism and heal its loneliness . . . (*An Experiment in Criticism*, pp. 137–38)

Elsewhere he suggests that myth goes beyond the expression of things we have already felt. It arouses in us sensations we have never had before, as though we had broken out of our normal mode of consciousness, and "possessed joys not promised to our birth." It shocks us more fully awake than we are for most of our lives.

But despite his intelligent remarks on these lines, about the liberating effects of creative myth, Lewis develops his own art in subservience to his own cosmology and devotional-moral set patterns, in which love and sympathy are not at a premium, but rather splitting, projection and hate—except in *Till We Have Faces*. One can see that in this he was yearning for order, in a world which seemed to threaten disorder from scientific hubris, from the inversion of values, and even sheer evil. The mediaeval cosmos Lewis studied as a mediaevalist depicted an intricately structured universe in which man occupied a definite and important link between the angels and the animal; the Arthurian legends also showed man to be a key member of a "company" brought togther to save earth from impending chaos and disorder. Lewis was influenced by such examples at a time when it seemed to him that man was reduced in status by science; he wished to see man in a divinely patterned universe.

I think we must say, however, there are other reasons why myth startles us—in the way Lewis acknowledges—out of our complacency. One is its emanation from the subjective life—and from the unconscious and body life. Beneath our rational and ordered ego-existence, we know we have impulses or fantasies to do with sexual possession of the mother, or murder of the father, or with our urge to eat our children, or to pursue revenge, or pull the temple down on ourselves.

But then, we also know that "the dreadful has already happened," that we are born and are thus condemned to die: "better never to have been born" (Sophocles) and "let the day perish in which I was born, and the night in which it was said 'There is a male child conceived'" (*Job* 3:3). We have all experienced moments of tragic despair when our suffering and mortality seem too terrible to us. We all need, at depth, to contemplate our being-unto-death, and to offer meanings to establish against it. These are the subjective spheres in which we experience the need to come to terms with our mortality and true joy lies in overcoming these feelings of the deepest dread.

If we turn with this kind of problem in mind to Lewis's myths, I believe we shall be seriously disappointed. A writer may understand the creative process, but the created pudding must be proved in the eating. Perhaps in the "Narnia" books, especially in The Last Battle, we are, at times, on the verge of the necessary gravity. But Lewis's solutions to all the existential problems, as I have tried to show, are childish: they are like the solutions attempted by the little boy in the Dawn Treader who seeks to save his mother from sickness and death. They resort to magic (and so manic denial) rather than a tragic engagement with reality.

While Lewis defines myth in his way as a living, creative art, his writing clings closely to the insistence that the Christian myth is the only one that is true. Thus, it can only be homiletic, and too literal to exert a truly creative power to lead us out of our normal mode of consciousness. In his critical writing he distinguishes between myth and allegory: once a story has a meaning tacked on it becomes allegory: we do not receive it concretely as a myth. But since behind Lewis's stories there is a universal unquestionable reality of spiritual structure, his art can never do more than reflect this. His writing is not thus often open to that 'enlargement' that love can bring, in generating sympathy. According to Lewis's definition, myth is a form that comes alive, moves into new areas, and can shake us up out of our conventionalities and dead ideas. The great myths he discusses, like Orpheus and Euridice, can do this: so can genuine creative writing at many levels. But Lewis's cannot because he can never do without a magic theocentric cosmology on which he must depend: the ultimate emperor must always be there, carrying out the emperor's deeper magic, God's plan, and whenever there is a perplexity or difficulty, more magic (like Aslan's) is available; and so insecure is Lewis that he must rely absolutely on this magic ultimately being effective.

The fate of the earth is being fought over between angels and demons; but we have the feeling whether we are reading "Narnia" stories or the space trilogy that the emperor's magic will, in the end, always overcome. So the fanciful fancies are never allowed to develop creatively beyond this scheme. They remain essentially propaganda for a particularly fixed (and at times inhumanly depersonalized) attitude to the world as is startlingly revealed by the Greeves's letters. It is a "cause," like Othello's, that has a black-and-white merciless and unrelenting conviction.

In the real world, however, and in the sphere of the subjective life and the unconscious life, there can be no such security—and we have to try to come to terms with this. There is only ambiguity and uncertainty (Sorge). Lewis's need for the emperor's magic is a mark of the deficiency of his independence in this existential way.

So in Lewis we have a perverse false solution to the problems of vulnerability. There is a deep sense of guilt and self-loathing, and his extreme dependence on the emperor's magic is a solution to this. But in the service of the emperor this guilt and sense of sin are projected over "enemies" in a paranoid-schizoid way, and attacked in them so that justified aggression becomes the focus of a false solution to the problem of life, and the problem of vulnerability is escaped.

His quest is not the pursuit of truth, self-knowledge, existential choice, or ethical living. It is simply aggressive assertion. One has to say that authoritarianism is often associated with an indulgent mental rage. It is not love, but idolized hatred, and the impulse to turn others into something else—to force them to become tractable, controllable, or to annihilate them. These are the solutions to life's problems of a deeply insecure but seethingly frustrated immature child. Since they are products of such rage, these fantasies fall short of that living myth that can move towards true solutions. Fairy tales like *Rapunzle* and *Cinderella* do become living myth, because, often in a terrifying way, they are unflinching about the more dreadful aspects of the world, from envy to mortality, and our anxiety.

Lewis's Ransom, in his space trilogy of fairy tales for adults, enacts some of his myths. Ransom, according to Sammons, was based on J. R. R. Tolkien, insofar as he is not Lewis himself. In any case, Ransom as hero is spun out of donship. Times have altered; but in Lewis's time there was a characteristic kind of academic sensibility, and its essence was emotional immaturity and naivety. If one reads the correspondence between Lewis and Greeves, one takes in this atmosphere of naive immaturity. I often have a sense, when reading such exchanges, especially the discussions of masturbation, sadistic fantasy, and gloatings on the bodies of women, of what a mature modern woman would think about these qualities of the male academic enclave. Women are careful what they say, and often do not speak on such matters: but what they would speak about, however sympathetic, would be something like the way George Eliot places the Reverend Edward Casaubon.

There is a thin trickle of emotion and an inadequacy in the real of passion: a deep guilt and loathing of emotion for which the playful sadism and murderous fantasies are a compensation. There is also an intense egoism, capable (as in Casaubon) of an erosive envy, and suspicion, and a cruel and insulting malevolence (as in Casaubon's will).*

The most disturbing aspect of this kind of donnish consciousness appears when it contemplates joy, the ideal, or the freely passionate. This is the problem of Charles Williams, with his combination of mysticism and sadistic fantasy,** or Lewis with his ideas from the classics of Pan-like behavior: the cries of Euan-oi-oi et cetera are combined with a corrupt desire to see a young woman teacher humiliated and her pupils discomforted. What sensual release did Lewis really wish to give these young creatures? One cannot escape the conclusion that the highest spiritual satisfactions in these fantasies are those of executing a minatory power over others.

This is not a minor aspect of the Lewis fables for the central events in the space fiction trilogy are extremely intense, sadistic fantasies, while in Narnia the main events are experiences of Aslan's velvet-clawed menace, the stripping of Eustace's flesh, the recurrent destruction of dehumanized enemies, the nightmarish horror of Tash, and the ultimate nightmare fantasy of the end of the world; and, all in all, the encouragement to believe in the paranoid-schizoid universe, and a self-righteous macho stance towards it.

The books appeal, no doubt, because of the unconscious material in them, as do all myths. If we compare them with the best of George MacDonald, we shall find that Lewis's use of the unconscious material is less successful than his—at least until Lilith. In MacDonald, though he failed in the end, the dynamics of hate, which arose from his intense grief in bereave-

---

*Cf. "an insufferable semi-lady scientific woman with a diploma from some tom-fool nursing college. . . ." Lewis in They Stand Together, (p. 476).
**Williams said "At bottom a darkness has always haunted me." Humphrey Carpenter says he "was a devoted lover but he also enjoyed the notion of inflicting pain." The Inklings, p. 80.

ment, are modified by love. In Lewis the anguish of loss was transformed by the experience of the sadism of an insane clergyman into a form of Christianized hate, and his solutions seem to me to belong to that tendency found in all religions, to be so absolute about the truth of one's own cause that one must seek to impose it on others, or to frighten them into acceptance, and to suppose that the stern authority one worships will vindicate such dealings with those who do not share one's beliefs. The impulse behind the "Narnia" books was to develop this kind of proselytizing ardor among children, and the adult fantasies seek to use the space fiction mode to put across the same message. Yet, when I relate the fantasies of the private mythology to the solutions indicated by the "upshot," I cannot but feel that they are hate solutions which solve nothing, but only tend to export the problem. There are a few exceptions, such as Digory's choice of the path of love, and the anguish endured through the complex story *Till We Have Faces*. But by my phenomenological analysis, I cannot help reaching the conclusion that the solutions subtly urged on the reader by Lewis's myths seem dangerous and perverse, tending to harden the soul rather than refresh it.

# Bibliography

This study concentrates almost exclusively on the fantasies and does not attempt a full account of Lewis's academic and theological works. For a full list of Lewis's work see *Light on C. S. Lewis*, ed. Jocelyn Gibb (London: Geoffrey Bles, 1965); *J. R. R. Tolkien: A Biography*, H. Carpenter (London: Allen and Unwin, 1977); *The Image of the City*, essays by Charles Williams, ed. Anne Ridler, (Oxford: Oxford University Press, 1958).

## Books by C. S. Lewis

*The Abolition of Man, or Reflections Upon Education with Special Reference to the Teaching of English in the Upper Forms of Schools*. Oxford: Oxford University Press, 1943.

*The Allegory of Love, a Study in Mediaeval Traditions*. Oxford: Oxford University Press, 1936.

*The Dark Tower and Other Stories*. Edited by Walter Hooper. London: Collins, 1977.

*Dymer, A Poem*. London: J. M. Dent, 1926.

*An Experiment in Criticism*. Cambridge: Cambridge University Press, 1961.

*A Grief Observed*. London: Faber and Faber, 1961.

*The Horse and His Boy*. London: Geoffrey Bles, 1954.

*The Last Battle*. London: The Bodley Head, 1964.

*Letters of C. S. Lewis*. Introduction by W. H. Lewis. London: Geoffrey Bles, 1966.

*The Lion, the Witch and the Wardrobe*. London: Geoffrey Bles, 1950.

*The Magician's Nephew*. London: Bodley Head, 1964.

*Mere Christianity* (*Broadcast Talks, Christian Behaviour* and *Beyond Personality*). London: Geoffrey Bles, 1952.

*Of Other Worlds: Essays and Stories*. Edited by Walter Hooper. London: Geoffrey Bles, 1966.

*Out of the Silent Planet*. London: Bodley Head, 1938.

*Perelandra*. London: Bodley Head, 1943; also published as *Voyage to Venus*. London: Pan Books, 1953.

*Poems*. Edited by Walter Hooper. London: Geoffrey Bles, 1964.

*Prince Caspian*. London: Geoffrey Bles, 1951.

*Reflections on the Psalms*. London: Geoffrey Bles, 1958.

*The Screwtape Letters*. London: Geoffrey Bles, 1942.

*The Silver Chair*. London: Geoffrey Bles, 1953.

*Spirits in Bondage: A Cycle of Lyrics.* (as "Clive Hamilton"). London: Heinemann, 1919.

*Surprised by Joy, the Shape of My Early Life.* London: Geoffrey Bles, 1955.

*That Hideous Strength, a Modern Fairy-Tale for Grown Ups.* London: Bodley Head, 1945.

*They Stand Together: The Letters of C. S. Lewis to Arthur Greeves, 1914–1963.* Edited by Walter Hooper. London: Collins, 1979.

*Till We Have Faces, a Myth Retold.* London: Geoffrey Bles, 1956.

*The Voyage of the Dawn Treader.* London: Geoffrey Bles, 1952.

## Biographies and Critical Works

Carpenter, Humphrey. 1978. *The Inklings. C. S. Lewis, J. R. R. Tolkien, Charles Williams and Their Friends.* London: Allen and Unwin.

Ford, Paul F. 1980. *Companion to Narnia.* New York: Harper and Row.

Gibb, Jocelyn, ed. 1965. *Light on C. S. Lewis.* London: Geoffrey Bles.

Gibson, Evan H. 1980. *C. S. Lewis: Spinner of Tales, a Guide to His Fiction.* Grand Rapids, Mich.: Eerdmans.

Gilbert, Douglas, and Clyde S. Kilby. 1973. *C. S. Lewis: Images of His World.* Grand Rapids, Mich.: Eerdmans.

Glover, Donald E. 1981. *C. S. Lewis, the Art of Enchantment.* Athens: Ohio University Press.

Green, Roger Lancelyn, and Walter Hooper. 1974. *C. S. Lewis, A Biography.* London: Collins.

Hannay, Margaret P. 1984. *C. S. Lewis.* New York: Ungar.

Heilaender, Gilbert. 1978. *A Taste for the Other: The Social and Ethical Thought of C. S. Lewis.* Grand Rapids, Mich.: Eerdmans.

Hillegas, Mark Robert. 1979. *Shadows of Imagination: the Fantasies of C. S. Lewis, J. R. R. Tolkien and Charles Williams.* Carbondale: Southern Illinois University Press.

Holmer, Paul L. 1977. *C. S. Lewis, the Shape of His Faith and Thought.* London: Sheldon Press.

Hooper, Walter. 1977. "Narnia, the Author, the Critic and the Tale," in *The Longing for a Form,* ed. Peter Schakel. Kent, Ohio: Kent State University Press.

Hooper, Walter. 1979. *Past Watchful Dragons.* London: MacMillan.

Howard, Thomas. 1980. *The Achievement of C. S. Lewis.* Wheaton, Ill.: Howard shaw.

Lewis, W. H. *The Diaries of Warnie Lewis.* Housed in the Wade Collection, Wheaton College, Wheaton, Illinois. There is also a typescript by Warnie Lewis entitled "C. S. Lewis: A Biography," the first draft for *Letters of C. S. Lewis,* which contains more biographical information.

Lindskoog, Kathryn. 1979. *The Lion of Judah in Never-Never Land.* Grand Rapids, Mich.: Eerdmans.

Purtill, Richard. 1974. *Lord of the Elves and Eldils: Fantasy and Philosophy in C. S. Lewis and J. R. R. Tolkien.* Grand Rapids, Mich.: Eerdmans.

Sammons, Martha C. 1980. *C. S. Lewis's Space Trilogy.* Winchester, Ill.: Cornerstone.

Sammons, Martha C. 1979. *A Guide Through Narnia.* Wheaton, Ill.: Howard Shaw.

Sayer, George. *A Critical Biography of C. S. Lewis.* Forthcoming.

Schakel, Peter J., ed. 1977. *The Longing for a Form.* Kent, Ohio: Kent State University Press.

Schakel, Peter J. 1979. *Reading with the Heart: the Way Into Narnia.* Grand Rapids, Mich.: Eerdmans.

Schakel, Peter J. 1984. *Reason and Imagination in C. S. Lewis: A Study of "Till We Have Faces."* Grand Rapids, Mich.: Eerdmans.

Vanaken, Sheldon. 1969. *A Severe Mercy: C. S. Lewis and a Pagan Love Invaded by Christ.* London: Hodder and Stoughton.

Walsh, Chad. 1979. *The Literary Legacy of C. S. Lewis.* London: Sheldon Press.

Wilson, A. N. 1990. *C. S. Lewis.* London, Collins.

## Other Relevant Works, Critical Studies and Books on Psychology

Bachelard, Gaston. 1964. *The Poetics of Space.* Boston: Beacon Press.

Bowlby, John. 1967. "Child Mourning and Psychiatric Illness." In *The Predicament of the Family,* edited by Peter Lomas. London: Hogarth Press.

Brewer, Derek. 1980. *Symbolic Stories.* Woodbridge, Suffolk, England: Brewer and Boydell.

Carline, Richard. 1968. *Draw They Must.* London: Arnold.

Chaloner, Len. 1963. *Feeling and Perception in Young Children.* London, Tavistock Press.

Fairbairn, W. R. D. 1952. *Psychoanalytical Studies of the Personality.* London: Tavistock Press.

Farber, Leslie H. 1966. *The Ways of the Will.* London: Constable.

Frankl, Viktor. 1969. *The Doctor and the Soul.* London: Souvenir.

Freud, Sigmund. 1955. *The Interpretation of Dreams.* London: Allen and Unwin.

Freud, Sigmund. 1904. *The Psychopathology of Everyday Life.* London: Fisher and Unwin.

Grene, Marjorie. 1965. *Approaches to a Philosophical Biology.* New York: Basic Books.

Grolnick, Simon O. and others. 1978. *Between Reality and Phantasy, Transitional Objects and Phenomena.* New York: Jason Aronson.

Guntrip, Harry. 1961. *Personality Structure and Human Interaction.* London: Hogarth.

Guntrip, Harry. 1968. *Schizoid Phenomena, Object-relations and the Self.* London: Hogarth.

Holbrook, David. 1964. *English for the Rejected*. Cambridge: Cambridge University Press.

Holbrook, David. 1971. *Human Hope and the Death Instinct*.

Hughes, Ted. 1970. *Crow*. London: Faber and Faber.

Jung, Karl et al. 1964. *Man and His Symbols*. London: Aldus Books.

Khan, Masud R. 1979. *Alienation in Perversions*. London: Hogarth.

Klein, Melanie. 1957. *Envy and Gratitude*. London: Tavistock.

Klein, Melanie. 1963. *Our Adult World and its Roots in Infancy*. London: Tavistock.

Klein, Melanie. 1932. *The Psychoanalysis of Children*. London: Hogarth.

Klein, Melanie, and Joan Riviere. 1938. *Love, Hate and Reparation*. London: Hogarth.

Laing, R. D. 1960. *The Divided Self*. London: Tavistock.

Lomas, Peter, ed. 1967. *The Predicament of the Family*. London: Hogarth.

Lomas, Peter. 1973. *True and False Experience*. London: Allen Lane.

MacDonald, George. 1858. *Phantases*. London.

MacDonald, George. 1871. *At the Back of the North Wind*. London.

MacDonald, George. 1872. *The Princess and the Goblins*. London.

MacDonald, George. 1882. *The Gifts of the Christ Child*. London.

MacDonald, George. 1882. *The Princess and Curdie*. London.

MacDonald, George. 1895. *Lilith*. London.

May, Rollo, Ernest Angel, and Henri F. Ellenberger. 1958. *Existence—a New Dimension in Psychiatry*. New York: Basic Books.

Naevestad, Marie von. 1979. *The Colours of Rage and Love*. Oslo: Universitetsforlaget.

Owst, G. R. 1933. *Literature and Pulpit in Mediaeval England*. Cambridge: Cambridge University Press.

Plath, Sylvia. 1966. *The Bell Jar*. London: Faber and Faber.

Plath, Sylvia. 1975. *Letters Home*. New York: Harper and Row.

Plath, Sylvia. 1982. *The Journals*. Edited by Ted Hughes and Frances McCullough. New York: Ballantine Books.

Polanyi, Michael. 1969. *Knowing and Being*. London: Routledge.

Stern, Karl. 1966. *The Flight from Woman*. London: Allen and Unwin.

Suttie, Ian D. 1935. *The Origins of Love and Hate*. London: Kegan Paul.

Tustin, Frances. 1981. *Autistic States in Children*. London: Routledge.

Ulanov, Ann Belford. 1981. *Receiving Woman*. Philadelphia: Westminster Press.

Ulanov, Ann Belford and Barry Ulanov. 1987. *The Witch and the Clown: Two Archetypes of Human Sexuality*. Wilmette, Ill.: Chiron Publications.

Winnicott, D. W. 1958. *Collected Papers, Throught Pediatrics to Psychoanalysis*. London: Tavistock.

Winnicott, D. W. 1965. *The Family and Individual Development*. London: Tavistock.

Winnicott, D. W. 1966. *The Maturational Processes and the Facilitating Environment*. London: Hogarth.

Winnicott, D. W. 1971. *Playing and Reality*. London: Tavistock.

Wolff, Robert Lee. 1961. *The Golden Key, a Study of the Fiction* of George MacDonald. New Haven; Conn.; Yale University Press.

## Articles

Biggs, R. A. 1985. "The Lion, the Witch and Plato." *The Times*, 20 April.

Fairbairn, W. R. D. 1929. "Fundamental Principles of Psychoanalysis." *Edinburgh Medical Journal* (June 1978).

Gordon, Rosemary. 1978. "D. H. Lawrence." *Journal of Analytic Psychology* 23, no. 3 (July): p. 259.

Holbrook, David. 1973. "The Problem of C. S. Lewis." *Children's Literature in Education*, no. 10 (March): p. 4.

Leavis, F. R. "Tragedy and the Medium." *Scrutiny* XII: p. 241.

Nesbit, E. 1908. "The Aunt and Annabel." In Blackie's Christmas Annual.

Prickett, Stephen. "What do the Translators Think They are Up To." *Universities Quarterly* 33, no. 3: pp. 263–64.

Robson, W. W. 1966. "C. S. Lewis." *The Cambridge Quarterly* 1, no. 3 (Summer): pp. 252–272.

Santayana, George. "Literary Criticism and Philosophy." *Scrutiny* V: p. 275.

VII *Magazine*. An Anglo-American Literary Review, devoted to the work of George MacDonald, G. K. Chesterton, C. S. Lewis, J. R. R. Tolkien, Charles Williams, Dorothy Sayers, and Owen Barfield. Edited by Barbara Reynolds. Published by Wheaton College, Illinois.

# Index